Baedeker's
VIENNA

Imprint

89 colour photographs
25 plans, 1 general map, 1 coat of arms, Underground (U-Bahn) railway plan, 1 large city map

Text: Dr Gerda Rob; additional text: Christa Sturm

Editorial work, Revision: Badedeker-Redaktion

English language edition: Alec Court

Cartography: Gert Oberländer, Munich; Hallweg AG, Berne (plan of city); Franz Kaiser, Sindelfingen; Cartographia, Budapest

General direction: Dr Peter Baumgarten, Baedeker Stuttgart

English translation: Babel Translations, Norwich

Updating and additional text: Barbara Cresswell, Alec Court

Source of illustrations: Albertina (1), Baedeker (1), Bildagentur Buonas Dias (1), Bildarchiv Preussischer Kulturbesitz (1), Bohnaker (1), dpa (22), Harenberg (3), Historia-Photo (8), Kurzentrum Oberlaa (1), Linde (3), Naturhistorisches Museum (1), Österreichisher Budestheaterverband (1), Österreich Werbung (2), Pfeifer (2), Prenzel (4), Rudolph (1), Uthoff (31), Weiner Fremdenverkehrsverband (5)

Following the tradition established by Karl Baedeker in 1844, sights of particular interest and hotels and restaurants of particular quality are distinguished by either one or two asterisks.

To make it easier to locate the various places listed in the "A to Z" section of the Guide, their co-ordinates on the large city map are shown at the head of each entry.

Only a selection of hotels, restaurants and shops can be given: no reflection is implied, therefore, on establishments not included.

In a time of rapid change it is difficult to ensure that all the information given is entirely accurate and up-to-date, and the possibility of error can never be entirely eliminated. Although the publishers can accept no responsibility for inaccuracies and omissions they are always grateful for corrections and suggestions for improvements.

4th Edition 1992

© Baedeker Stuttgart Original German edition

© 1992 Jarrold and Sons Ltd English language edition worldwide

© 1992 The Automobile Association
United Kingdom and Ireland

US and Canadian edition Prentice Hall Press

Distributed in the United Kingdom by the Publishing Division of The Automobile Association, Fanum House, Basingstoke, Hampshire, RG21 2EA

The name *Baedeker* is a registered trademark
A CIP catalogue record for this book is available from the British Library.

Licensed user: Mairs Geographischer Verlag GmbH & Co.,
Ostfildern-Kemnat bei Stuttgart

Reproductions: Golz Repro-Service GmbH, Ludwigsburg

Printed in Italy by G. Canale & C. S.p.A – Borgaro T.se – Turin

ISBN 0–13–063660–6 US and Canada
     0 7495 0408 0 UK

Contents

The Principal Sights at a Glance

Preface

This Pocket Guide to Vienna is one of the new generation of Baedeker city guides.

Baedeker pocket guides, illustrated throughout in colour, are designed to meet the needs of the modern traveller. They are quick and easy to consult, with the principal sights described in alphabetical order and practical details about opening times, how to get there, etc., shown in the margin.

Each guide is divided into three parts. The first part gives a general account of the city, its history, population, culture and so on; in the second part the principal sights are described; and the third part contains a variety of practical information designed to help visitors to find their way about and make the most of their stay.

The new guides are abundantly illustrated and contain numbers of newly drawn plans. At the back of the book is a large city map, and each entry in the main part of the guide gives the co-ordinates of the square on the map in which the particular feature can be located. Users of this guide, therefore, will have no difficulty in finding what they want to see.

Facts and Figures

Arms of the
City of Vienna

General

Vienna is both the capital of the Republic of Austria and one of neutral Austria's nine provinces. It is the seat of the Austrian President, the Federal Government, the supreme administrative governmental bodies and of local government for the province of Vienna.
Despite its peripheral location in present-day Austria, it is very much the political, economic, intellectual and cultural hub of the Republic.

Capital

Located in northern Austria, the city is encircled by the province of Lower Austria and, at an altitude of 558ft (170m), it lies on latitude 48°14′N and longitude 16°21′E.
Most of the city extends along the right bank of the Danube and it is bordered in the W by the Vienna Woods.

Situation

Vienna is situated at the junction of the oceanic and continental climatic regions; the winter temperatures, on average −1.4°C, hardly ever fall below −5°C and the summer temperatures are rarely in excess of 30°C, averaging at 20°C. Rain showers are frequent, especially in the summer, but not persistent. There is an almost constant light breeze which has been called the "Wiener Wind".

Climate

Vienna, like most large cities, has its share of environmental problems. A five-year scheme to improve water purity was started in the mid-1980s at an estimated cost of 224 million schillings, linking more suburban districts to the public water system. The municipal utilities have been converted to use natural gas and oil to reduce sulphur emission and improve the air quality. Waste incineration plants have been equipped with filters to reduce levels of toxic emissions. These measures are to be extended to other sectors by the city's environment department, concentrating on pollution caused by vehicle exhaust fumes, domestic heating and industry.

Ecology

The projects undertaken for this programme are designed to benefit the environment and quality of life in the city. The leisure area created on Danube Island has already proved a great success. On a similar scale, the woods and meadowland to the N and S of the city are to be developed and new woodland areas created. During the next ten years 500 acres/200ha of woodland will be established in the Favoriten, Simmering, Floridsdorf, Donaustadt and Liesing districts. In 1987, as part of this project, Viennese school children began planting a wood in the 22nd district to commemorate the 65,000 Jewish citizens of Vienna who died in the holocaust. The wood will be indicated

The Green Programme

◀ *View of the Cathedral over the roofs of Vienna*

by a memorial stone. The recreational area at Wienerberg-Ost in the Favoriten district is almost complete.

Four new parks were created in 1987 alone, in the 10th, 14th, 16th and 19th districts. Residents, local committees and district councils have all been involved in the redevelopment of existing parks such as Schönborn Park and the Denzel-Gründen. Other projects to enlist the support of residents include a scheme to encourage firms to buy protective supports for trees in exchange for free advertising space; a competition, "Vienna in Bloom", with generous prizes, and advice and grants from the city's department of gardens and parks.

Cleaning the Danube

The Danube is heavily polluted and cleaning the Viennese waterways poses one of the greatest environmental problems to the city and provincial authorities alike. In 1985 the Austrian government resolved to clean the Danube and its tributaries. The paper industry is one of the main contributing factors to the level of pollution, filtering only 40% of 1 million tons of waste produced each year.

The cleaning operation is only part of a larger project to restore the landscape along the river. Work has already begun on the Eastern National Park which is to extend from the Lobau to the Czechoslovakian border. Indigenous plant-life will be reintroduced into the Lobau and arable fields will be returned to meadowland. After attempts to establish beaver colonies on the river banks were successful, The European terrapin and fish otter, once native to this area, will also be reintroduced.

The area cannot be entirely reverted to its natural state and the oil tanker wharf at Lobau will be retained. The construction of an additional wharf at the Albern docks has been prevented, however, by the installation of new cargo handling equipment.

Area and population

With a total area of 160 sq. miles (415km²) Vienna falls within the middle range of European capitals.

Its population has declined in numbers since the First World War. In 1910 Vienna still had a population of 2·1 million but today it has only 1·5 million inhabitants. The negative growth rate is due as much to a higher annual death rate (c. 21,000) than birth rate (c. 16,000), as to the migration of 32,000 people out of the city, compared with the 31,000 who moved to the city. The Inner City has been particularly hard hit by depopulation and in 20 years has lost a third of its residents. The province of Vienna has also been affected; at present ranking as the most heavily populated province, it is expected to drop to third place in the next 30 years. The trend is a migration from East and South Austria, which borders mainly on socialist states, to western Austria and the neighbouring economies of Bavaria, Switzerland and North Italy.

City Districts (Stadtbezirke)

The city is divided into 23 Districts: I City Centre, II Leopoldstadt, III Landstrasse, IV Wieden, V Margareten, VI Mariahilf, VII Neubau, VIII Josefstadt, IX Alsergrund, X Favoriten, XI Simmering, XII Meidling, XIII Hietzing, XIV Penzing, XV Rudolfsheim-Fünfhaus, XVI Ottakring, XVII Hernals, XVIII Währing, XIX Döbling, XX Brigittenau, XXI Floridsdorf, XXII Donaustadt and XXIII Liesing.

District I, the City Centre, corresponds to the historic city of Vienna. Districts III–IX, developed from outlying villages, are now termed "Inner Districts", while districts X–XIX, the former

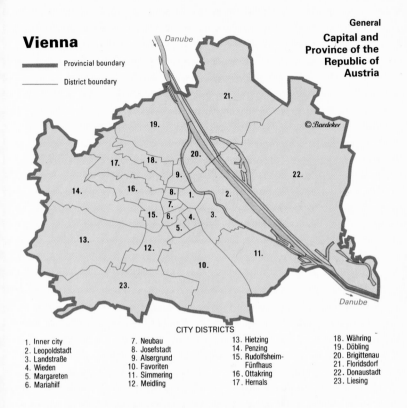

Vienna

━━━━━ Provincial boundary

───── District boundary

Danube

21.

19.

© *Baedeker*

18.

17. 20.

9.

16. 8. 1.

14. 7. 2.

15. 6. 4. 22.

5. 3.

13.

12. 11.

10.

23.

Danube

CITY DISTRICTS

1. Inner city	7. Neubau	13. Hietzing	18. Währing
2. Leopoldstadt	8. Josefstadt	14. Penzing	19. Döbling
3. Landstraße	9. Alsergrund	15. Rudolfsheim-Fünfhaus	20. Brigittenau
4. Wieden	10. Favoriten	16. Ottakring	21. Floridsdorf
5. Margareten	11. Simmering	17. Hernals	22. Donaustadt
6. Mariahilf	12. Meidling		23. Liesing

suburbs outside the Gürtel, the outer ring road, are the "Outer Districts". In a broader sense districts II and XX, together with the fringe districts XXI–XXIII, also belong to the Outer Districts. The smallest district (Josefstadt) covers an area of ¾ sq. mile (1·8km²) while the largest (Donaustadt) is 40 sq. miles (102km²) in extent. The most thinly populated district is the City Centre with 19,000 inhabitants and the most densely populated is Favoriten with 146,000.

Every district has its own individual character. The 3rd district (Landstrasse) is known as the diplomatic quarter; the 4th (Wieden) and the Inner City as the most fashionable; the 5th (Margareten), 6th (Mariahilf) and 7th (Neubau) represent the growth of the middle classes; trade and industry have been established, factories built and workers' settlements placed next to residential complexes. Vienna's largest shopping street crosses the Mariahilf district; the picturesque but somewhat neglected Spittelberg quarter in the 7th district is being renovated. The quiet 8th district (Josefstadt) retains its traditional role as the civil servants' district; the 9th district (Alsergrund) is Vienna's academic quarter with many clinics, hospitals and sanatoria. The 10th (Favoriten), 11th (Simmering), 12th (Meidling) and 15th (Rudolfsheim-Fünfhaus) districts are home to the blue-

11

collar workers, the lower income bracket and tenement dwellers and is the most densely populated area. The 16th (Ottakring) and 17th (Hernals) stretching to the Vienna Woods are similar to these neighbouring districts; Ottakring is also in the process of renovation. The 18th (Währing) is a popular residential area containing one of Vienna's loveliest parks, the Türkenschanzpark. The park extends through Gersthof and Pötzleinsdorf to the wooded hills bordering the city. The 13th (Hietzing) and the 19th (Döbling) districts contend for the title of Vienna's most beautiful suburb. Elegant villas surround Schönbrunn Palace in Hietzing, where even the municipal buildings have a dignified air. Döbling, by contrast, is a collection of old wine producing villages and country inns which has attracted wealthy residents. Liesing, the 23rd district which borders on Hietzing, is a group of sleepy villages set in rolling hills, to which Rodaun belongs, at one time the home of Hugo von Hofmannsthal.

On the other side of the Danube Canal is the 2nd district (Leopoldstadt) in the past the home of Balkan traders, Turks and Jews from the eastern Mediterranean and Poland. It includes the Prater Park, the trade fair exhibition site, the large sports stadium and the track for trotting races. Many new buildings have sprung up around the canal. Next to this is the 20th district (Brigittenau) with drab tenements and fortress-like municipal buildings. Beyond the Danube is Floridsdorf, the 21st district, a workers' quarter where allotment gardens nestle under factory chimneys. In the neighbouring 22nd district, Donaustadt, a new cityscape has been created called "Transdanubien", dominated by United Nations City and Austria-Center, the Danube Tower and Danube Park.

Renovating the Old City

The age of Vienna's buildings is immediately apparent and statistics prove that Vienna has the greatest proportion of residential properties over 70 years of age than any other city of its size in the world. The latest tally shows that 30 out of 100 dwellings were built between 1881 and 1918. As magnificent as the façades may be, the sanitation facilities of many buildings do not meet modern-day standards, for example 30,300 dwellings have no running water at all, where the "Bassena", the communal tap on the stairway, is still in use. The modernisation of residential properties is one of the most important tasks facing the city authorities in the framework of the renovation programme. Several projects are being planned and implemented; the Spittelberg district has already undergone successful renovation. The project for the Ottakring district also includes the creation of parks and green spaces.

Administration

Both a district and a province, Vienna also plays a dual role in administrative terms. The District Council, consisting of 100 members elected for five years, is at the same time the Provincial Council and the elected Mayor heads both authorities. The Provincial Senate, the effective Government, is composed of the Mayor, two Deputy Mayors and 915 office-holding Councillors.

In order to decentralise the administration the 23 districts have their own representatives who elect one of their number to act on their behalf. Since 1987 the representatives have been granted greater autonomy: every district has a budget to provide its own maintenance and services to parks and gardens,

View from the Town Hall (Rathaus) tower

environmental protection, street and road repairs, civic culture, etc. Residents are being given a greater say in the decisions which affect their immediate environment.

Vienna is the headquarters of a great many international organisations: UNIDO (the United Nations Industrial Development Organisation), IAEA (the International Atomic Energy Agency), the UN High Commission for Refugees, ICEM (International Committee for European Migration) and OPEC (Organisation of Petroleum Exporting Countries). IAEA has 80 and UNIDO has 86 permanent delegations of member countries in the city. The Commission of the European Community has plans to establish a representative body in Vienna.

International organisations

Population and Religion

In the Middle Ages Vienna, with a population of 20,000, was already one of the largest German-speaking cities. The influx into the city was at its height between 1880 and 1910 when the population figures soared from 592,000 to 2 million. The newcomers were mainly from Bohemia, Moravia, Hungary and Galicia and when, at the turn of the century, over 60% were non-German-speaking, Vienna became a gigantic melting-pot for ethnic and religious minorities.
After the Second World War those coming to settle in Vienna were chiefly refugees from Hungary and Czechoslovakia, most of whom have since become Austrian citizens. Since 1960 it has mainly been Yugoslav immigrant workers who have sought to settle permanently in Vienna.

Population

Of Vienna's 160,000 registered foreigners, most are Yugoslavs, Turks, Germans, Poles and North Americans. Among the smaller foreign groups there are many students from Arabic-speaking countries, from Africa and the Far East.

Religion

Seventy-four per cent of the Viennese are Roman Catholic, 7·5% Protestant and 0·5 Jewish. In addition there are congregations of the Old Catholic, Greek, Serbian, Russian and Bulgarian Orthodox Churches, and of the Armenian Church, Methodists and Mormons.

Vienna is also the seat of a Roman Catholic Archbishop.

The year 1979 saw the building of an Islamic centre and mosque for the city's 50,000 Muslims.

Transport

Vienna is situated at the intersection of important N–S and E–W routes, at a point where the Alpine Foreland merges with the Hungarian Plain. In the S, W and NW the encircling hills, with their woods and meadows, penetrate deep into the residential areas while the flat plain extends beyond the city in the E and NE.

A 12½ mile (20km) stretch of the Danube flows through E Vienna, splitting off Districts XXI and XXII from the rest of the city. This ranks as an international waterway and its banks are Federally administered.

The Danube is an important artery for international goods transport and in 1989 accounted for 7·7 million tons on the Austrian stretch of the river. Ships carry agricultural produce, timber, foodstuffs and animal feed, solid fuels and oil products, ores, building materials, fertilisers and chemicals. The Danube is growing in importance as an international waterway: the Cernavoda–Constanta Canal has reduced the route to the Black Sea by some 185 miles/300km and the completion of the Rhine-Main-Danube Canal during the 1990s will establish a navigation link to the major industrial areas of western Europe and to the North Sea, presenting new economic opportunities for Austria.

The Danube, Austria's only navigable river, accounts for over 10% of the country's carriage of export goods.

Port

The port at Vienna had already established the city as an important trade centre in the 10th and 11th c. Nowadays its location is significant as a turntable for international trade and transport between eastern and western Europe and it is the most advanced port in Austria.

The port is situated in the SE corner of the city and is divided into three sections: the grain docks at Albern, general cargo and bulk goods at Freaudenau and the oil docks at Lobau. The trans-shipment of oil at Lobau is 1·1 million tons; of iron, paper, oil barrels, building materials, diverse fuels and container cargo is 755,000 tons at Freudenau and 123,000 tons of grain at the Albern docks. In the duty free zone, the turnover of goods stored by foreign firms and transport companies and the handling of cars and goods vehicles amounts to 92,000 tons.

Airport

Schwechat, Vienna's international airport, is 11¼ miles (17km) from the city centre, to the E of the location of Schwechat itself and handles over 80% of Austria's incoming and outgoing air traffic.

At present 37 airlines and 61 ancillary transport firms use the airport, carrying over 3·8 million passengers, 52,800 tons of freight and over 6·7 tons of mail annually.
Since 1977 there has been an Underground station at the airport, connected by fast trains with Wien-Rennweg, Wien-Mitte and Wien-Nord.

Railway stations

European rail services from all points of the compass converge on Vienna, although not all at one central station.
Vienna has three main railway stations:
Westbahnhof (West Station) takes trains coming from W Austria and Western, Central and Northern Europe.
Südbahnhof (South Station) and Ostbahnhof (East Station) handle trains from S Austria, Italy, Yugoslavia, Greece, Warsaw and Moscow.
Trains from N Austria and Czechoslovakia arrive at Franz-Josefs-Bahnhof.

Urban rail transport

Commuters in particular are efficiently and speedily catered for by the rail network (117 miles (187km)) operated by Austrian Railways within the city, with its 39 stations and 30 halts.
Tramways, S-bahn, Underground, Express railways and municipal buses serve a network of about 400 miles/650km. Every year they carry more than 590 million passengers.
In autumn 1982 the so-called basic network of the Underground had been completed and now has four routes, U1, U2, U4 and U6. New sections, including the U3, are under construction.
The "Silver Arrows" of the Underground reach top speeds of 50m.p.h. (80km.p.h.) and run at an average speed (including stops) of 22m.p.h. (35km.p.h.).

Karlsplatz Station, part of Vienna's urban transport network

Roads

The Underground stations are closely supervised at night and are generally considered to be safe.

Vienna's first urban motorway is the partially completed "Gürtelautobahn", the ring road that runs round the S and SE part of the city (A23), linking the S motorway with the (A22).
The W motorway (A1 – Westautobahn) from the W edge of the city leads to Salzburg and the Austrian border, while the S motorway (A2 – Südautobahn) departs in the direction of Wiener Neustadt and Graz. The A21 links the W and S motorways S of the city. The A4 leads in an easterly direction S of the Danube to Schwechat.

Other major roads (Bundesstrasse) out of Vienna:
Highway   1 – to Linz, Salzburg
            3 – to Krems, Wachau
            4 – to Horn, Lower Austria
            9 – to Hainburg
          10 – to Bruck/Leitha
          12 – to Mödling, Baden
          14 – to Klosterneuburg
          16 – to Eisenstadt, Burgenland
          17 – to Semmering, Steiermark
       230 – to Laxenburg

Culture

Vienna is one of the world's greatest metropolises from the cultural point of view and in terms of the number of international figures in the artistic world who gather there, particularly musicians. No other city has been the home of so many great composers nor of so many chamber ensembles, orchestras and choirs.
Many works of great value are on show in its more than 100 national and private museums and some 120 galleries while the Brueghel Collection, one of Europe's greatest collection of paintings, is here in Vienna, together with one of the world's most extensive collection of graphics and the largest number of Albrecht Dürer's drawings assembled in one place. The collection of incunabula in the National Library is the third largest in the world.
About 2·9 million visitors a year pass through the city's museums. The prime attraction for sightseers is Schönbrunn Palace (over 1·3 million visitors), closely followed by the Museum of Fine Arts, the Imperial Apartments in the Hofburg and the Austrian Gallery in the Upper Belvedere.

Universities

The University of Vienna, founded in 1365 as Alma Mater Rudolphina, is currently attended by 100,000 students, engaged on studies in all the classic faculties. It enjoys an exemplary reputation in the fields of medicine, psychology, physics and technical studies.
Vienna also has universities for Technical, Veterinary and Agricultural studies and the study of Economics, the latter is attended by as many as 23,500 students.

Academies and colleges

The Academy of Fine Art, the Academy of Diplomacy, the College of Applied Arts and the Academy of Music and Dramatic Art are all of international standing.

The Albertina – the world's most important collection of graphic art

Artists who have lectured at the Academy include Arik Brauer, Wolfgang Hollegha, Markus Prachensky, Friedensreich Hundertwasser, Anton Lehmden, Josef Mikl and Arnulf Rainer, while at the Academy of Music celebrated musicians, singers and actors are on the teaching staff.

The Austrian Academy of Science is located in Vienna. It has 26 institutes and 31 specialist commissions.
It is divided into two classes, that of philosophical and historical sciences and that of mathematical and natural sciences. Each class has 33 members as well as 60 correspondent members from abroad and 40 correspondent members within Austria.

Academy of Science

The foremost of the libraries in Vienna are the Austrian National Library with 10 important leading collections – encompassing 2·5 million volumes – and the University Library with about 2 million volumes. The most extensive specialist collection is that of the Technical University with 800,000 volumes.

Libraries

Vienna's many theatres (see Practical Information – Theatres) can seat about 16,000 in total and their annual audience figures amount to close on 3·3 million.
The Burgtheater heads the dramatic league. The home of the great classics, it has become a byword among German-speaking peoples for the excellence of the German spoken on its stage.

Theatres, orchestras

17

The Vienna State Opera (Staatsoper) ranks among the three most important opera-houses in the world. It has international opera stars on its permanent staff and can call on the top names among performing artistes and conductors for guest performances. The Vienna Philharmonic gives its concerts in the Staatsoper and the Great Hall of the Musikverein, while the Vienna Symphonic performs in the Konzerthaus. The city has a further six orchestras, 28 chamber music ensembles and 20 choirs. Over 700,000 a year enjoy the music on offer in Vienna's many concert halls.

Music

The court choir was founded during the reign of Maximilian I in 1498 and for many years the "chapel choir" was financed directly by the Emperor. The choir had its heyday during Vienna's classical period when Mozart, Haydn and Beethoven composed unrivalled Masses; Joseph Haydn was a member of the choir from 1740 to 1749, as was Franz Schubert from 1808 to 1813. There are now four choirs, two spend most of the time touring and one choir sings Mass every Sunday at the chapel of the Hofburg. There are 24 boys in each choir; after their voices have broken they join the Viennensis Choir.

Vienna Boys' Choir

Vienna is a centre of journalism, producing 24 newspapers, including six daily and 18 weekly papers, and 1412 magazines and journals.

The Press

Commerce and Industry

The emergence of Austria as a small republic after the collapse of the Habsburg Empire in 1918, lost Vienna, in its peripheral location, much of its standing as a world power in commercial terms. Today Vienna owes its status as the place where commercially East meets West mainly to good bilateral trading relationships.
Many foreign and multi-national companies and banks are represented in Vienna as Austria's capital, and crucial decisions of far-reaching importance are taken here at the sessions of OPEC, the Organisation of the Petroleum Exporting Countries.

International status

Vienna is the hub of Austria's administration, commerce, industry and money market.
In relation to the size of the province, Vienna has the greatest proportion of workplaces in Austria. There are over 66,000 employers (excluding 1278 agricultural and forestry-related businesses); a quarter of all Austrians work in Vienna. Of the 741,000-strong workforce (including 65,000 immigrant workers), 3450 are engaged in the basic goods sector, 220,290 in industry and commerce and 517,160 in service industries. 71,336 are in the direct employ of the city.

Centre of the Austrian economy

For 200 years industry in Vienna has centred on the processing of imported and local raw materials. The sector with the greatest turnover is food and drink, followed by electrical industries, chemicals, mechanical engineering and steel construction, ironware and metal goods, as well as the clothing industry. Currently Viennese industry has a gross annual product valued at over 82 billion schillings.

Industrial tradition

◀ *The Vienna Philharmonic performing in the Musikvereinsgebäde*

Commerce and Industry

The Viennese themselves are also skilled craftsmen when it comes to the production of fashion accessories, lace, petit-point, luxury leather goods and gold and silverware.

Tourism

In 1989 6,900,000 hotel bookings were registered in Vienna, of which 5,595,000 were foreign visitors. The largest proportion of guests (22%) come from Germany, followed by Italian visitors and Austrians.

Prominent Figures in Viennese History

After studying at the Vienna Academy Amerling travelled across half Europe and it was Thomas Lawrence in London and Horace Vernet in Paris who had the decisive impact on his work. The son of a filigree-worker, Amerling became the portrait-painter most sought after by the nobility in his time.

Friedrich von Amerling (1803–87)

Amerling's most famous picture, "Emperor Francis I", hangs in the Marie-Antoinette Room at the Palace of Schönbrunn. Many of his other works are on show in the Historical Museum in the city of Vienna (see entry).

Beethoven, who was born in Bonn, was 22 years old when he came to Vienna where he remained until his death. His misanthropy was notorious. He stood aloof from society and never became a real Viennese although it was here that he found patrons and friends such as Archduke Rudolf and Princes Lichnowsky and Kinsky. Temperamentally never at his ease, he felt impelled frequently to move house. Of the many houses he lived in the most famous is No. 6 Probusgasse. Here he drafted in 1802, as his deafness worsened, his tragic "Heiligenstadt Testament".

Ludwig van Beethoven (1770–1827)

The majority of Beethoven's works were composed in Vienna, all nine symphonies receiving their first performances here. The Ninth (Choral) Symphony was first performed in 1824 at a great concert in the Kärntnertor Theatre.

Brahms settled in Vienna only in 1869 when the Gesellschaft der Musikfreunde invited him to become conductor of their concerts. Brahms's symphonies were originally offered to the public in Vienna, the Second and Third Symphonies receiving their first performances from the Vienna Philharmonic. His greatest success, however, came when his "German Requiem" was performed in the city. Brahms's work is considered to be the culmination of the Viennese Classical tradition in music. He is buried in the central cemetery.

Johannes Brahms (1833–97)

Ludwig von Beethoven

Johannes Brahms

Sigmund Freud

Prominent Figures in Viennese History

Charles VI (1685–1740)

More a Spaniard than an Austrian, the Emperor Charles introduced strict Spanish Court ceremonial to Vienna. In 1713 he promulgated the Pragmatic Sanction under which his daughter Maria Theresa was allowed to succeed him.

Buildings erected in Vienna during the reign of Charles VI include the Karlskirche, the Court Library, the Winter Riding School, the Palace of Schönbrunn, Prince Eugene's Belvedere (see entries), numerous palaces for the nobility and several new churches for the religious Orders.

Elisabeth I (1837–98)

Elisabeth, a Wittelsbach Princess, became Empress when she married Emperor Franz Joseph I in 1854. She also became Queen of Hungary in 1867. The marriage was basically intended to favour German interests in Austria. There were four children, Rudolf, the heir to the throne, and three daughters.

Elisabeth I, or Sissi as she was commonly known, was richly talented, artistic, sporting and capricious. Her aversion to strict Court etiquette drove her to spiritual loneliness. After her son, Crown Prince Rudolf, committed suicide in the hunting-lodge at Mayerling, she led a restless life, travelling constantly. In 1898 she was the victim of an attack by the anarchist Luccheni in Geneva.

The magnificent apartments of the Empress in the Hofburg and in the Palace of Schönbrunn are on show (see entry).

Johann Bernhard Fischer von Erlach (1656–1723)

J. B. Fischer von Erlach was born in Graz. After studies in Rome in the ambit of Bernini he became Imperial Court Building Superintendent. He is rated Austria's greatest Baroque architect.

He discovered a synthesis between Italian exuberance and Viennese charm, between French Early Classicism and Late Ancient style. His façades are not stiff or rigid; they are always dynamic.

Fischer von Erlach's masterpieces in Vienna are the Karlskirche, the Palace of Schönbrunn, the early parts of Prince Eugen's Winterpalais, Trautson and Neupauer Palaces, parts of the Schwarzenbergpalais and the Hofbibliothek which his son completed (see entry).

Francis II (I) (1768–1835)

With the Emperor Francis II the Holy Roman Empire of the German Nation came to an end. On account of the foundation of the Rhenish Confederation he abdicated as Roman Emperor in 1806 and from 1804 onwards he had assumed the title of Emperor Francis I of Austria.

The first Emperor of Austria participated in a variety of coalitions against France but gained no benefit. Finally Napoleon I moved into Schönbrunn, and in 1810 Francis I found himself obliged, for purely political reasons, to marry his daughter Marie Louise to the Corsican adventurer. The marriage took place in the Augustinerkirche (see entry); Napoleon did not himself attend the ceremony.

Franz Joseph I (1830–1916)

Franz Joseph I, Austria's penultimate Emperor and at the same time King of Hungary, came to the throne when 18 years old. He reigned for 68 years. In the course of his long reign there were military defeats in 1859 and 1866, the settlement of differences with Hungary, the formation of the Triple Alliance, the annexation of Bosnia and Herzogovina, and the outbreak of the First World War.

Vienna became bigger thanks to the Emperor's plans for enlarging the city, more beautiful when the Ringstrasse was laid out, and more important thanks to his support for the Arts. In his personal affairs the Emperor was dogged by misfortune; his brother Maximilian of Mexico was executed by a firing-squad in 1867, his son Crown Prince Rudolf committed suicide in 1889, Empress Elisabeth was stabbed to death in 1898, and Franz Ferdinand the heir to the throne was assassinated in 1914 in Sarajevo.

Sigmund Freud revolutionised the realm of psychology. At a time when the monarchy was collapsing and all was in tumult, he analysed human failure and dreams, developing a method based on response to suppressed traumatic experiences.
The father of psychoanalysis was a professor at the University of Vienna. Taking into account the significance of the unconscious he influenced our understanding of the human mind, of the relationship between mind and body and psychiatry.
Freud's apartment, 19 Berggasse, has become a museum (see Practical Information – Museums).

Sigmund Freud (1856–1939)

Franz Grillparzer, Austria's most important playwright, came from an old-established Viennese bourgeois family. He was a civil servant, rising to the rank of Hofrat, going into the "Herrenhaus" (Upper Chamber) in 1871. Although essentially he had his roots in early-nineteenth-century middle-class culture he tried to lead the way towards a new style distinct from Romanticism. He became the classic author in the theatres of Vienna. In 1816 he made his début with "Die Ahnfrau" (The Ancestress) at the Burgtheater. In 1888 the rebuilt theatre opened with his "Esther". In 1955 a performance of his "König Ottokars Glück und Ende" (King Ottokar's Prosperity and Demise) was given to mark the opening of the reconstructed theatre.

Franz Grillparzer (1791–1872)

Joseph Haydn, the son of a wheelwright, begun his career at the age of eight as a cathedral chorister in Vienna. He is considered the founder of the symphony and himself wrote more than one hundred works in the new style.
Even during his lifetime Haydn was recognised and famous. He served first as Musical Director to Prince Esterhazy, later scoring notable successes in Paris (Paris symphonies) and in London (London symphonies). He returned to Vienna in 1797. He

Joseph Haydn (1732–1809)

Joseph Haydn

Franz Grillparzer

Emperor Franz Joseph I

was a successful man who composed two more of his finest oratories in his own house 19 Haydngasse (see entry). "The Creation" was first performed in Vienna in 1798 to be followed by "The Seasons" in 1801.

Johann Lukas von
Hildebrandt (1668–1745)

Lukas von Hildebrandt was the second outstanding architect of the Viennese High Baroque period. He was born in Genoa, settling in Vienna a decade after Fischer von Erlach. Though they were on good terms, great rivalry developed between these two gifted men as they strove to win the favour of their patrons.

An outward sign of the interplay between these two great talents is evident in various buildings which, reflecting the changing taste of their patrons, are partially by one and partially by the other.

Hildebrandt's masterpieces are his palaces for Prince Eugene, above all the Belvedere (see entry).

Hugo von Hofmannsthal
(1874–1929)

Hugo von Hofmannsthal, whose Jewish forebears came from Bohemia and Milan, was a genuine product of cosmopolitan Austria. He became famous as an author, writing plays and libretti for Richard Strauss's operas.

His play "Der Schwierige" (The Bore) belongs to the repertoire of the Viennese theatre. His "Jedermann" (Everyman) is one of the great attractions of Salzburg.

Gustav Klimt (1862–1918)

Gustav Klimt belonged to that group of progressive artists who in 1897 broke away from the Künstlerhaus Verein and, as the "Secession", sought new developments.

As a painter Klimt is considered to be the main representative of the Viennese Jugendstil (Art Nouveau). He also had a major influence on the Wiener Werkstätte (Viennese Workshops). Several of his works of art are in the 19th and 20th c. Austrian Gallery in the Upper Belvedere (see Belvedere-Schlösser). His monumental "Beethoven Frieze" can be seen in the Secession building.

Franz Lehár (1870–1948)

Franz Lehár was the outstanding personality in the second great age of operetta after 1900. Lehár, who was born in Hungary, was active in all centres of the monarchy as a military bandmaster.

"The Merry Widow" received its first performance in Vienna in 1905. It was followed by "The Count of Luxemburg" (1909), "Gypsy Love" (1910), "Frasquita" (1922) and "Paganini" (1925). After his 25th work for the stage he decided to write for the theatre in Berlin. He returned to Vienna only for his last two operettas "The World is Beautiful" and "Giuditta".

Maria Theresa (1717–80)

Charles VI's eldest daughter was the first woman to succeed to the throne of the Holy Roman Empire of the German Nation. This woman "with the heart of a king" had to defend her country against France, Prussia, Saxony and Bavaria. Despite three wars which were energetically waged she lost Silesia to Frederick the Great, King of Prussia.

Maria Theresa, who married Francis Stephen of Lorraine, was a thoroughgoing Baroque personality. She had 16 children and with immense energy and a vibrant passion for reform she reorganised the "House of Austria" and filled its empty treasury.

Wolfgang Amadeus Mozart   *Johann Nestroy*   *Ferdinand Raimund*

Wolfgang Amadeus Mozart was born in Salzburg where he became the Archbishop's Musical Director in 1769. He came to Vienna in 1781 and it was here that he wrote his great operas: "Il Seraglio" (Die Entführung aus dem Serail) first performed in 1782, "Marriage of Figaro" in 1786, "Così fan tutte" in 1790 and "The Magic Flute" in 1791. Only "Don Giovanni" and "La clementia di Tito" received their premières in Prague.

Wolfgang Amadeus Mozart (1756–91)

Mozart, who was adulated as a child, met with disappointments and successes in Vienna. The disappointments were mainly of ä financial nature. Nine weeks after the first performance of "The Magic Flute" Mozart died; he was buried in an unmarked pauper's grave in St Marx's cemetery.

Johann Nestroy, a raffish student, opera-singer, comic improviser and theatre manager, became famous for his farces. He portrayed the lowest social classes brilliantly and fought against the social ills of the time. He was, in many respects, at the opposite end of the scale to Ferdinand Raimund whose imaginary dream world he brought back to reality. His greatest success in Vienna was "Lumpazivagabundus".

Johann Nestroy (1801–62)

Nikolaus Pacassi was Maria Theresa's Court Architect and her favourite. Overwhelmed with commissions he was the busiest architect of his age. Pacassi was responsible for completing the Palace of Schönbrunn, the reconstruction of the Theresianum and Hetzendorf Palace: he built the Gardekirche (see entry) and the Kärntnertor Theatre. Nearly all the major 18th c. public buildings in Vienna were reconstructed, enlarged or restored under his direction.

Nikolaus Pacassi (1716–90)

Ferdinand Raimund, whose real name was Jakob Raimann, found scope for his dramatic and poetic talents in the Josefstädter Theatre in Vienna. He took the old Viennese fairy-tale and magical play and gave it a poetic form, thus founding a genuine folk drama. After Raimund had been bitten by a dog suspected of rabies he shot himself in a fit of depression.

Ferdinand Raimund (1790–1836)

The repertoire of the Burgtheater today includes some of his plays: "Der Verschwender" (The Spendthrift), "Der Bauer als Millionär" (The Peasant as a Millionaire) and "Alpenkönig und Menschenfeind" (King of the Mountains and Misanthropist).

Prominent Figures in Viennese History

Eugene, Prince of Savoy
(1663–1736)

France refused to let Prince Eugene join the French Army because of his diminutive stature. So he first became an Abbé, entering Austria's service as a soldier only in 1683. He rose to the rank of Field-Marshal, becoming Commander-in-Chief in the war against Turkey in 1697, President of the Court Council of War in 1703 and Viceroy in the Austrian Netherlands in 1714. Among his triumphs are numbered victories over the Turks at Zenta, Peterwardein and Belgrade as well as successes in the War of the Spanish Succession. Prince Eugene was the Councillor of the Emperors Leopold I, Joseph I and Charles VI, and is considered to be the true creator of Austria's status as a Great Power. The Belvedere Palace provided a fitting surrounding for this great man (see entry).

Egon Schiele (1890–1918)

A protégé of Gustav Klimt, Egon Schiele, a pupil of the Academy, specialised in life studies and drawings. At first an adherent of the Jugendstil, he later developed an entirely personal style and took his place at the head of Viennese Expressionistic avant-garde.

In his short life Schiele produced some 2,000 drawings and water-colours. His most important works are to be found in the Austrian Gallery in the Upper Belvedere (see entry) and in the Museum of the 20th Century (see entry).

Franz Schubert (1797–1828)

Franz Schubert was born in Vienna. He was a composer who was able to express himself in a wide variety of musical forms. Beginning as an assistant to his father who was a schoolmaster, he became "the master of the 'Lieder'".

His life was short, but as well as suffering from poverty and anxiety he also enjoyed satisfying friendships, with authors such as Bauernfeld and Grillparzer and with the painter Moritz von Schwind. He wrote 600 "Lieder", 8 symphonies, 6 Masses, numerous pieces for piano and for chamber ensemble, overtures, operas, musical comedies and choruses.

The most impressive of his symphonies are "The Unfinished" and "The Great C Major". His song-cycles are in the repertoire of every major Lieder-singer.

Moritz von Schwind
(1804–71)

Moritz von Schwind, a fresco-painter and pupil of the Viennese Academy, worked for a few years in Vienna but was disappointed by his lack of success. So in 1847 he went to Munich where he taught in the Academy.

Returning in 1863 to Vienna for a few years he painted the fresco-cycles in the State Opera. This theatre was bombed and gutted by fire in 1945, but the originals of Schwind's scenes from famous operas can still be seen in the foyer and the Loggia. Other frescoes by Schwind are to be found in the dome of the Austrian Gallery in the Upper Belvedere (see Belvedere-Schlösser).

Johann Strauss (Father)
(1804–49)

As composer and conductor, Johann Strauss, together with his contemporary Josef Lanner, created the new form of the Viennese waltz in the second quarter of the 19th c. Strauss was first viola-player in Lanner's Quartet, formed his own dance band in 1825 and developed it into a large orchestra. He made concert tours to Germany, Paris and London. In 1835 he was appointed Musical Director of the Court.

The "Radetzky March" is probably his most popular composition.

Johann Strauss possessed exceptional charm, temperament and inventiveness. He was only 19 when, against his father's wish, he made his Viennese début with his own orchestra. Five years later he took over his father's famous orchestra and toured half Europe before going on to the USA.

Johann Strauss (Son)
(1825–99)

He was called the "Waltz King" because he made the Viennese waltz world-famous. It was only later in life that he turned to operetta. He scored his first major success with "Die Fledermaus" (The Bat) in 1874, followed by "The Gypsy Baron" in 1885 and "Wiener Blut" (Viennese Blood) in 1899.

Strauss composed his waltz "The Blue Danube" at 54 Praterstrasse. It is now the home of the Strauss Museum (see Practical Information – Museums).

The history of Viennese operetta begins with Franz von Suppé, who was Musical Director at three Viennese theatres. Suppé began by composing comic operas including "Die Schöne Galathee" (Beautiful Galathea). Then, under Jacques Offenbach's influence, he wrote "Fatinitza", the first of his operettas to be performed in Vienna, and "Boccaccio" came just a little later. These are among the finest examples of classical operetta.

Franz von Suppé (1819–95)

History of Vienna

5000 B.C.	First indications of human settlement.
2000 B.C.	Indo-Germanic settlements on the NW wooded slopes.
800 B.C.	Celts settle on what is now the site of the "Hoher Markt".
15 B.C.	The Celtic town of Pannonien is occupied by the Romans. "Vedunia" becomes the Roman "Vindobona".
2nd c. A.D.	Vindobona, a fortress with a garrison of 6,000 legionaries, expands, becoming a rectangular walled enclosure on the site of the present "Hoher Markt".
3rd c.	Vindobona is a city with a population of 20,000.
c. 400	The Celts destroy the Roman city.
8th c.	Bajouarii found, around present-day Vienna, their first small settlements. The names of these end in -ing; among them are Penzing, Ottakring, Grinzing.
799	Charlemagne founds the Carolingian province.
976–1246	Austria under Babenberg rule.
1030	Emperor Conrad II is besieged in Vienna by the Hungarians.
1042	Emperor Henry VI holds a Council at Vienna.
c. 1135	Babenbergs win suzerainty over Vienna.
1147	The Wienerische Kirche (Viennese Church) is erected on the square in front of St Stephen's Cathedral.
1156	Duke Henry II, "Jasomirgott", Duke of Ostarichi, transfers his residence from Regensburg to Vienna. The first palace, Am Hof, is built.
c. 1180–98	The city becomes larger, and the city wall is reconstructed.
c. 1190	Planning of the moat.
c. 1198–1204	The Teutonic Order of Military Knights is summoned to Vienna.
1190	Coins are minted in Vienna.
1200	Consecration of the Schottenkirche (Scots Church).
1220	The Ducal Court moves into a new palace on the site of the present-day Stallburg.
1221	Vienna is granted the status of a city with the right to hold a market.
1237	For the first time Vienna becomes an Imperial Free City, a distinction it forfeits in 1239.
1246	The Babenberg line becomes extinct.

Granting of the status of Imperial Free City.	1247
Rule of the Bohemian King Přemysl Ottokar II.	1251–76
Rudolf of Habsburg is elected King of Germany, taking the title of Rudolf I. He lays claim to Austria as a former Imperial part of the feudal empire. Přemysl Ottokar II refuses to do homage.	1273
Regency of King Rudolf I after the decisive defeat of Ottokar of Bohemia.	1278–82
Founding of the University of Vienna.	1365
Vienna's population grows to 40,000 in the course of this century.	15th c.
The city's privileges confirmed.	1412
Vienna becomes the seat of the Holy Roman Empire of the German Nation.	1438
The Hungarian King Matthias I Corvinus holds sway over Vienna for a short while.	1485–90
Emperor Maximilian I expels the Hungarians from Vienna. Vienna sides with the Reformation.	1493–1519
The double wedding between the children of Vladislav and the grandchildren of Maximilian constitutes the foundation of what will become the Danube monarchy.	1515
The failure of a popular uprising is followed by the Bloody Assizes of Wiener Neustadt.	1522
Execution of Caspar Tauber, the first martyr of the Wars of Religion.	1524
The Turkish Siege leads to the erection of a massive circle of permanent defences.	1532–1672
The Jesuits arrive in Vienna and spearhead the Counter-Reformation.	1551
Protestant services are forbidden: Vienna has become a Catholic city once again.	1577
The "monastery offensive": many monasteries and churches are built by Franciscans, Dominicans, Capuchins, Barnabites, Discalced Carmelites and Servites.	c. 1600–38
The Thirty Years' War brings the Bohemians and the Swedes to the gates of Vienna (1645).	1618–48
Vienna is attacked by plague. The dread pestilence claims 30,000 victims in a very short period.	1629
Grand Vizier Kara Mustafa with 200,000 men lays siege to the city which is defended by no more than 20,000 under the leadership of Count Starhemberg. Vienna is delivered from the overwhelming Turkish army by a relieving force under the Polish King Sobieski.	1683
Prince Eugene of Savoy, as Imperial Field-Marshal, gains victories over the Turks and French. This restores Austria to the	1683–1736

status of a Great Power, and its capital gains lustre as "Vienna gloriosa".

1740–80	When Maria Theresa comes to the throne in 1740 160,000 people are resident within its fortifications. The Empress lays the foundations of present-day culture and institutes the system of central government.
1744–49	The Palace of Schönbrunn is built.
1754	First population census: it reveals that Vienna has 175,000 inhabitants.
1780–90	Joseph II develops Vienna as a world city in accord with the concepts of Enlightened Absolutism, leading the capital into the Industrial Era.
1782	Pope Pius VI in Vienna.
1783	Reform of the city's government: appointment of a Chief Magistrate.
1800	Vienna has a population of 231,000.
1804	The French besiege Vienna.
1806	Under pressure from Napoleon, Francis II has to abdicate as Holy Roman Emperor. Henceforth he is simply Emperor of Austria.
1809	Napoleon takes up residence in the Palace of Schönbrunn. The siege of Vienna leads to the financial collapse of the State.
1814–15	The Congress of Vienna, renowned for its glittering festivities, debates under the presidency of Prince Metternich with a view to establishing a new order in Europe (the "Restoration") after Napoleon's defeat.
1830	Danube floods. Vienna's population has swollen to 318,000.
1831–32	Cholera epidemic.
1848	Revolution in March against Prince Metternich's régime. Though the Revolution is put down by Prince zu Windischgrätz it leads to Metternich's retirement and the abdication of Emperor Ferdinand I.
1848–1916	Franz Joseph I is Emperor of Austria.
1857	Plan of the Ringstrasse area (partially opened in 1865) and razing of the fortifications.
1872–73	Building of the New Town Hall.
1890	The suburbs are incorporated in the city (11–19 Districts).
1900	Brigittenau becomes the 20th District.
1918	Collapse of the Dual Monarchy and abdication of the last Austrian Emperor, Charles I. Vienna becomes the Federal capital. Formerly the seat of government of a State with a population of 50 millions made up of 12 nationalities it becomes overnight simply the capital of a minor country with a population of 6·6

million. This diminution in size leads to immense political problems within the State. Vienna is surrounded by a belt of hideous modern blocks of flats which were built to relieve the social problems thrown up by this so-called "second foundation era".

Vienna becomes an administrative region within the German Reich. The pan-Germanic interlude costs the lives of 200,000 Viennese inhabitants. Fifty-two air raids and 10 days of fighting in the city itself leave 21,000 houses destroyed and 86,000 dwellings uninhabitable. 120 bridges are blown up and 3,700 gas and water mains are smashed.   1938

The Red Army occupies the city.   1945

Austrian State Treaty. After 10 years of occupation the city, which had been divided up into zones administered by the victorious Allies, celebrates the freedom it gains thanks to the Treaty.   1955

Vienna becomes the seat of the Atomic Energy Authority.   1956

John F. Kennedy, President of the USA and Nikita Kruschev, Chairman of the Soviet Council of Ministers, meet here for the first time on 3 and 4 June 1961.   1961

Vienna becomes the seat of UNIDO.   1967

Construction of an Underground railway begins.   1969

Opening of UNO City.
President Carter of the USA meets Leonid Brezhnev, President of the Presidium of the Supreme Soviet of the USSR.   1979

In the parliamentary elections the SPÖ loses its absolute majority. The Federal Chancellor, Bruno Kreisky, resigns; the new Chancellor is Fred Sinowatz (SPÖ). Vienna celebrates the "Turkish Year" (1683–1983), the 300-year existence of the Viennese Coffee House. – U.N. Conference on human rights in Vienna. – Pope John Paul II in Vienna on the occasion of the Austrian Catholic Conference.   1983

The 30th anniversary of the signing of the Austrian State Treaty is marked by a meeting of the Foreign Ministers of the countries which concluded it.   1985

The conference centre "Austria Center Vienna" is opened in April, increasing the conference facilities in the capital by almost 20%.   1987

Death of the former Czarina Zita of Habsburg, aged 96, the last Empress of Austria and Queen of Hungary; she is buried in the Capuchin vault amid great public sympathy (1 April).
Opening of the new Underground line U6 (October).   1989

In connection with the centenary of the birth of the painter Egon Schiele, exhibitions of his work are held in Vienna.   1990

Vienna in Quotations

Fynes Moryson

Wien the metropolitan City of Austria, is a famous fort against the Turkes . . . It is dangerous to walke the streetes in the night, for the great number of disordered people, which are easily found upon any confines, especially where such an army lieth neere, as that of Hungary, governed by no strict discipline.

An Itinerary, 1617

Lady Mary Wortley Montagu

The streets are very close and so narrow one cannot observe the fine fronts of the Palaces, tho many of them very well deserve observations, being truly magnificent, all built of fine white stone and excessive high. The Town being so much too little for the number of the people that desire to live in it, the Builders seem to have projected to repair that misfortune by claping one Town on the top of another, most of the houses being of 5 and some of them of 6 storys. You may easily imagine that the streets being so narrow, the upper tooms are extream Dark, and what is an inconveniency much more intolerable in my Opinion, there is no house that has so few as 5 or 6 familys in it. The Apartments of the greatest Ladys and even of the Ministers of state are divided but by a Partition from that of a Tailor or a shoe-maker . . . Those that have houses of their own let out the rest of them to whoever will take 'em; thus the great stairs (which are all of stone) are as common and as dirty as the street. 'Tis true when you have once travelled through them, nothing can be more surprizingly magnificent than the Apartments. They are commonly a suitte of 8 or 10 large rooms, all inlaid, the doors and windows richly carved with Gilt, and the furniture such as is seldom seen in the Palaces of sovereign Princes in other Countrys: the Hangings of the finest Tapestry of Brussells, prodigious large looking glasses in silver frames, fine Japan Tables, the Beds, Chairs, Canopys and window Curtains of the richest Genoa Damask or Velvet, allmost covered with gold Lace or Embroidery – the whole mad Gay by Pictures and vast Jars of Japan china, and almost in every room large Lustres of rock chrystal . . . I must own I never saw a place so perfectly delightful as the Fauxbourgs of Vienna. It is very large and almost wholly compos'd of delicious Palaces.

Letter to Lady Mar. 8 September 1716

Hester Lynch Piozzi

The streets of Vienna are not pretty at all, God knows; so narrow, so ill built, so crowded, many wares placed upon the ground where there is a little opening, seems a strange awkward disposition of things for sale; and the people cutting wood in the streets makes one half wild when walking; it is hardly possible to pass another strange custom, borrowed from Italy I trust, of shutting up their shops in the middle of the day; it must tend, one would think, but little to the promotion of that commerce which the sovereign professes to encourage, and I see no excuse for it *here* which can be made from heat, gaiety, or devotion.

Observations . . . in the Course of a Journey, 1789

This is one of the most perplexing cities that I was ever in. It is extensive, irregular, crowded, dusty, dissipated, magnificent, and to me disagreeable. It has immense palaces, superb galleries of paintings, several theatres, public walks, and drives crowded with equipages. In short, everything bears the stamp of luxury and ostentation; for here is assembled and concentrated all the wealth, fashion and nobility of the Austrian empire, and everyone strives to eclipse his neighbour. The gentlemen all dress in the English fashion, and in walking the fashionable lounges you would imagine yourself surrounded by Bond Street dandies. The ladies dress in the Parisian mode, the equipages are in the English style though more gaudy; with all this, however, there is a mixture of foreign costumes, that gives a very motley look to the population in the streets. You meet here with Greeks, Turks, Polonaise, Jews, Sclavonians, Croats, Hungarians, Tyroleans, all in the dress of their several countries; and you hear all kinds of languages spoken around you . . . here the people think only of sensual gratifications.

Washington Irving

Letter to his sister, 10 November 1822

A clever thing said by Lord Dudley, on some Vienna lady remarking impudently to him, 'What wretchedly bad French you all speak in London!' 'It is true, Madame, (he answered), we have not enjoyed the advantage of having the French twice in our capital.'

Thomas Moore

Diary 1829

Vienna from A to Z

Suggestions for making the most of a short stay in Vienna may be found under the heading "Sightseeing Tours" in the Practical Information section at the end of this guide book.

Note

*Akademie der Bildenden Künste (museum)

C4

The Akademie der Bildenden Künste (The Academy of Fine Arts) is an institution of international importance for the training of painters, sculptors, graphic artists, stage-designers and architects. It also has a major print collection and impressive picture gallery.

Peter von Strudel, the founder of the Academy, started the first art school in his house called "Strudelhof" in 1692. He was inspired by Italian examples. In 1876 it transferred to new premises on the Schillerplatz; they were designed by Theophil Hansen in Italian Renaissance style. They were severely damaged in 1945, but have been restored.

Among former pupils of the Academy are such Viennese painters as Friedrich von Amerling, Ferdinand Georg Waldmüller, Leopold Kupelweiser, Moritz von Schwind, Egon Schiele, Albert Paris Gütersloh, Ernst Fuchs, Wolfgang Hutter, Rudolf Hausner and Anton Lehmden. Professors of the architecture faculty have left their mark on the appearance of the city; practically all the architects responsible for the buildings on the Ring were professors at the Academy, including Theophil Hansen, who also designed the Musikvereinsgebäude and the Parliament (see entries). In more recent years, Professors Friedensreich Hundertwasser (see Hundertwasser Haus) and Fritz Wotruba (1907–1975) (see Wotruba Kirche) have added their own creations.

Adolf Hitler applied for admission to the Academy in 1907, but he failed the entrance examination.

Location
1, Schillerplatz 3

Underground station
Karlsplatz (U1, U2, U4)

Bus
59A

Trams
1, 2, D, J, 62, 65

Print Room

Before going up to the Print Room on the mezzanine, visitors should pause on the ground floor and take a look at the Aula, a classical hall for ceremonies with an arcaded gallery all round. On its ceiling is a painting by Anselm Feuerbach, "The Fall of the Titans".

The Print Room, adjacent to the Library on the mezzanine, has a collection of 30,000 drawings and water-colours, 25,000 engravings and etchings, unique Gothic architectural drawings from the Clerk of the Works' office at St Stephen's Cathedral, more than 300 nature studies by Friedrich Gauermann and 415 water-colours of flowers by the miniature-painter Michael Daffinger.

Opening times
Mon. & Wed. 10 a.m.–noon;
Tues. & Thur. 2–6 p.m.;
Feb., Easter, & July–Oct., only by prior arrangement.

Admission free

◀ *Plague Pillar in the Graben*

Akademie der Bildenden Künste

Picture Gallery

Opening times
Tues., Thur., Fri. 10 a.m.–
2 p.m., Wed. 10 a.m.–
1 p.m. & 3–6 p.m., Sat.,
Sun. 9 a.m.–1 p.m.

The Picture Gallery (west wing of the first floor) was originally intended as a "teaching aid" in order to train students in observation and feeling for style. However, the Academy was not only a school of art but also an institution and thus during the 18th c. the collection was increased by "accepted works". These were pictures which every student had to submit when applying to be a member of the Academy. In 1822 when the stock of pictures was increased by the acquisition of the collection of the late President of the Academy, Anton Graf Lamberg-Sprinzenstein, the first step towards the foundation of a gallery of international importance had finally been taken. Even today, when the collection is being increased by purchase and by gifts, the picture gallery of the Academy is characterised by the fact that at least one work of almost all the artists associated with it is included.

Rooms 1, 2 and 3 are used for administrative purposes.

Room 4: 15th and 16th c.; Dutch and German artists.
Examples of 15th c. painting include a panel by Simone da Bologna depicting the Holy Trinity and Saints, as decoration for a late 14th c. altarpiece, and the "Miracle of St Nicholas" (c. 1455) by Giovanni di Paolo, probably also from an altar. Dierck Bouts's "Coronation of the Virgin" represents early Dutch art of the 15th c. One of the most important works in the collection is a triptych by Hieronymus Bosch (after 1504) of the "Last Judgment between Heaven and Hell". An important early work by Hans Baldung-Grien is "The Holy Family in the Open Air" (c. 1512). "The Holy Family" and "Lucretia" (1532) are major works by Lucas Cranach the Elder.

Room 5: 16th c. and Baroque; Italian and Spanish artists.
The classical ideal of Italian Renaissance painting is captured in the "Madonna and Child with Angels" (c. 1480) from the workshop of Botticelli. Pictures of the Venetian School include the "Reclining Venus" from the workshop of Giorgione and one of Titian's last works "Tarquin and Lucretia" (c. 1575). "The Deliverance of Peter" (c. 1650) by Mattia Preti and "Still Life" (1675) by Giuseppe Antonio Recco represent the Italian Baroque; works of the Spanish Baroque include sketches by Carreno de Mirandas for an altarpiece of the First Mass of St John (c. 1666) and Murillo's "Boys Playing Dice".

Room 6: 17th c.; Flemish artists.
Works by Peter Paul Rubens, with the magnificent sketches for his ceiling-painting (subsequently destroyed by fire) for the Jesuit Church in Antwerp. Van Dyck, who worked as an independent artist in Rubens' studio, is represented by a self-portrait and the sketch of an "Assumption of the Virgin". "Paul and Barnabas in Lystra" (1645) is by Jacob Jordaens, also associated with Rubens.

Rooms 7–9: 17th c.; Dutch artists.
Works by David Vinckboons, Pieter Codde, Dirck Hals, Adriaen van Ostade, Cornelis Bega and Cornelis Saftleben typify Dutch genre painting. Architectural paintings are by Hendrick C. van

Vliet and Jan van der Heyden. Portraits include Pieter de Hooch's "Dutch Family" (c. 1660) and Rembrandt's "Young Woman in an Easy Chair" (1632). Landscapes include works by Jan van Goyen, Jacob van Ruisdael and Cornelis Vroom and some Italianised landscapes; the still-life works are by Jan Weenix and Jan Davidsz de Heem.

Room 10: 18th c.
Works by Giovanni Battista Tiepolo, Alessandro Magnasco and Gianpaolo Pannini. The paintings of Francesco Guardi: eight Venetian "Vedutas" and two altarpieces, are among the greatest works of art in the Academy's collection. The "Artist's Studio" (c. 1747) is a major work of Pierre Gubleyras. Austrian painting includes a portrait of the Empress Maria Theresa (1759) by Martin Van Meytens, a director of the Academy, and works by Daniel Gran, Franz Anton Maulbertsch and Johann Martin Schmidt (Kremser Schmidt), the last of the great Baroque painters.

Room 11: 19th and 20th c.; Austrian artists.
Works by Friedrich Heinrich Füger, Johann Peter Krafft, Hubert Maurer and Josef Abel represent Austrian Classicism. Biedermeier painting is represented by Ferdinand Georg Waldmüller, Friedrich von Amerling and Josef Danhauser, whose painting "The Pupils' Room" shows a classroom in the former academy building.

Room 12: Student collection and temporary exhibitions.
Works by Herbert Boeckl, Fritz Wotruba, A. P. Gütersloh, Sergius Pauser, Franz Elsner, Gustav Hessing and by previous professors of the Academy, including Friedensreich Hundertwasser, Anto Lehmden, Josef Mikl and Arnulf Rainer.

** **Albertina** (art gallery)   C4

The Albertina possesses 45,000 drawings and water-colours, about 1½ million printed sheets of graphic material covering a period of half a millennium and 35,000 books – it is the world's most comprehensive collection of graphic material.
The collection was founded in 1768 by Maria Theresa's son-in-law, Duke Albert of Saxony-Tescha. Since 1795 it has been housed in the former Taroucca Palace. Between 1801 and 1804 the building was altered by Louis von Montoyer.
The Albertina as we know it today resulted from the amalgamation, after the First World War, of the collections of Duke Albert and the print room of the Imperial Library. The holdings are so rich and vast that normal exhibition is not possible. Instead only a portion of the collection can be shown at one time, and the displays are changed throughout the year. It is, however, between March and October that the choicest examples are on show:
Dürer: "The Hare", "Madonna with all the Animals", "Praying Hands", and "The Large Piece of Turf". Raphael: "Madonna with the pomegranate". Rubens: The portraits of his family.
*For conservation reasons some parts of the collection are accessible only to researchers. There is, however, no catalogue.

The drawings are classified under national schools.

Location
1, Augustinerstrasse 1

Underground station
Karlsplatz (U1, U2, U4)

Trams
1, 2, D, J (Ring), 62, 65, L

Opening times
Mon., Tues., Thur.
10 a.m.–4 p.m., Wed.
10 a.m.–6 p.m., Fri.
10 a.m.–2 p.m., Sat. & Sun.
10 a.m.–1 p.m.
Closed on Sun July–Aug.

A memorial against war and Fascism by the Austrian artist Alfred Hrdlicka was erected on the Albertina platz in 1988.

Drawings

Albertina

Albertina: Figures in the entrance hall

German School after the 15th c. – 145 drawings by Dürer, who is more fully represented in the Albertina than anywhere else, works by Holbein the Elder, Baldung Grien, Cranach the Elder, Altdorfer, Kölderer, Menzel, Spitzweg, Feuerbach, Liebermann, Nolde and Kollwitz.

Austrian School, from the 18th c. onwards, including von Rottmayr, Troger, Kremser-Schmidt, Schwind, Daffinger, Amerling, Alt, Gauermann, Makart, Klimt, Schiele and Kubin.

Italian School, from the Early Renaissance onwards, including Pisanello, Fra Angelico, Lippi, Mantegna, Leonardo, Titian, 43 drawings by Raphael, Michelangelo, Tintoretto, Veronese, Guardi, Canaletto and Tiepolo.

Flemish School, from the 15th c. onwards, including drawings by Van Leyden, Brueghel the Elder, de Momper, Van Dyck and a collection of sketches by Rubens.

Dutch School, city schools from the 17th c. onwards, including drawings by Both, Asselijn, Van Goyen, Ruysdael, De Hooch and 70 drawings from all Rembrandt's creative periods.

French School, from the 16th c. onwards, including examples of work by Clouet, Bellange, and Callot, choice drawings by Poussin and Lorrain, works by Watteau, Liotard and Fragonard, and by Picasso, Matisse and Chagall.

English School, from 1650 onwards, with drawings by Hogarth, Reynolds, Gainsborough and Romney.

The Special Collections, available only to experts, include architectural drawings (8,000 sheets), miniatures, views of Austria and Vienna, historic prints, illustrated books, Japanese woodcuts and posters and collections of sketch books (including those belonging to Waldmüller, Stifter, Gauermann, Schwind and Schiele).

The Print Collection (woodcuts, copperplate engravings, etchings, screen-prints, lithographs and metal cuts) includes the world's largest collection of 15th c. single-sheet xylographs, Dürer's woodcuts and copper engravings, Rembrandt's etchings, original work by Menzel, woodcuts by Munch, first impressions by Goya and works by Picasso and Chagall. The majority of the collection consists of original graphics. Special collections, which may only be viewed by researchers, include historical papers and collections of playing cards, caricatures, illustrated books and portfolios, views, posters and original printing plates from the time of Dürer.

Print Collection

The Albertina also houses the Austrian Film Museum (film shows, but no exhibitions). Programmes can be found in the daily papers and weekly brochure of events (see Practical Information – Events).

Film Museum

Performances
Oct.–May, Mon.–Fri., 6 and 8 p.m.

Albrechtsrampe   C4

The ramp is now just the remains of the old, once-mighty Augustinian priory, on the site of some former city fortifications. The bastion was destroyed in 1858, and the ramp that remained was severely damaged by bombing in 1945. It was converted into open-air steps in 1952. The ramp is dominated by an equestrian statue (1899) by Kaspar von Zumbusch of the Field-Marshal Archduke Albrecht (1817–95), the victor of the battle of Custozza (1866).

Location
1, Albertinaplatz

Underground station
Karlsplatz (U1, U2, U4)

Trams
1, 2, D, J (Ring)

By the "ground floor" of what remains of the ramp stands the Danubius Fountain (also called the "Albrecht Fountain"). It, too, has survived only in a fragmentary state. The fountain was a gift to the city of Vienna from Franz Joseph I, and when it was unveiled in 1869, the allegorical figures of Danubius and Vindobona in the middle were surrounded by 10 more figures in alcoves. All of white Carrara marble, they personified the Rivers Theiss, Raab, Enns, Traun, Inn, Save, March, Salzach, Mur and Drau.
Most of the figures have been returned to their alcoves.

Danubius Fountain

Altes Rathaus (Old Town Hall; Museum of Austrian Resistance)   B4

The Old Town Hall, opposite the Böhmische Hofkanzlei (see entry), houses the archive of the Austrian Resistance Movement. In the Resistance Museum are exhibits illustrating the active revolt against Austrian Fascism (1934–38) and of the resistance and persecution under the National Socialists in Austria (1938–45). A memorial can be found at No. 6 Salztorgasse five minutes away.
Although the decision to set up the Museum of Austrian Resistance in the Old Town Hall had little to do with the history of the

Location
1, Wipplingerstrasse 8
Staircase 3

Underground stations
Stephansplatz, Schwedenplatz (U1, U4)

Bus
1A, 2A, 3A

39

Amalienburg

Opening times
Mon., Wed., Thur. 8 a.m.–
5 p.m. (Memorial room Mon.,
Wed., Thur. 9 a.m.–
5 p.m.)

building, there are nevertheless parallels. The Old Town Hall was originally the house of a rebel, Otto Heimo. After Emperor Albrecht I was murdered in 1309 a number of influential Viennese citizens including Heimo resolved to resist the new Habsburg rulers. However the plot was discovered, the conspirators punished and their property confiscated. Duke Frederick the Fair gave Heimo's house to the municipality in 1316.

The building remained the town hall until 1885 and during this time was on several occasions altered, enlarged and partly rebuilt. It received its Baroque façade about 1700 and the portals with the sculptures of "Fides publica" and "Pietas" by Johann Martin Fischer are also 18th c. The Andromeda Fountain with a lead relief of Perseus and Andromeda in the courtyard is one of Raphael Donner's last works, dating from 1740 to 1741.

Amalienburg

See Hofburg

Am Hof   B4

Location
1st District

Underground stations
Stephansplatz (U1),
Schottentor (U2)

Buses
1A, 2A, 3A

Trams
1, 2, D, T

Am Hof is the largest square in the city centre. Since the transfer of the Saturday Flea Market to the Naschmarkt (see entry) it has lost much of its colour and bustle, but is of great historical significance.

The Romans set up camp on this site (remains of buildings may be seen at Am Hof 9, open: Sat., Sun. and public holidays 11 a.m.–1 p.m.). The Babenbergs judged this the right place to build their first palace (1135–50), and Walther von der Vogelweide sang the glories of the glittering festivities there: "That is the wondrous court at Vienna" (plaque on wall of Länderbank 2). Later the Ducal Court was replaced by the Mint of the ruling princes.

In 1667 the Corinthian column with the bronze figure of the Virgin treading the serpent underfoot was erected in the middle of the square. The four putti symbolise the Virgin's protection against war, plague, hunger and heresy.

Church of the Nine Choirs of Angels

The square is dominated by the remarkable Early Baroque W façade of the former Jesuit church dedicated to the Nine Choirs of Angels. In 1782 Pius IV pronounced his blessing "Urbi et Orbi" from the balcony above the entrance. It was from the same balcony that Emperor Francis II proclaimed the dissolution of the Holy Roman Empire of the German Nation in 1806. The Gothic rectangular church was built in the 14th c., reconstructed in the Baroque style in the 17th c. and provided, probably by Carlo Carlone, with its façade which dominated the square in 1662. Inside, the organ-casing is notable, as are the Maulbertsch frescoes (second side-chapel on the left), the Lady Chapel altar, and the ceiling-paintings by Andrea Pozzo in the Ignatius Chapel.

Fire Service Museum

The former Burghers' Armoury (Am Hof 10), built in the 16th c., later enlarged and extensively rebuilt in 1731–32, now houses the headquarters of the Vienna Fire Brigade and the Fire Ser-

Am Hof: The "Nine Choirs of Angels" church

vice Museum. (Open: Sun. and public holidays 9 a.m.–noon, admission free.) The development of the Vienna Fire Brigade is brought to life with a display of fire engines, fire-fighting equipment, uniforms, figures, documents and paintings.

Among the more noteworthy houses around Am Hof is the Märkleinische House at No. 7, named after its original owner who commissioned it to be built from 1727–30 to a design by Lucas von Hildebrandt. The Urbanihaus (No. 12) is a Baroque building housing the Urbanikeller, a well-known Viennese wine tavern.

Noteworthy buildings

The Palais Collalto (No. 13) was built in 1680; the façade towards Am Hof was redesigned in 1715 and 1725, the façade on the Schulhof re-fashioned in a classical style in 1804. A tablet on this building commemorates the fact that Mozart made his first public appearance here in 1762.

Annakirche   C4

The Church of St Anne in Annagasse was built in the 15th c. in the Gothic style. It was founded by Elisabeth Wartenauer, the wife of a burgher of Vienna. In the 17th c. the original church was rebuilt, and in 1715 it was refurbished in the Baroque style. It belonged successively to the Poor Clares and to the Jesuits, before being handed over in 1897 to the Oblates of St Francis of Assisi.

Location
1, Annagasse 3b

Underground station
Stephansplatz (U1)

The church has a ceiling-painting and a picture above the High Altar, both by Daniel Gran. The 1505 wood-carving of Anne, above the first altar on the left, is ascribed to the Nuremberg Master, Veit Stoss.

Devotion to St Anne has deep roots in Vienna. The church has in its keeping as a precious relic the hand of the Saint in a rich Baroque setting.

Annagasse

Annagasse, which turns off right from Kärntnerstrasse (see entry), is a narrow thoroughfare which is a reminder of what Vienna looked like in the 18th c. The lane existed as early as the 14th c., when it was called "Pippingerstrasse", and there was a chapel already on the site now occupied by the Annakirche.

There are some fine old houses here: the 17th c. Esterhazy Palace (No. 2), Kremsmünsterhof (No. 4), Herzogenburgerhof (No. 6), Maibergerhof (No. 7), Deybel or Täuberlhof, which was a school for artists and engravers before the Academy of Fine Arts (see entry) was opened, Zum Blauen Karpfen (Blue Carp House, No. 14), now a hotel, and Zum Römischen Kaiser (the Roman Emperor, No. 16).

Augarten   A5

Location
2, Obere
Augartenstrasse 1–3

Bus
5A

Trams
31, 32, N

The Augarten is a 140 acre (52ha) park between the Danube Canal and the Danube. In it still stand the ruins of the Alte Favorita, the Augarten Palace and Josephsstöckl.

The park was laid out as an Imperial pleasure garden in the 17th c., and reconstructed in 1712 to plans by Jean Trehet. In 1775, at the desire of Emperor Joseph II, it was opened to the people of Vienna "as a place dedicated to the enjoyment of all men".

The Alte Favorita, Leopold I's garden palace, was set on fire by the Turks in 1683. Joseph I had the Garden Pavilion erected on part of the ruins, and it was here that from 1782 the famous musical matinées took place, under the direction first of Mozart, then also of Beethoven.

The Augarten porcelain manufactory is at present housed in the former Garden Pavilion. It was founded in 1718 and has belonged to the city since 1924. Its traditional dinner-services, bearing the names Pacquier, Liechtenstein, Prince Eugene and Maria Theresa are known the world over. The most popular articles made for export are porcelain Lippizaner horses in the various haute école positions and Viennese types based on original models dating back to the era of Maria Theresa.

Augartenpalais and Josephsstöckl

Since 1948 the Augarten Palace has been the boarding-school for the Vienna Boys' Choir.

A Privy Councillor had the proud mansion built towards the end of the 17th c., to plans produced by Johann Bernhard Fischer von Erlach. In 1780 it was purchased by Emperor Joseph II who, however, personally preferred to reside in the modest Kaiser-Joseph-Stöckl. The latter was built for him in 1781 by Isidor Carnevale. Nowadays this building houses the "transitional" members of the Vienna Boys' Choir, that is to say choristers who have to move on when their voices have broken.

In 1782 Pope Pius VI, stayed in Josephsstöckl.

*Augustinerkirche   C4

The Church of the Augustinians is externally without decoration, but it was once the scene of great weddings. In 1810 the
Archduchess Marie Louise was married here to Napoleon I,
who was so short of time that he had to be represented by a
proxy. In 1854 Emperor Franz Joseph wedded Elisabeth (Sissi)
of Bavaria here, and in 1881 the legendary and unfortunate
Crown Prince Rudolf married Stefanie of Belgium.
The church was built for the Augustinian Canons. Between
1330 and 1339 Dietrich Ladtner von Pirn constructed an aisle-
less oblong church in Gothic style. The aisle-less choir was
added about 1400, and the tower was built on in 1652. The
Chapel of St George dates from 1351, and the Loretto Chapel
from 1724. The church was refurbished in Baroque style later,
but all this was swept away in 1785 when J. F. Hetendorf von
Hohenberg carried out a restoration, bringing back the Gothic
style.

Walking round the church in a clockwise direction visitors will
note – in addition to the features mentioned below – the icon to
the left of the entrance, the chancel and the High Altar.

The Loretto Chapel was once adorned with silver, but that had
to be melted down during the Napoleonic Wars. The beautiful
wrought-iron railing dates from the 18th c.

Location
1, Augustinerstr. 3

Underground station
Stephansplatz (U1)

Bus
1A, 2A, 3A

Trams
1, 2, D, T (Ring)

Tour

Loretto Chapel

The Augustinerkirche: its unadorned exterior, its Gothic interior

Heart Vault	In the Heart Vault the hearts of the Habsburgs are contained in small silver urns. The earliest is the heart of Matthias who died in 1619. Here rest the hearts of 9 emperors, 8 empresses, 1 king, 1 queen, 14 archdukes, 14 archduchesses and 2 dukes.
Chapel of St George	The Chapel of St George was built in the 14th c. by Duke Otto the Merry as a meeting-place for the knightly Order of St George. Later it was converted into a mortuary chapel, and the victor of Kolin, the Imperial Count Daun, lies buried here, as does Maria Theresa's Physician, Gerard van Swieten. The marble tomb of Leopold II (1799) is empty. The Emperor lies in the Imperial Vault in the Kapuzinerkirche (see entry).
Christinendenkmal	The Christinendenkmal is a monument opposite the entrance. It is considered to be the most important piece of sculpture in the church. Antonio Canova's famous marble tomb for the Duchess of Saxony-Tescha, the daughter of Maria Theresa, dates from 1801 to 1805. Beneath the apex of the flat pyramid up against the surface of the wall, the spirit of blessedness bears the Archduchess's medallion. Her body, however, lies in the Imperial Vault in the Kapuzinerkirche (see entry).
Organ	The organ, like the pews, comes from the Schwarzspanier-kirche (The Black Spaniard Church) which was destroyed in a storm. This organ was used at the first performance of Bruckner's Mass in F minor. The organ was restored between 1974 and 1976.

Bäckerstrasse   B5

Location 1, Off Lueck **Underground** Stephansplatz (U1)	In this street where bakers once lived and worked visitors will find old mansions and ancient doorways with coats of arms and signs on houses that have been handed down over the ages.
Buses 1A, 2A	Among the more notable houses are: No. 7 with a courtyard with Renaissance arcading and, on the first floor, a small collection of fine metalwork which the Viennese painter F. Amerling brought together. No. 8 is the former Seilern Palace which was built in 1722 in J. L. von Hildebrandt's style. No. 12 dates from the 15th and 16th c. and has a remarkable Renaissance oriel on its first floor. Once upon a time the house was called "Wo die Kuh am Brett spielt" (Where the cow plays chequers) and was painted all over. No. 14 was built in 1558, and altered in 1700. The Baroque residence at No. 16 was built in 1712 and formerly housed a tavern called the "Schmauswaberl", a much-loved eating-place for the students of the nearby university as the food was left over from the court kitchens and very cheap.

---

*Baden (near Vienna) (spa)

Baden Railway from Oper	Baden is a spa at the foot of the Valley of the Helenen. Its sulphur springs were known to the Romans as Aquae Pannonicae. Especially in the early 19th c. it was a popular resort

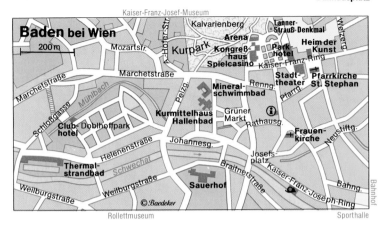

Kaiser-Franz-Josef-Museum

Rollettmuseum — Sporthalle

for Viennese society. Here Mozart wrote his "Ave Verum" for the choirmaster of the parish church, and Beethoven spent 15 summers here at 10 Rathausgasse, working on his Ninth Symphony which he completed in 1823–24. Schubert, Liszt, Raimund, Stifter, Alt, Daffinger, Waldmüller and Schwind were frequent visitors to Baden. Lanner, Ziehrer and Strauss gave concerts in the Spa Gardens, and it was near here that Grillparzer composed "Das Goldene Vliess" (The Golden Fleece). Today people go to Baden to bathe in the large hot baths in Helenenstrasse, to attend the open-air performances in the Summer Arena in the Spa Park and to gamble in the Casino. Interesting sights are a Trinity Column (1714) in the main square, the Town Hall (1815) and the "Imperial House" (1792), where the Emperor resided each summer from 1803 to 1834.

Regional Railway
from Südbahnhof (R10)

Bus
from Westbahnhof
Bus Station

Distance
12½ miles (20 km) S

Ballhausplatz   B4

For more than 250 years Austrian history was made and suffered at Ballhausplatz; today the seat of the Austrian Government and of its Ministry of Foreign Affairs is at Ballhausplatz 2. Austria's foreign policies were not resolved in the ministry but at Ballhausplatz according to Robert Musil in his novel "The Man Without Qualities".

Location
1st District

Underground station
Volkstheater (U2)

Bus 2A

Trams 1, 2, D, J

Bundeskanzleramt (Office of the Federal Chancellor)

The Office of the Federal Chancellor, formerly the Privy Court Chancellery, was erected here between 1717 and 1719 to plans by Lucas von Hildebrandt. It was enlarged by Nikolaus Pacassi in 1766 and made even bigger when the State Archive Building was added in 1902. After damage in the war, restoration was completed in 1950.
In 1814 and 1815 the Congress of Vienna met here for its deliberations after Napoleon's downfall. It was here, too, that the ultimatum to Serbia which led to the outbreak of the First

The Office of the Federal Chancellor in the Ballhausplatz

World War was conceived, and here, also, that Federal Chancellor Dollfuss was murdered in his office in 1934. In 1938 Federal Chancellor von Schuschnigg concluded his famous farewell address with the words: "May God protect Austria". In 1940 Baldur von Schirach, Hitler's Governor in the Vienna District, moved into Ballhausplatz. The Federal Government and Ministry of Foreign Affairs have been housed here once more since 1945.

Basiliskenhaus   B5

Location
1, Schönlaterngasse 7

Underground station
Stephansplatz (U1)

The Basiliskenhaus, formerly also called the "House with the Red Cross", is known to have existed as early as 1212. It is one of the oldest houses in Vienna. It was damaged by bombing in 1944, and has been restored in 16th c. style.

There is a sandstone figure of a basilisk in a niche in the second storey of the façade. Legend has it that a monster, which had been disgorged by a hen, lived here in a fountain; its poison is supposed to have brought disease and death to many people until a brave man held a mirror up to the monster, which was so shocked at its appearance that it burst!

Beethoven-Denkmal (Monument)   C5

Location
1, Beethovenplatz

The Beethoven Monument is the work of the Westphalian sculptor Kaspar von Zumbusch and dates from 1880. It stands in a little square in front of the Akademisches Gymnasium, founded by the Jesuits in 1552, and which is one of the oldest and best humanistic schools in Vienna; former pupils include Arthur Schnitzler and Peter Altenberg.

Underground station
Stadtpark (U4)

At the feet of the seated figure of the composer may be seen Prometheus in chains with the eagle pecking at his flesh. On the right stands Victory proffering a triumphal wreath, and all round are nine putti, representing Beethoven's nine symphonies. Formerly Beethoven's statue faced away from the River Wien, but since the little river was covered over it has faced the water.

Belvedere-Schlösser (palaces)

C5

There are two Baroque palaces built for Prince Eugene, the Unteres (Lower) Belvedere and the Oberes (Upper) Belvedere. They now house the three museums of the Austrian Gallery.

Location
Unteres Belvedere:
3, Rennweg 6
Oberes Belvedere:
3, Prinz-Eugen-Str. 27

With the Château of Versailles in mind, Prince Eugene, who defeated the Turks, had a summer residence built on the abandoned slope of the Glacis by the Rennweg. Work began in 1700, and Lucas von Hildebrandt devoted 10 years to what was to be his masterpiece. In 1716 the Unteres Belvedere, where Prince Eugene actually lived, was completed. It was only in 1724 that the Oberes Belvedere with its reception-rooms was finished. It stands on higher ground. Montesquieu remarked, in connection with this building, that it was pleasant to be in a country where the lower orders were better housed than their master. The two palaces are linked by a magnificent garden. Dominique Girard, a landscape-gardener from Paris, designed them in accord with Hildebrandt's over-all concept of a terraced park laid out along an axis with cascades and symmetrical flights of stairs and with hedges and paths forming the sides. The sculptures adorning the pools lead symbolically up from the bottom. At the foot we see the Underworld with Pluto and Proserpina in the bosquets, then Neptune and Thetis, the deities of water, in the area where the cascades play, together with Apollo and Hercules. From the terrace in front of the Oberes Belvedere there is a wonderful view down over the garden which drops away, and out over the towers of Vienna and heights of the Vienna Woods. S of the Oberes Belvedere is an Alpine Garden.

Underground stations
Karlsplatz (U1, U2, U4)
Taubstummengasse (U1)

Tram
D, 71

Opening times
for all museums Tues.–Sun.
10 a.m.–4 p.m.
Son et Lumière in summer
daily 9.30 p.m.

After the death of the Prince who remained a bachelor all his life, his heiress – "frightful Victoria", as the Viennese called her – sold off the entire property without a second thought. The Imperial Court acquired the buildings and the gardens in 1752. Franz Ferdinand, the heir to the throne, lived in the Belvedere between 1894 and 1914, and he was living here at the time of his tragic visit to Sarajevo.

Alpine Garden

Opening times
Daily 9 a.m.–4.30 or
6 p.m.

It was in the Marble Chamber of the Oberes Belvedere that, on 15 May 1955, the Foreign Ministers of France, Great Britain, the Soviet Union, the United States and Austria signed the Austrian State Treaty which restored Austria's independence.

A tablet in the curator's wing of the Upper Belvedere commemorates the death here of Anton Bruckner in 1896. The Emperor had placed the quarters at the disposal of the Court Organist and Composer as a mark of his respect.

The history of the palace is recounted in a Son et Lumière open-air presentation in the park in front of the Oberes Belvedere on summer evenings.

From the Upper Belvedere there is access to the Alpine Garden (see Botanical Gardens).

Museum mittelalterlicher österreichischer Kunst

Location
Unteres Belvedere (entry
through the Österreichisches
Barockmuseum)

The Museum of Austrian Art from the Middle Ages is housed in the Orangery of the Unteres Belvedere. The collection includes masterpieces of sculpture and panel-painting from the end of the 12th c. to the early 16th c., though there is some emphasis on 15th c. works. The oldest exhibit is the Romanesque Stammerberg Crucifix. It dates from the end of the 12th c. and is thought to be the oldest surviving example of Tyrolean wood-carving.

The collections of the museum are divided into five sections.

Section 1: Works by the "masters of the altar-pieces", including four stone figures by the Salzburg Master of Grosslobming (*c.* 1415–20) and a Madonna and Child on a throne (end of the 12th c. and the second oldest exhibit in the museum).

Section 2: The outstanding exhibits are the Crucifixion scenes, the so-called "Wiltener Crucifixion" and the centre panel of Conrad Laib's 1449 Crucifixion reredos.

Section 3: Here may be seen five pictures by the Tyrolean painter and carver Michael Pacher and seven pictures by Rueland Frueauf the Elder. Among the works by Pacher owned by the museum are parts of the High Altar from the Franciscans' Church in Salzburg.

Section 4: Important exhibits include a pair of pictures: "Pietá" and "The Adoration of the Kings"; they once formed part of the

Lower Belvedere Austrian Baroque Museum

1 Ticket Office
2 Portraits
3 Rottmayr, Altomonte
4 Gran, Troger; Giuliani
5 Kremser-Schmidt
6 Disciples of Troger and Maulbertsch
7 Marble Cabinet
8 Marble Hall: Figures by Donner
9 Baroque Sculpture

Ambraserhof

Entrance

10 Dormer Gallery
11 Maulbertsch Gallery
12 Funerary reliefs
13 Maria-Theresa Gallery
14 Grotesques
15 Maulbertsch Cabinet
16 Marble Gallery
17 Hall of Mirrors (Gold Cabinet)
18 Early Classicism

original reredos in four sections of the Schottenkirche in Vienna and date from 1469.

Section 5: As well as Marx Reichlich's pictures of the Life of the Virgin and parts of the Waldauf reredos (from near Hall), the pictures by Urban Görtschacher, including an "Ecce Homo" of 1508, are especially noteworthy.

Österreichisches Barockmuseum

The Austrian Baroque Museum has been housed since 1923 in Prince Eugene's residence, the Unteres Belvedere. It contains a collection of paintings and sculptures from the great age of the Baroque style in Austria executed between 1683 and 1780. The museum was re-opened in 1953 after the Second World War and rebuilt in 1974.

Location
Unteres Belvedere

The most important rooms in the museum are:
The Rottmayr Room (Room 3): Johann Michel Rottmayr painted figures like those of Rubens in bright, light colours. On show are two of his early works, "The Praising of the Name of Jesus" and "The Sacrifice of Iphigeneia". The picture "Susannah and the Elders" in the same room is by Martin Altomonte.

Kremser-Schmidt Collection (Room 5): Martin Johann Schmidt devoted himself almost exclusively to religious painting, but there are two of his secular paintings here. "Venus in Vulcan's Forge" and "The Judgment of Midas" were the two works he painted when he sought admission to the Viennese Academy.

Marble Hall (Room 8): This two-storey-high chamber with its extremely rich stucco decoration and its painted ceiling by M. Altomonte which depicts the Triumph of Prince Eugene, the conqueror of the Turks, is the finest room in the Unteres Belvedere. In the middle stand the original figures made by George Raphael Donner for the Providentia Fountain in the Neuer Markt (see entry).

Donner Gallery (Room 10): In what used to be Prince Eugene's bedroom, with a painted ceiling by M. Altomonte, may be seen Donner's reliefs for the piscina at St Stephen's Cathedral, statuettes of Venus and Mercury, statues of Charles VI and of a nymph.

Maulbertsch Gallery (Room 11): Franz Anton Maulbertsch brought the Austrian Baroque tradition to its culmination. Some notion of the power of his monumental paintings is given by such works of his as the "Allegory of the Jesuits' Mission to the Whole World" and "Saint Narcissus".

Maulbertsch Cabinet (Room 15): Here hang some small-scale pictures and sketches by Maulbertsch.

Marble Gallery (Room 16): The former audience chamber portrays, like the Marble Hall, the Apotheosis of Prince Eugene. The life-size figures of Greek deities in the alcoves are the work of the Venetian artist Domenico Parodi.

Hall of Mirrors (Room 17) also called the Gold Chamber: This is a grandiose room with massive mirrors in golden frames which

View from the Palace Gardens over the Lower Belvedere

seem to make the room go on and on for ever. Here stands Balthasar Permoser's "Apotheosis of Prince Eugene", a marble sculpture carved in Dresden in 1721. It was commissioned by Prince Eugene himself.

Österreichische Galerie des 19. und 20. Jahrhunderts

Location
Oberes Belvedere

Opening times
Tues.–Sun. 10 a.m.–4 p.m.

This Gallery which is housed in the Upper Belvedere is devoted to Austrian art of the 19th and 20th c. It offers an excellent survey of Austrian artistic endeavour from the end of the Baroque era to the present day, taking in the art of the early 19th c., of the period when the Ringstrasse was being developed, and the so-called "Jugendstil", the characteristic Austrian version of Art Nouveau which developed at the end of the 19th c. The collection was started in 1916, and it has had its present form since 1953.

Ground Floor

On the ground floor (left of the vestibule) may be seen pictures by Friedrich Füger, the chief representative of Austrian Classicism, by the portrait-painter Johann Baptist Lampi and by Barbara and Peter Krafft.

First Floor

The 19th c. gallery is housed on the first floor. The most important rooms in the East Wing are: Room 1: Works by Moritz von Schwind (1804–71), including "Kaiser Max auf der Martinswand", "Party Game", "The Man cutting Bread", and "The Painter's Daughter". There are also landscapes by Friedrich Gauermann ("Althauser Lake" and "Landscape near Miesenbach") and by Stifter.

Upper Belvedere

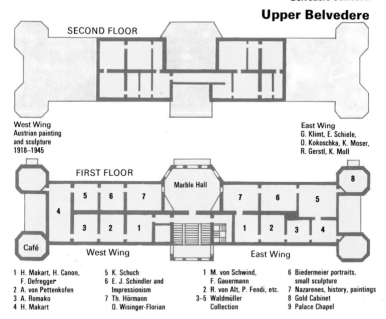

SECOND FLOOR

West Wing
Austrian painting
and sculpture
1918–1945

East Wing
G. Klimt, E. Schiele,
O. Kokoschka, K. Moser,
R. Gerstl, K. Moll

FIRST FLOOR

Marble Hall

West Wing   East Wing

Café

1 H. Makart, H. Canon, F. Defregger	5 K. Schuch	1 M. von Schwind, F. Gauermann
2 A. von Pettenkofen	6 E. J. Schindler and Impressionism	2 R. von Alt, P. Fendi, etc.
3 A. Romako	7 Th. Hörmann O. Wisinger-Florian	3–5 Waldmüller Collection
4 H. Makart		

6 Biedermeier portraits, small sculpture
7 Nazarenes, history, paintings
8 Gold Cabinet
9 Palace Chapel

Room 2: Paintings of the Biedermeier period (1815–48). Most noteworthy are Rudolf von Alt's genre scenes and works by Peter Fend.

Rooms 3, 4 and 5: The Waldmüller Collection. Ferdinand George Waldmüller (1793–1865) was the most important Viennese master in the early 19th c. He painted portraits, landscapes, still-lifes and genre pictures. He was famous for his consummate skill in the handling of light. A Waldmüller canvas recently realised 4½ million Austrian schillings (about £135,000) at auction in the Dorotheum. The Gallery has examples of his work, including his "Corpus Christi morning", "The Monks' Soup" and "Perchtoldsdorf Peasant Wedding".

Room 6. Early 19th c. portraits. Friedrich von Amerling was the portrait-painter favoured by the nobility and the middle classes with a sense of their own importance. He painted such works as "Emperor Francis I", "Group Portrait of Rudolf von Arthaber with his children" and "Girl in a straw hat".

The most noteworthy rooms in the West Wing are:

Room 3: Anton Romako Room. This collection of pictures offers a cross-section of the production of this capricious artist (1832–89). It is devoted mainly to portraits and scenes of everyday life. The picture "Admiral Tegetthoff at the sea battle of Lissa" is particularly noteworthy.

Room 4. Hans Makart Room. As well as large formal pictures such as "The Triumph of Ariadne", "Modern Love" and "The

Five Senses", the brilliant sketches, portraits and genre pictures by Hans Makart (1840–84) should also be looked at.

The 13 rooms on the second floor house the 20th c. Gallery. The most important artists represented are:

Gustav Klimt: On show are pictures and landscapes by the Master of the Vienna Secession (1862–1918). Among the most important works are "The Kiss", "The Picture of Fritza Riedler" and "Adele Block-Bauer sitting".

Egon Schiele: This artist (1890–1918) was not an adherent of the Vienna Secession and was in fact fully appreciated only after his death. His picture "The Family" is one of his major works, dating from the year he died.

Oskar Kokoschka: Works from all periods of this artist's life (1890–1980). One of the earliest paintings is "Child with the Hands of his Parents" and one of his last "Amor and Psyche".

Botanischer
Bus
1A, 2A,

Blutgasse (District)   B5

The Blutgasse District, just behind St Stephen's Cathedral (see entry) is one of the oldest and most interesting parts of the city. The medieval houses, forming a complex of seven old buildings (others in Fähnrichshof, houses Nos. 3–9), were restored and improved in 1965 in exemplary historical fashion. Where lovers of Schubert used to meet in the café whose name was altered to "Zur lustigen Blunze", there are now dwellings and artists' studios.
The name "Blutgasse" (Blood Lane) is without historical warrant. According to legend, however, when the French Chivalric Order of the Knights Templar was dissolved here, so many Templars were slain that the narrow lane ran with their blood.

Location
1, Off Singerstrasse

Underground station
Stephansplatz (U1)

Bus
1A, 2A, 3A

The Blutgasse District also has one of Vienna's special architectural features: the "Durchhäuser" (passage houses). The passages lead through one or more courtyards to the next street, passing from Blutgasse through picturesque galleried courtyards (the Viennese "Pawlatsch") into Fährichshof and further into Singerstrasse.

Durchhäuser

Böhmische Hofkanzlei   B4

The buildings of the former Bohemian Court Chancellery now serve as the seat of the Constitutional and Administrative Court.
The original building dates from 1710 to 1714. J. B. Fischer von Erlach designed this Baroque palace, and Lorenzo Mattielli was responsible for the many sculptures. In 1752 Maria Theresa commissioned Matthias Gerl to enlarge the building. The build-

Location
1, Wipplingerstrasse 7

Underground station
Stephansplatz (U1)

◀ *The Upper Belvedere, Prince Eugene's ceremonial palace*

ing was badly damaged in the war, and large-scale reconstruction was necessary (1946–51). A pedestrian passage was added in 1948.

Botanischer Garten (botanical gardens) C5

Location
3, Mechelgasse 2

Underground station
Südtirolerplatz (U1)

Tram: 71, D

Opening times
Mid April–mid Oct. daily
9 a.m.–dusk.

The chief attractions of the Botanical Gardens are its cacti and succulents and its orchids as well as the important collection of Australian plants housed in the Sundial House.

The garden, originally only for medicinal plants, was laid out by Maria Theresa in 1757 on the advice of her physician, G. van Swieten. There is a tradition that when one of the plants failed to bring the Empress any relief in an illness she ordered the physician and botanist Nikolas von Jacquin to forget about the medicinal plants and turn the place into a botanical garden.

Alpine Garden

Adjoining the Botanical Gardens on the S (entrance from Upper Belvedere) is a large Alpine Garden, with a comprehensive display of rare plants. (Open: Apr.–June, Mon.–Fri. 10 a.m.–6 p.m.; Sat., Sun. and public holidays 9 a.m.–6 p.m.; July–Sept., Mon.–Fri. 10 a.m.–4 p.m.; Sat., Sun. and public holidays 9 a.m.–4 p.m.)

Bundeskanzleramt

See Ballhausplatz.

Bundessammlung alter Stilmöbel (period furniture museum) C3

Location
7, Mariahilferstrasse 88

Underground station
Mariahilferstrasse (U2)

S-Bahn station
Westbahnhof
6, 6D, S50

Trams
5, 6, 8, 9, 18, 52, 58

Opening times
Tues.–Fri. 9 a.m.–4 p.m., Sat.
9 a.m.–noon.

The Federal Furniture Collection contains precious furniture and tapestries from the former Imperial palaces. The Republic loans Imperial furnishings to official buildings where appropriate. The furnishings on show are divided into two sections. In the first part may be seen Court furniture from the Early Baroque era to the time of the Empire. The most important exhibit is the Schlosshofer Room which belonged to Prince Eugene of Savoy.

In the second section the 19th c. Imperial throne is on show, together with Joseph II's writing-desk and Francis I's bedroom. Fifteen rooms have been set out in original early 19th c. style (with a music-room, a drawing-room, etc.).

Guided tours every hour on the hour.

Burggarten (park) C4

Location
1, Opernring/Burgring

Underground station
Mariahilferstrasse (U2)

In 1809 Napoleon had the bastions of the Burg blown up which meant that at last there was room for an Imperial garden, generally called the "Promenade". Later the Neue Burg (see Hofburg) was erected on part of the site. The Burggarten has

The Staircase in the Burgtheater ▶

Burgtheater

Bus
3A, 57A

Trams
1, 2, 52, 58, D, J

Mozart Memorial

Emperor Francis I Statue

Franz Joseph I Memorial

been open to the public since 1919. Attempts by young people to win the right to walk on the grass by organising sit-down strikes have so far been in vain.
In the park stand famous monuments to Mozart, Francis I and Franz Joseph I.

The Mozart Memorial of 1896 is a master-work in marble by Victor Tilgner. The plinth is embellished with the various musical members of the Mozart family and with two reliefs from "Don Giovanni". The monument used to stand in Albertina-Platz, was seriously damaged in the last war, taken away and then, in 1953, after full restoration re-erected in the Burggarten.

The equestrian statue of the Emperor Francis I, by Moll, was erected in 1781 in the Paradiesgartel on the bastion. It was later moved to the present spot.

During the Emperor's lifetime Vienna had no statue of Franz Joseph I, and then the Republic was not interested in erecting one. This memorial was erected as late as 1957, almost as an act of subversion. To general surprise, there were no unfortunate political consequences.

**Burgtheater   B4

Location
1, Dr-Karl-Lueger-Ring 2

This theatre, "Die Burg" as the Viennese call it, is the stage with the richest traditions in the German-speaking lands. For a long

The "Burg", the theatre with the richest German-speaking tradition

time it was also the most important. The Classical style of the Burgtheater and the German spoken by the players exerted a decisive influence on the development of the German stage, and even now an engagement to play at the Burgtheater is still a high point in the artistic career of an actor or actress.

The theatre was built in 1751 with the agreement of the Empress Maria Theresa. It has had the status of a Court and national theatre since 1776. The theatre moved to new premises in 1888. These had been built on the Ring, to designs by C. von Hasenauer and Gottfried Semper.

When the Viennese voiced criticisms of the new theatre, Gottfried Semper retorted that "every theatre has to be rebuilt after 60 years or it is bound to burn down after that period". Right on time the Burgtheater was burned down in 57 years, when it caught fire in 1945. The auditorium was completely destroyed, and it was not until 15 October 1955 that the theatre could reopen with Grillparzer's "König Ottokars Glück und Ende" (King Ottokar's Prosperity and Demise).

The building is 445ft (136m) long and the middle section is 320ft (95m) across. The height of the façade is 88ft (27m). In the auditorium there are seats for 1,310 and standing room for 210. The exterior of the Burgtheater is impressive on account of the numerous decorative figures, colossal groups, scenes and busts by the sculptors Tilgner, Weyr and Kundmann.

The interior has costly decoration in the French Baroque style. The staircase has frescoes by Gustav and Ernst Klimt and by Franz Matsch.

The theatre is open for ten months in the year. The price of seats is high. The stage has excellent technical facilities, but the scenery dock is situated away from the building, in the "Arsenal". This means that the scenery has to be transported to and from the theatre on a low-loader.

Underground stations
Rathaus, Schottentor (U2)

Trams
1, 2, D, T (Ring), 37, 38, 40, 41, 42, 43, 44

Viewing
by arrangement
(tel. 51 44 40)

---

*Carnuntum (open-air museum)

The little market town of Petronell lies in part on the site once occupied by the Roman city of Carnuntum. This city which formed round the legionary camp a mile or so (2km) away had in its prosperous days a population of 50,000 and was more important than Vindobona. It was in Carnuntum that Septimius Severus had himself proclaimed Emperor, and Diocletian convened an Imperial Conference here. In 375 Carnuntum was successfully stormed by warriors belonging to the Quadi tribe. The remains of the Roman city uncovered by excavation are now an open-air museum. The foundations of houses may be seen, together with the ruins of a palace, a 45ft (14m) high gate, the Heidentor (Pagans' Gate), the so-called second amphitheatre with 1,300 seats (2nd c.), and the remains of a hypocaust and bathhouse with pavement mosaics.

Of the legionary camp there remain the ruins of a tower and the foundations of the first amphitheatre (late 2nd c.). Open-air performances are given here in summer.

Location
near Petronell
26 miles (42 km) E of Vienna

S-Bahn
S7

Bus
Bus route from Wien-Mitte Bus Station

Note
The Carnuntum site and open-air museum are to be turned into an extensive archaeological park

---

Danube (Donau)   A6

The Danube, which is almost 330 yards (300m) wide, flows for 15 miles (24km) through Vienna from NW to SE. In times past

History of river

this, the second largest river of Europe, brought great problems to the city. The river meandered considerably – every rise in its level caused catastrophic flooding and it often formed new channels. Naturally the first efforts to control the waters were concentrated on the channels nearest the city and in 1598 the so-called "Danube Canal" was regulated. This flowed for 10 miles (17km) between Nussdorf and Praterspitz; it was navigable and commercially important. With the introduction of larger vessels and with the growth of Vienna along the right bank of the main river and its expansion on the plain to the E it became necessary to regulate the main stream. Between 1868 and 1876 the river was straightened and provided on the E with a 550 yard (500m) wide flood channel. Further measures, begun in 1975 and now almost finished, will complete the protection against flooding. Parallel to the main river a relief channel, the "New Danube" has been excavated in what had been a useful flood-plain, forming an elongated island, called "Spaghetti Island" (see Danube Island). The Danube is now in four parts; the main stream, the New Danube, the Danube Canal and the Old Danube, the last named being made up of the cut-off remains of various arms of the old course of the river.

Redevelopment Area

Below the Reichsbrücke the river is flanked by broad meadows which have been converted into a park-like area in the Prater and in the Lobau have been declared a nature reserve. From here to the Czech border the Eastern National Park is to be established. Within an over-all civic plan Vienna will convert the Danube area into a scenically attractive region.

Bridges and Ferries

The river is spanned by two railway bridges, Nordbahn- and Stadtlauer Ostbahnbrücke; four road bridges, Nordbrücke, Floridsdorfer Brücke (renovated 1977–8), Reichsbrücke, which collapsed in 1976 and was fully restored by 1980, and the Praterbrücke as well as two service tunnels. There are also two small ferries.

Port

See Facts and Figures, Transport.

Danube Island (Donauinsel)   A6

Location
Between Klosterneuburg and the oil port Lobau

Vienna has to thank the scheme for the regulation of the Danube for the creation of Danube Island which lies between the relief channel, the New Danube, and the main river. The island extends over 1,730 acres (700ha) and includes woodland areas of grass, stretches of water and several kilometres of bathing beaches. The island consists of three sections.

North Section

S-Bahn station
Strandbäder (S1, S2, S3)

Bus
33B

Trams
31, 32

Ferry
DDSG landing-stage Nussdorf

This is a paradise for yachtsmen and surfers, as the wind coming from the Vienna Woods blows most strongly here. There are surfing schools and yacht harbours; bicycles can be hired as can rowing, paddle and electric boats (motor boats are not permitted on the New Danube). There are good facilities for swimming and sunbathing and, as in the other parts of the island, restaurants and cafeterias.
There are parking facilities at the main access point (via Langenzersdorf); at the N yacht harbour (via Scheydgasse); on the

Überfuhrstrasse and by the Floridsdorfer bridge. There are cycle paths on the Floridsdorfer bridge, on the Jedleseer foot-bridge and on the main access road.

Central Section

As befits their function as a flood barrier, the banks of Danube Island are reinforced with boulders and concrete, but in a few places suitable for bathing a layer of fine gravel covers the stones and there are special areas with shallow water for children. Full-size football pitches, an 880 yard (800m) long water ski lift and a water chute are available and there is a school for diving, sailing and canoeing. Further attractions include a roller-skating rink and a "fun" cycle area. Cyclists can reach the island via the Nordbahn and Brigittenauer bridges; the Reichs-brücke, the Praterbrücke and weir 1. There are parking facilities by the Reichsbrücke and in Raffineriestrasse.

S-Bahn station
Strandbäder (S1, S2, S3)

Underground station
Donauinsel (U1)

Buses
80B, 91A, 18A

South Section

Here there are facilities for naturists and the handicapped. A 1,650 yard (1500m) long cyclodrome provides a venue for cycle, roller-skating and wheelchair races. Sites are available for summer barbecues and anglers can find peaceful spots for their sport (a fishing permit is necessary) – some of the best fishing in Vienna is from the banks of the Danube. The "Toter Grund" (dead ground) with its pools and reeds is a protected area in this part of the island.
There are parking facilities along the left bank of the New Danube with display boards showing the number of free spaces.

S-Bahn stations
Lobau, Stadtlauerbrücke (S80)

Buses
18A, 80B, 91A

Tram 21

Ferries
at the Lindmayer and Ronesch restaurants (R bank), WALULISO (New Danube); also for cyclists.

Visitors can reach the south section of the island by ferry from the right bank of the Danube at Lindmayer's restaurant (Damm-haufen 50) and visit the "Peace Pagoda" at the same time. The pagoda was erected at the restaurant by Elisabeth Lindmayer, the proprietor's daughter, who is a Buddhist. In 1982 two monks of the Michidatsu Fujii order visited her; members of their order had already erected some 70 peace pagodas in Japan, Sri Lanka, India and the US during their pilgrimage for world peace.
Elisabeth Lindmayer had the first peace pagoda in Europe erected on the banks of the Danube in 1983. The bell-shaped pagoda is a monument rather than a temple and contains an almost 3m/10ft high seated statue of Buddha under a dome decorated with a band of ornaments and reliefs.

Peace Pagoda

Three brochures of the individual sections of Danube Island and their facilities are available from the tourist information office (see Practical Information, Tourist Information) or in the City Information Office at the Reichsbrücke on the left bank of the New Danube.

Note

---

*__Demel__ (café)   B4

Demel was once the Royal and Imperial pastry-cook's. Now it is the choicest and most expensive café in Vienna. All cooked

Location
1, Kohlmarkt 14

Demel's, formerly pastry-cooks to kings and emperors

Underground station
Stephansplatz (U1)

Bus
2A

Opening times
Mon.–Sat. 9 a.m.–7 p.m.,
Sun. 10 a.m.–7 p.m.

dishes and cakes are prepared by hand to traditional recipes. In the kitchen machinery is hardly used at all. The waitresses, who are called "Demelinerinnen" (Demel's young ladies) in a famous song by G. Bronner and H. Qualtinger, still wear modest black dresses and address customers almost impersonally in a very formal language which is used only here. Here they say "Haben schon gewahlt . . . ?" (Has Madam already made her choice . . . ?).

Demel was founded in 1785 by a pastry-cook by the name of Ludwig Dehne, was acquired by Christoph Demel in 1857 and now belongs to a Swiss company.

About 60 years ago A. Kuh wrote an essay with the title "Demel and Lenin". His anxiety that Demel might fall a victim to democracy was without foundation. It was precisely in Demel that the Socialist politicians set up their exclusive Club 45.

Note that in Demel customers have to make their own choice at an enormous buffet. They then take a number, and waitresses bring to their table whatever has been selected.

Deutschmeisterdenkmal (monument)   B4

Location
1, Deutschmeisterplatz

Underground station
Schottenring (U2, U4)

Bus 40A

Trams 1, 2, D, T

In 1896, to celebrate and honour the second centenary of the Viennese garrison regiment, the K. und K. Hoch- und Deutschmeister Nr. 4 (The Fourth Royal and Imperial High and German Masters), money was raised for a memorial. It was inaugurated in 1906.

Johann Benk made the bronze figures. Under an ensign bearing the standard of the regiment are gathered "Vindobona", and "Landshut Grenadier" and the "true comrade". Two reliefs recall the regiment's baptism of fire at Zenta in 1696 and the Battle of Kolin of 1757. In the course of the first 200 years (before the First World War, of course) the regiment lost 407 officers and 18,511 men.

On 1 November 1918 Egon Erwin Kisch formed the "Red Guard" in front of this memorial, and Franz Werfel, too, spoke at the mass meeting held at the same time.

Deutschordenshaus and Deutschordenskirche B4

The buildings round two inner courtyards extend back as far as Stephansplatz (see entry) and Domherrenhof.

The Teutonic Order was called to Vienna by Duke Leopold VI at the beginning of the 13th c. The Order started constructing its premises, which probably included a chapel, a little later. In the 14th c. the Gothic church dedicated to St Elisabeth was incorporated into the buildings. In 1667 Carlo Carlone erected a new building which included a church. Between 1720 and 1725 this building was given the appearance which it has kept to the present day. The architect was Anton Erhard Martinelli.

The church was remodelled between 1720 and 1722, to harmonise with the 14th c. Gothic work. It was restored in 1868 and 1947.

In the Middle Ages the Teutonic Order was devoted to colonial and military activity. Now it is a spiritual Order concerned with religious matters and also with service in hospitals and the care of the young and the old. Since 1923 the High Masters of the Order have always been priests of the Order.

Location
1, Singerstrasse 7

Underground station
Stephansplatz (U1)

Opening times
Daily 10 a.m.–noon; Tues., Wed., Fri., Sat. also 3–5 p.m.

The interior of the church is decorated with coats of arms and banners. Among the most precious objects are the Flemish reredos (1520) and the epitaph of Jobst Truchsess von Wetzhausen (1524).

Church

The Treasury of the Order is in four rooms. Room 1: Insignia of the Order and coins. The enthronement ring of High Master Hermann von Salza which is on show dates from the 13th c.

Treasury

Room 2: Chalices and other Mass vessels dating from the 14th to the 16th c. Also cutlery made of exotic materials.

Room 3: Art collection of the High Master Archduke Maximilian III (1602–18): silver and gold reliefs, ornaments, Oriental parade arms, clocks, astronomical equipment.

Room 4: Miniatures, rosaries, precious glasses, armour and 15th c. panel-paintings.

Dogenhof B5

The Dogenhof (Doge's Palace) is a typical example of architectural taste at the end of the 19th c. It is inspired by the Ca d'Oro in Venice and is decorated with a stone lion of St Mark.

Emperor Franz Joseph I wanted to designate for each of the various ethnic groups in the monarchy a specific part of Vienna and to let them create there an environment in which they would feel at home. Thus an Italian colony was supposed to

Location
2, Praterstrasse 70

Underground station
Nestroyplatz (U1)

Bus
5A

grow up in Leopoldstadt. Not a lot came of the idea, and the Dogenhof stands now as a rather odd historical curiosity amid the other houses on Praterstrasse.

*Dominikanerkirche (officially the Rosary Basilica ad S. Mariam Rotundam) B5

Location 1, Postgasse 4	This church was promoted to the rank of a "minor basilica" in 1927, bearing the name "Rosary Basilica ad S. Mariam Rotundam".
Underground stations Stephansplatz, Schwedenplatz (U1)	The Dominicans were called to Vienna in 1226 and they consecrated their first church as early as 1237. After a series of fires work began on the construction of a Gothic church between 1283 and 1302. This suffered severe damage in the First Turkish Siege of 1529. The present church, the third, was built between 1631 and 1632. It is the most important Early Baroque church in Vienna. The frescoes, High Altar and the chapels are especially noteworthy.
Bus 1A	
Trams 1, 2	
Frescoes	The frescoes in the nave are by Matthias Rauchmiller (17th c.); those in the crossing are by Franz Geyling (1836), and those in the choir by Carpoforo Tencala (1676). All the wall- and ceiling-paintings in the side-chapels date from the 17th c.
High Altar	The subject of the picture above the High Altar, "The Virgin as Queen of the Rosary" by Leopold Kupelwieser (1839), refers to the institution of the Festival of the Rosary by Pope Gregory XIII.
Chapels	The chapels date from the 17th and 18th c. The oldest is the Thomas Aquinas Chapel with a painting above the altar dated 1638. The most important is the Vincent Chapel. Its altar-piece, "St Vincent raising a man from the dead", was painted by Françoise Roettiers in 1726.

*Dom- and Diözesanmuseum (museum) B5

Location 1, Rotenturmstrasse 2 (Entrance 6 Stephansplatz)	The Cathedral and Diocesan Museum stands in Zwettlerhof, adjacent to the Archbishop's Palace. Founded in 1932, it was remodelled in 1973 and extended in 1985. It displays religious art from the Middle Ages to the present day.
Underground station Stephansplatz (U1)	The Treasury contains the most valuable items from St Stephen's (see entry – Stephansdom), including two Syrian glass vessels of the 13th and early 14th c., the St Andrew's Cross reliquary and an important 14th c. reliquary which was refashioned in 1514. Mementoes of Duke Rudolph IV the Benefactor, who had the church rebuilt in Gothic style, include the Chapter Seal, an antique medieval cameo and his portrait and funeral shroud. Other valuable exhibits include a monstrance with a pattern of rays by Ignaz Würth (1784), enamelled 12th c. tablets (with scenes from the Old Testament), a Carolingian 9th c. evangelistary with all its sides decorated with representations of the Evangelists, and the sword of St Ulrich (10th c.). Pre-eminent among the Gothic painted panels are the Upper St Veit Altar, based on a sketch by Dürer, and the "Man of Sorrows" by Lukas Cranach. Among Gothic sculptures are a relief of the "Descent from the Cross" and the Erlach and Therberg Madonnas (14th c.). The most valuable of the many
Bus 1A	
Opening times Wed.–Sat. 10 a.m.–6 p.m., Sun. and public holidays 10 a.m.–1 p.m.	

15th and 16th c. sculptures are the Madonna of the Shrine (early 15th c.) and the Anna Selbdritt group by Veit Stoss. Pictures from the 16th, 17th, 18th and early 19th c. complete the exhibits. The most noteworthy Baroque works are by Paul Troger ("St Cassian"), A. Maulbertsch ("Golgotha"), Kremser-Schmidt ("St Sippe") and Jan von Hemessen ("Christ bearing the Cross").

*Donaupark

The Danube Park occupies 250 acres (1 million m²) and is thus the second largest park in Vienna. It was laid out in 1964 in connection with the Vienna International Garden Show (WIG '64) at a cost of 7 million schillings (about £250,000).

The Danube Park Railway, a narrow-gauge line, runs round the gardens. There is an artificial lake (Lake Iris) on the bank of which stands a theatre which seats 4,000. A chair-lift follows a triangular course between the Old and the New Danube, offering wonderful views of the entire park and the office towers of UNO-City (see entry) which is adjacent.

The Danube Tower is 825ft (252m) high, which makes it the tallest building in Vienna. It was opened in 1964. Its weight is 17,600 tons, and it is 100ft (31m) in diameter at the base. Two express lifts climb to 540ft (165m) in 45 seconds. They lead to the viewing-chamber and to the two revolving restaurants. The rates at which they revolve round the axis of the tower can both be regulated so that a cycle takes either 26, 39 or 52 minutes.

Location
22, Danube/Old Danube

Underground station
Alte Donau (U1)

S-Bahn station
Strandbäder

Buses
90A, 91A, 92A; 20B

Opening times
Tower: lift until 11 p.m.

Opening times
Restaurants:
11.30 a.m.–3 p.m. and
6–11 p.m.

Dorotheum   C4

The Dorotheum is one of the largest pawnbroking institutions in the world. The Viennese call it either "Tante Dorothee" or just "Pfandl" (The Pawn). It occupies a block of buildings erected by E. von Förster along the lines of a Baroque palace between 1898 and 1901.

There are 2,400 auctions a year, dealing with over 600,000 objects. In Vienna alone the Dorotheum has 16 branches. In the main building there are sections for furniture, carpets, pictures, small objects, furs, objets d'art, stamps, books and jewellery. The four major art auctions, in March, June, September and November, attract experts from all over the world (see Practical Information – Auction Rooms).

The origins of the Dorotheum go back to 1707 when the Emperor Joseph I founded an office for pawnbroking. It was moved in 1787 into the Dorothea Monastery which was empty at the time. These premises later underwent large-scale reconstruction.

Location
1, Dorotheergasse 17

Underground station
Stephansplatz (U1)

Bus
2A

Opening times
Regular auctions: see
Practical Information –
Viewing: Mon.–Fri.
10 a.m.–6 p.m., Sat.
9 a.m.–noon

Dreifaltigkeitskirche   B3

The Dreifaltigkeitskirche, dedicated to the Holy Trinity, is commonly called the "Alserkirche" in Vienna. It stands opposite the front of the General Hospital, and sick people and those on the way to recovery used to hang up thousands of votive tablets in the cloister and in the Antony Chapel.

Location
8, Alserstrasse 17

Underground station
Schottentor (U2)

The church which was completed in 1727 was taken over by the Minorites in 1784. In its exterior form it is an Early Baroque building with a façade flanked by twin towers and a high domed roof. Inside visitors find a cruciform plan with side-chapels to the left and right. Through the cloister on the right is the way to the Antony Chapel, and the church is the centre in Vienna of the devotion to St Antony.

The furnishing of the church dates primarily from the 18th and 19th c. An exception to this generalisation is the "Weeping Madonna" by the Spanish Baroque Master, Pedro de Mena y Mendrano. He carved this bust out of mahogany and pine in 1662–63; it may be seen in the Johann Nepomuk Chapel. There is a wooden Crucifix, larger than life-size, in the third chapel from the entry on the right; it dates from the 16th c. In 1827 the body of Beethoven was brought to this church. One year later, just a few weeks before his own death, Schubert wrote the hymn "Glaube, Liebe, Hoffnung" (Faith, Love and Hope) for the consecration of the church's bells.

*Ephesos-Museum   C4

Location
1, Heldenplatz, Neue Burg

Underground station
Mariahilferstrasse (U2)

Trams
1, 2, D, J

Opening times
Mon. and Wed.–Fri.
10 a.m.–4 p.m.
Sat., Sun. 9 a.m.–4 p.m.

The Ephesos-Museum was opened in 1978 in the Neue Burg (see Hofburg); entrance behind the Prince Eugene Monument. It is the only museum between Istanbul and London which possesses a collection of finds from the ancient trading city on the coast of Asia Minor. Excavations by the Austrian Archaeological Institute which are still continuing have brought interesting finds to light, among them statues, architectural fragments, reliefs and bronzes. The exhibits from the Aegean island of Samothrace were dug up between 1873 and 1875. Particularly interesting is a model of Ephesus which fills an entire room and was made with countless little pieces of wood. The model cost 1·3 million schillings (about £40,000).

Sculpture Collection

Among the most remarkable exhibits in the Sculpture Collection are:
The bronze of an athlete (Roman copy of a Greek original, second half of the 4th c. B.C.).
Parthian Memorial, a nearly 130ft (40m) long frieze with life-size figures in relief commemorating Lucius Verus (who died in A.D. 169), who ruled with Emperor Marcus Aurelius. It was erected after the victorious conclusion of the war against the Parthians (161–165).
"Hercules fighting with the Centaurs", "Boy with a Goose" (Roman copy in marble of an Hellenistic original).

Architectural Remains

Among the architectural remains the following are especially interesting:
Fragments of the altar of a Shrine to Artemis (4th c. B.C.), of an octagon (second half of the 1st c. A.D.), of a so-called "Round House" (second half of the 1st c. A.D.) and of the Great Theatre (mid 1st c. A.D.) with erotic reliefs and a frieze of masks.

Finds from Samothrace

Exhibits from the island of Samothrace: Victory figures, pediment sculptures (from the Hellenistic Hieron), Ionic capitals (from the Ptolemaion), frieze of lotus fronds (from the Arsinoeion) and a gable-end from the Propylon.

Fiakermuseum

Fähnrichshof

See Blutgasse

Fiakermuseum   B3

In the "Fiakerhaus", built 1952, the Viennese landau-drivers
have set out in three rooms an exhibition tracing in prints,
photographs, pictures and models, the 300-year history of their
trade.
The first licence for a carriage to ply for hire was granted in
Vienna in 1693, 71 years later than in Paris. Towards the end of
the 19th c. there were, however, 70 ranks. A hundred years ago
a 3 mile (5km) ride in a landau cost only about 1½ guilders. All
the same, that provided a large enough income and Viennese
landau-drivers paid for the Schrammel brothers to take music
lessons, while the Fiaker Ball, with "Fiaker Milli" as queen of
the dance was the high point of the carnival. Today there are
only about three dozen "Fiaker". They ply for hire in Stephansplatz, in front of the Albertina in Augustinerstrasse and in Heldenplatz, taking visitors round the sights of the city centre. A
few drivers still wear the traditional costume of Pepita trousers,
a velvet jacket and a hard hat called a "Stösser".
The bronze in the garden of the Fiakerhaus is a reminder of the
project to erect a "Fiaker Fountain" commemorating Vienna's
landaus; it was finished at the beginning of the war but was
never set up.

Location
17, Veronikagasse 12,
second floor

S-Bahn station
Alserstrasse (9, 9D)

Tram
2

Opening times
1st Wed. in month
10 a.m.–1 p.m.

Admission free

Sightseeing in a Viennese "Fiaker" – a sight in itself

Figarohaus   B5

Location
1, Schulerstrasse 8 (Entrance
in Domgasse 5)

Underground station
Stephansplatz (U1)

Bus
1A

Opening times
Tues.–Sun.
9 a.m.–12.15 p.m.,
and 1–4.30 p.m.

Figarohaus stands on Schulerstrasse which leads out of
Stephansplatz (see entry). For three years, from 1784 to 1787,
Mozart lived here with his wife and son in a typical Old Viennese house near St Stephen's Cathedral (see entry). These
were his happiest years, and it is here that he wrote "The
Marriage of Figaro". For a short while Beethoven was his pupil,
and it was while he was resident here that Mozart was
appointed Imperial Chamber Composer.

Mozart lived on the first floor of what was then called "Came-
sina House", and his rooms have been set out as a permanent
memorial. Visitors can see the room (with a fine stucco ceiling)
where Mozart worked, pictures and prints, figurines and the
first German libretto of "The Marriage of Figaro".

* Franziskanerplatz   C5

Location
1, Singerstrasse/
Weihburggasse

Underground station
Stephansplatz (U1)

Bus
1A

Franziskanerplatz with the Franciscan monastery and church
has 17th and 18th c. buildings all round and is one of the most
attractive old squares in Vienna.

The Moses Fountain, with its base like the jaws of a lion, used to
stand in the courtyard of No. 6 Zum grünen Löwen (The Green
Lion). Johann Martin Fischer designed the lead statue of Moses
striking water from the rock. In 1798 it was placed on the base of
the fountain which had been brought here.

The country coaches used to set out from the former Zum
grünen Löwen in the days of Emperor Joseph. It was possible
to travel 100 miles and more out of the city into the country by
these coaches.

Franziskanerkirche (officially St Jerome)

The Church of St Jerome at present standing on this idyllic
old-world square is the only church in Vienna to possess a
Renaissance façade. The interior is, however, decorated and
fitted out in the Baroque style.

A 14th c. Poor Clares convent formerly occupied the site where
this church was constructed between 1603 and 1611. Father
Bonaventura Daum was responsible for the designs of the new
building. The tower was added in 1614.

In the interior the High Altar by Andrea Pozzo dating from 1707
is particularly notable as is a venerated picture of the Madonna
and Child from about 1550 which probably came from Grün-
berg in Bohemia. Behind the altar is the monks' choir which is
reached by passing through the sacristy.

The Capristan Altar (second altar on the left) with a painting the
"Martyrdom of St Capristan" by Franz Wagenschön. The Francis Altar (fourth altar on the left) with a picture of the church's
Patron Saint by Johann George Schmidt. The Crucifixion Altar
(third altar on the right) with a "Crucifixion" by Carlo Carlone
(first half of the 18th c.).

The carved Baroque organ of 1643 is the oldest organ in
Vienna. It has folding doors which are in part painted, in part
carved, with the figures of saints on them.

According to legend, the Madonna on the reredos, popularly called the Madonna with the Axe, was being struck down by iconoclasts, but the axe remained firmly attached. Soldiers took this indestructible image of the Virgin with them on their campaign against the Turks and ascribed to it their victory at Pest in Hungary.

Freyung

B4

The Freyung is a triangular space near the Schottenkloster (see entry – Schottenstift). The name Freyung ("free place") refers to the fact that, like St Stephen's (see entry – Stephansdom), it had the right of receiving and protecting any who were being pursued, except those who had shed blood. In olden days a Punch and Judy Show stood on Freyung, and later on there was a gallows where quick justice was meted out to traitors. Mountebanks, hucksters and sweetmeat-sellers had their pitches here. It was only in the 17th and 18th c. that the buildings were erected which form the setting for Freyung today: Palais Ferstel (No. 2), Harrach Palace (No. 3) and Kinsky Palace (No. 4), the latter was built between 1713 and 1716 by Johann Lucas von Hildebrandt.

Location
1st District

Underground station
Schottentor (U2)

Bus
1A

Trams
1, 2, D, T (Ring)

Austria-Brunnen (Austria Fountain)

In the middle of the square is the Austria Fountain which is a work of Ludwig Schwanthaler. It was cast by Ferdinand Miller in the Munich bronze-foundry and unveiled on Freyung in 1846. Its allegorical bronze figures represent Austria and the main rivers of the monarchy as it then existed, the Po, Elbe, Weischsel and Danube.
There may be some truth in the Viennese chronicles which state that Alma von Goethe, the granddaughter of the poet, was the model for the figure of Austria at the age of seventeen, shortly before her death.
After the bronze figure was completed, Schwanthaler is said to have had it filled with cigarettes in Munich to smuggle them into Vienna. The figure was set in place so quickly on arrival, however, that he never had the chance to "empty" Austria and the cigarettes may still be there to this day.

Palais Ferstel

The Palais Ferstel, which Heinrich Ferstel, architect of the Votivkirche (see entry) and the University (see Universität), built in 1856–60 for the National Bank, has a distinct Italianate air. For years the building was neglected but has been restored exactly as it was in the elaborate "Ringstrasse" style as an exclusive venue for conferences and banquets. A glass-roofed shopping arcade containing the fountain of the Danube sprites by Anton Fernkorn, leads to the Herrengasse.

The Café Central (open: Mon.–Sat. 10 a.m.–11.30 p.m.) was reopened in 1986 in the Palais Ferstel. On entering the café from Herrengasse the visitor will find himself greeted by the writer Peter Altenberg – not, of course, in person but as a life-size model. Altenberg was a regular patron and often gave as his address "Vienna 1, Café Central".

Café Central

Other "regulars", who brought renown to the café and turned it into a Viennese institution, were Egon Friedell, Franz Werfel, Stefan Zweig, Karl Kraus, Leo Trotzky and Alfred Polgar, who even wrote a theory on the Café Central.

Today the café displays its wonderful vaulted ceiling and beautifully restored marble columns to visitors who may find it a pleasant place to stop and relax from the rigours of sightseeing.

Gardekirche "Zum gekreuzigten Heiland"   C5

Location
3, Rennweg 5a

Underground station
Karlsplatz (U1, U2, U4)

Tram
71

The Guards' Church dedicated to the Crucified Saviour stands on Rennweg, as do the Belvedere Palaces (see entry). It has been the Polish national church since 1897.

It was built during Maria Theresa's reign by Nikolaus Pacassi to serve as the church of the Imperial Hospital. In 1782 it was handed over to the Polish Life Guards. It was altered again between 1890 and 1898. The painting above the High Altar in the attractive central section of the building with its light Late Rococo decoration is by Peter Strudel and dates from 1712. Strudel was the founder of the Akademie der bildenden Künste (see entry).

Gartenpalais Liechtenstein   B4

Location
9, Fürstengasse 1

Bus
40A

Tram
D

The Summer Palace in Fürstengasse is accounted one of the most beautiful Baroque buildings in Vienna. The valuable Liechtenstein Picture Gallery was taken to Vaduz during the Second World War.

Domenico Martinelli put up the building between 1691 and 1711 for Johann Adam Andreas, Prince of Liechtenstein. The sculptural decoration is by Giovanni Giuliani, and the frescoes in the interior are by Andrea Pozzo, Antonio Belluci and Johann Michael Rottmayr. The ceremonial marble staircases are imposing.

Since 1979 the Museum of Modern Art has been here, as well as the former Hahn Collection and pictures on permanent loan from the Ludwig Collection (from Aachen) and the Austrian Ludwig Foundation.

Museum of Modern Art

Opening times
Daily (except Tues.)
10 a.m.–6 p.m.

Highlights of this exhibition of international art from 1900 to the present day are the "modern classicists" – with works by Picasso, Kupka, Nolde, Schlemmer, Lipschitz, Kirchner, Pechstein, Klimt, Schiele and Kokoschka. Jawlensky and Marc represent the "Blue Rider" group. Non-figurative painters include Itten, Leger, etc. Abstract art is represented by Delaunay, Wotruba and others; works by Lehmden, Fuchs, Hutter and Hausner are examples of Surrealism.

Also to be seen are examples of "Nouveau Realisme", Pop art and Photo-realism.
A branch of the Museum of Modern Art is the Museum des 20. Jahrhunderts (see entry) housed in the pavilion of the 1958 Brussels World Fair.

Geymüller-Schlössl (Sobek Collection) (museum)

This small palace was built in 1808 for the banker J. Heinrich Geymüller. It is now the home of the Sobek Collection of old Viennese clocks, and is a separate department of the Austrian Museum of Applied Arts.

There are seven rooms decorated in the Empire and early 19th c. style. On show are 200 clocks – old Viennese pedestal clocks, case clocks and wall clocks. The oldest are Baroque clocks, but most of the exhibits come from the period 1780–1850.

Location
18, Pötzleinsdorfer Str. 102

Tram 41

Opening times
Mar.–end Nov., Tues., Wed.
11 a.m.–3.30 p.m. (Mon., Thur.
notice required); Sun. 3 p.m.
guided tour.

Graben   B4

Graben, a wide-open space which is half street and half square, is the hub of the great city of Vienna. In 1950 it was the first place to have fluorescent lighting. In 1971 it became the first pedestrian zone, and soon afterwards cafés took over for the summer months what was formerly a major thoroughfare.
Graben was once the city moat round the Roman camp, then it became the flower and vegetable market, and from the 17th c. on it was the scene of Court festivities.
There are two old fountains, the Joseph Fountain and the Leopold Fountain. Both were altered many times. Lead figures were added by Johann Martin Fischer in 1804.
Of the numerous Baroque buildings that once surrounded Graben in the 18th c. only the Bartolotti-Partenfeld Palace (No. 11) remains.
Also of interest at Graben are the subterranean Art Nouveau toilets. They were built in 1905 by Adolf Loos and have been renovated to reveal their true glory. The cubicles are lined with wood and marble panels and have gilded fittings.

Location
1st District

Underground station
Stephansplatz (U1)

Buses
1A, 2A, 3A

*Plague Pillar

In the middle of Graben stands the famous Plague Pillar. This 70ft (21m) tall Baroque pillar (also called the "Trinity Pillar") owes its existence to a vow made by Emperor Leopold I. He swore that when the plague ceased he would pay for the erection of a pillar which would reach up to the heavens.
The plague of 1679 cost 75,000 Viennese their lives, other estimates even 150,000. The first plague pillar was erected in 1679, too. The construction of the definitive Plague Pillar was begun by Matthias Rauchmiller in 1681, continued after his death, which occurred in 1686, by J. B. Fischer von Erlach, and completed in 1693 by Locovico Burnacini. The figure of the Emperor kneeling in prayer is the work of Paul Strudel, that of the Trinity was modelled by Johann Kilian of Augsburg.

Griechenbeisl

Neidhart Frescoes

Opening times
Tues.–Sun. 9 a.m.–
12.15 p.m.; 1 p.m.–4.30 p.m.

In 1400 a wealthy cloth merchant, Michael Menschein, had the great hall decorated on the first floor of the house at Tuchlauben 19 (near the Graben square) with frescoes depicting the Minnesänger Neidhart's poetry. In 1715/16 the house was refashioned in the Baroque style and most of the paintings were destroyed and the rest covered with a thick layer of plaster. The frescoes were discovered by accident during renovation work in 1979 and took three years to restore. They are the oldest profane wall paintings in Vienna and an important example of popular art in the late Middle Ages. The walls of the 15×7·50m/50×25ft hall were originally completely covered; the frescoes depict typical scenes from Neidhart's songs in the cycle of the four seasons.

*Griechenbeisl (inn)   B5

Location
1, Fleischmarkt 11

Underground stations
Stephansplatz, Schwedenplatz
(U1)

Bus
2A

This historic inn with the figure of "lieber Augustin" on the façade, was called "Zum roten Dach" (The Red Roof Inn) in the 15th c., becoming "Griechenbeisl" in the 18th c. Pilsner Urquell was first served here in 1852. Among the many famous persons to frequent the inn were Wagner, Strauss, Brahms, Waldmüller, Grillparzer and Nestroy.

It has been proved that Mark Twain wrote "The Million Pound Note" in a room at Griechenbeisl. The walls of the Mark Twain

Griechenbeisl, an historic inn, with "Lieber Augustin" on the façade

Room are completely covered with the autographs of famous artists.

There is no definite proof that it was in the seven little vaulted rooms which are full of all manner of curious objects that some anonymous ballad-singer wrote the mocking song "lieber Augustin" in 1679 while the plague was raging outside.

Grinzing

With its old houses and lanes, nestling in gardens and vineyards, the name "Grinzing" still is to many people all over the world synonymous with "Viennese Heurige".

Location
19th District

Tram
38

The word "Heurige" has two meanings: wine made from grapes most recently gathered and thus new wine, but also the place where that wine is drunk. Places which are open have branches of fir over their entrances, and a sign is hung out. Genuine "Heurige" serve only their own wine, and they are open each year for only from three weeks to a maximum of six months. (Generally they use the self-service system.)

The big Heurige in Grinzing and the so-called "Nobel Heurige" are for the most part only pseudo-Heurige. They serve cold and hot meals, and their wines often come from Lower Austria.

The little village of Grinzing is first mentioned in records in 1114. It was destroyed by the Turks in 1529 and there was a great fire in 1604. The village was destroyed again by the Turks in 1683 and in 1809 by the French. Nowadays there is another

Grinzing, synonymous with the Viennese "Heurige"

type of destruction, caused by the erection of buildings on the vineyards.

In order to counter this building it is possible for individuals to purchase 1 square yard (1m^2) of Grinzing with a vine. The vine is given a name-plaque, the purchaser receiving a certificate and declaration of ownership. Among owners of Grinzing vines are Kurt Waldheim, Jimmy Carter, Leonard Bernstein and Sophia Loren.

Gumpoldskirchen

Location
Between Mödling and Baden

Südbahn station
Gumpoldskirchen (S1, R10)

Bus
From Wien-Mitte Bus Station

Distance
11½ miles (18 km) S

Amid the vineyards, at the foot of Anniger, lies Gumpolds-kirchen, which is famous for its wine. There is evidence that wine has been made here for a thousand years, perhaps even for twice as long. Gumpoldskirchen wines – Zierfandler, Rot-gipfler and Neuburger – were the first alcoholic beverages to take the air in the Zeppelin and graced the choice table on the occasion of the crowning of Queen Elizabeth II in London.

Visitors generally go to Gumpoldskirchen to drink the new wine in inns and pubs. The Renaissance Town Hall and the picturesque old houses of the burghers are also noteworthy.

Haarhof   B4

Location
1, Between Naglergasse and Wallnerstrasse

Underground station
Stephansplatz (U1)

Opening times
Adler Collection,
Wed. 5–7 p.m. in winter months

This tiny lane acquired its name which means "Hair Yard" because originally flax-sellers used to live here. The city ditch used to pass through here.

Since 1683 No. 1 has housed the Wine Cellar of the Dukes of Esterhazy.

No. 4 houses the collection of the Adler Heraldic and Genealogical Society. It has a collection of painted coats of arms, family trees and pedigrees, impressions of seals and some 80,000 family insignia.

Haydn Museum   C3

Location
6, Haydngasse 19

Underground station
Pilgramgasse (U4)

Bus 57A

Trams
52, 58

Opening Times
Daily (except Mon.) 9 a.m.–
12.15 p.m. and 1–4.30 p.m.

Joseph Haydn acquired the single-storey house in the little street known as Steingasse (which later received the name Haydngasse) in 1793. He lived here until his death, and it was here he wrote his oratorios "The Creation" and "The Seasons". When he died in 1809 shortly after the second occupation of Vienna by the French, Napoleon ordered the posting of a Guard of Honour outside his house.

The museum here was opened in 1899. Among the objects on display are letters, manuscripts and personal possessions as well as two pianos and the deathmask of the composer.

Also in the house is a memorial room to Brahms, with memen-toes and furniture from the composer's last home and a pic-torial record of his later life and works.

Heeresgeschichtliches Museum   D5

Location
3, Arsenalstrasse, Objekt 1

The Museum of Army History is housed in the oldest building in Vienna to have been designed specifically as a museum. It

Museum of Army History: the exterior and some of the exhibits

contains valuable collections of militaria and historical relics concerned with the history of the army and of warfare in Austria from the outbreak of the Thirty Years' War to the First World War.

It was Emperor Franz Joseph I who commissioned the museum, and Ludwig Förster and Theophil Hansen erected between 1850 and 1857 a building inspired by Byzantine architectural styles.

Ground Floor

On the ground floor are the Hall of the Field-Marshals, the Navy Room to the left, the Emperor Franz Joseph Room and the Heavy Artillery Room to the right.

The Hall of the Field-Marshals contains 36 life-size marble statues of Austrian rulers and military commanders.

The Navy Room has an impressive collection of model ships which recount the history of the Imperial (later the Royal and Imperial) Navy. The exhibits include a model of the "Novara" which circumnavigated the globe and a model of a longitudinal section (to a 1:25 scale) of the Austrian Navy's First World War battleship "Viribus Unitis" which was launched in 1911.

The Franz Joseph Room recalls the era of the Emperor with portraits, the insignia of the family Orders, pennants and uniforms. In an adjoining room stands the motor car in which the heir to the throne, Archduke Franz Ferdinand, and his wife tragically lost their lives when attacked by an assassin in Sarajevo on 28 June 1914. Other mementoes are the Archduke's uniform, pictures and documents.

Underground station
Südtirolerplatz (U1)

S-Bahn station
Südbahnhof
(S1, S2, S3)

Buses
13A, 69A

Trams
D, O, 18

Opening times
Daily (except Fri.) 10 a.m.–4 p.m.

The Heavy Artillery Room has a display of the monarchy's heaviest guns from the period between 1859 and 1916. The most impressive is an M16 15in (38cm) motorised howitzer.

First Floor
The first floor houses the Commemorative Rooms; the Radetzky Room and the Archduke Charles Room are on the right, and on the left is the Prince Eugene Room and the Maria Theresa Room.

The Hall of Fame is a domed chamber with frescoes illustrating the most important military events in Austrian history.

The Radetzky Room is devoted to the period between Napoleon's downfall and the 1848 Revolutions and to the memory of Field-Marshal Radetzky. Relics of the Duke of Reichstadt, Napoleon's son, are displayed in a showcase.

The Archduke Charles Room recalls the Napoleonic era by means of pictures by Peter Krafft. There is a hot-air balloon (a "Montgolfière") which was captured from the French and a Russian officer's greatcoat which Napoleon is said to have worn when he was exiled to Elba.

The Prince Eugene Room has a display of weapons and armour from the period of the Thirty Years' War and the wars against the Turks. There are also 15 battle scenes by the Court Painter, Peeter Snayer. Mementoes of Prince Eugene include his breastplate, his Marshal's baton and his shroud.

The Maria Theresa Room illustrates the events of the War of the Spanish Succession and the last wars against the Turks. The Turkish Tent of State was probably captured at Peterwardein in 1716. The mortar did great service at the Siege of Belgrade in 1717. The central showcase shows the institution of the Order of Maria Theresa after the Battle of Kolin in 1757.

The Artillery Halls, Objekte 2 and 17, contain the largest collection of guns in the world. Most of them date from the 16th and 18th c.

*Heiligenkreuz (monastery)

Distance
19¼ miles (34km) SW

Bus
From Wien-Mitte Bus Station (1092, 1093, 1094)

The prettiest route to Heiligenkreuz goes through the village of Perchtoldsdorf with its vineyards and Trinity Pillar by J. B. Fischer von Erlach on the Main Square, the friendly little town of Mödling and through the Hinterbrühl Valley (with an underground grotto by the lake and the historic Höldrichsmühle Inn).
The Cistercian Monastery of Heiligenkreuz was founded in the 12th c., and the main buildings date from the 17th c. The monastery church is Romanesque and has important stained glass dating from about 1300. The rich carving in the choir is by Giovanni Giulani (1707).
In the chapter-house may be seen the gravestone of Frederick II, the last Babenberg Duke. Visitors who take the conducted tour are also shown the Early Gothic cloister with more than 300 marble pillars.
In the Monastery Museum (West wing of the courtyard) illustrations dating from the 13th c. to the 16th c. are on show, together

Heiligenkreuz: Trinity Pillar in the monastery courtyard

with about 150 clay models by the Venetian Baroque sculptor Giulani (1663–1744) who resided in the monastery as a "house guest" ("familaris") from 1711 until his death.

The hunting-lodge of Mayerling, today a Carmelite nunnery, lies 6 miles (10km) away. In 1889 it was the scene of the tragedy when Crown Prince Rudolf and Mary Vetsera perished.

Mayerling

Heiligenkreuzerhof

B5

The present Heiligenkreuzerhof complex, consisting of the abbey church, the prelacy, the counting-house and the courtyard, lies in the old and now totally refurbished Schönlaterngasse District (see entry). The Heiligenkreuzerhof was erected between 1659 and 1676 at the behest of the Abbots of the Monastery of Heiligenkreuz (see entry). Considerable alterations were made in 1746 when the complex took on the appearance it has at present. The counting-house was not built until 1754. The Baroque painter Martino Altomonte lived here in the monastery until his death in 1745. He spent his declining years here, paying rent and painting a fresco without payment, but he did dine at the Abbot's table.

Location
1, Schönlaterngasse 5

Underground station
Stephansplatz (U1)

Bus
1A

The Bernhard Chapel near the prelacy is used for weddings and is one of the most beautiful of Vienna's churches. The picture above the High Altar, by Altomonte, dates from 1730.

*Heiligenstadt

Location
19th District

Underground station
Heiligenstadt (U4)

S-Bahn station
Heiligenstadt (S9)

Tram
D, 37

Heiligenstadt, incorporated in Döbling in 1892, is the oldest and the prettiest of the Viennese wine-producing villages. Its narrow, winding streets have helped to keep it free from too much bustle. In the area around Probusgasse and Armbrustergasse it is still possible to see how the place used to look, with its vineyards and Empire and early 19th c. houses. St Jacob's Church (3 Pfarrplatz) was built in Romanesque times on Roman foundations; although frequently destroyed, altered and rebuilt, it is still worth seeing.

Beethoven stayed in Heilingenstadt on several occasions; in 1802 while working at 6 Probusgasse on his Second Symphony, he wrote his "Heiligenstadt Testament", a letter to his brothers Carl and Johann which he never sent. The house is under the administration of the Vienna City Historical Museum. (Open: Tues.–Sun. 10 a.m.–12.15 p.m., 1 p.m.–4.30 p.m.) In 1817 he was once more living in Heilingenstadt, this time at 2 Pfarrplatz, where he worked on his Pastoral Symphony.

*Historisches Museum der Stadt Wien (museum)   C4

Location
4, Karlsplatz 8

Underground station
Karlsplatz (U1, U2, U4)

Buses
4A, 59A

Trams
1, 2, D, J, 62, 65.

Opening times
Tues.–Sun. 9 a.m.–
4.30 p.m. (2nd floor:
closed noon–1.15 p.m.)

The Vienna City Historical Museum stands on Karlsplatz. The Vienna City Council decided to transfer it there from the New Town Hall on the occasion of the 80th birthday of Theodor Körner, the Federal President. It was opened in 1959, but Körner was no longer alive, having died in 1957.

The exhibits on show in the museum display particularly clearly the history of the city of Vienna. All exhibits are numbered.

Ground Floor
Neolithic Period–Time of the Tribal Migrations. Finds from the Stone Age, Bronze and Iron Ages and the time of the Tribal Migrations. The most important exhibits are a painted Sequani gravestone (2nd c.; 1/28), a Roman altar (1/20) and an ancient treasury (1/12).

Middle Ages and Late Middle Ages. Views of the city and plans illustrating its development. The Albertinischer Plan (1/79) is considered to be the oldest plan of the city of Vienna. There are stone fragments and valuable architectural remains from St Stephen's Cathedral. These were removed during restoration and carefully preserved. Among them are an Early Gothic Anna Selbdritt (about 1320; 1/40), three larger-than-life-size pairs of Princes (about 1360–65; 1/43), Gothic stained glass from the Duke's Chapel (1/49) and the remains of an altar of lime wood (14th c.; 1/73).

Collection of weapons from armouries and arsenal. Among the exhibits are suits of armour, shields, spears and halberds, and also the oldest Italian horse-armour (1/82) and the funeral arms of Emperor Frederick III (1/77).

First Floor
History of Vienna in the 16th c. It was a warlike century, and so exhibits include weapons, armour, such as the gilt armour of Imperial Princes (2/30), ensigns, orders and battle pictures.

Counter-Reformation to the Great War against the Turks. The life of Vienna in the 17th c. is represented in portraits,

Historical Museum of the City of Vienna

From 1780 to the Present Day

SECOND FLOOR

SECOND FLOOR
1 Pompeian Salon
2 First half of the 19th c.
3 Second half of the 19th c.
4 1848 Revolution
5 Grillparzer's Apartments
6 Theatre
7 Model of city as in 1898
8 Loos's living-room
9 Otto Wagner
10 Painting about 1900
11 First half of the 19th c.

From 1500 to 1780

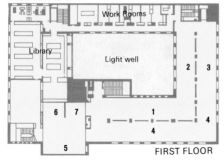

FIRST FLOOR

FIRST FLOOR
1–4 History of the City from the 16th to the 18th c.: weapons, Turkish Siege; views of city, pictures, porcelain, etc.
5 Model of the Inner City in 1852–54
6–7 Castle of Laxenburg

Neolithic Period to 1500

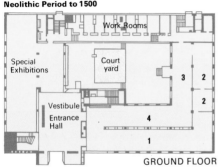

GROUND FLOOR

GROUND FLOOR
1 Prehistory, Roman period, Tribal Migrations
2–4 Middle Ages (maps of the city, views, architectural fragments from St Stephen's Cathedral, stained glass), Weapons and armour

medallions, coats of arms and etchings and engravings. An exceptional suit of armour (2/44) recalls the Thirty Years' War, and the Turkish ensigns (2/81–83) are mementoes of Prince Eugene's victory over the Turks at Zenta.

The transition from Baroque to Classicism and City life in the 18th c. The views of Vienna by Delsenbach (2/108–110) are particularly interesting, as are the guild booths (2/132–137), the old house signs and traders' signs (2/162, 187–194) and the Baroque paintings, sculptures and prints (2/141 onwards).

Second Floor

Napoleonic Era. Medallions from the reign of Francis II (3/37). The Caprara-Greymüller Empire Salon. This "Pompeian Salon" with its gold, white and pastel shades, tells us about the environment in which the nobility lived about 1800.

The Congress of Vienna, the early 19th c. (Biedermeier period), pre-1848 period and Revolution. There are a great number of paintings here with all the Viennese painters of the Biedermeier period represented (Fendi, Schindler, Danhauser, Gauermann, Rieter, Waldmüller and Amerling). There are displays of the fashions of the day (3/101), glass and porcelain (3/21), a survey of Viennese Biedermeier period social games (3/58), Lanner's giraffe piano (3/69) and Fanny Elssler's butterfly grand piano (3/81/2). The time of the Revolution is evoked in prints and paintings, and weapons of the National Guard are on show (3/103–123).

Foundation period (i.e. mid 19th c.). This is illustrated by portraits and relics, in handicrafts and busts. Theatrical life of the period is evoked, too.

Franz Grillparzer's Apartments. When the house at 21 Spiegelgasse was demolished, everything was brought here and the apartments were set up with careful attention to detail. The living-room of the architect Loos. This is one of the most outstanding examples of Viennese interior design from the early 20th c.

Jugendstil (Viennese Art Nouveau). The most important exhibits include paintings by Klimt (3/191–193) and Schiele (3/205–209) and designs by Kolo Moser (3/198, 225, 226/1, 228/10–12). There is also a sculpture by Rodin (3/231).

Vienna between the wars and during the Second World War. Documentation concerning the history of the period and modern art. There are works by Wotruba (3/237, 238) Kokoschka (3/240), Herbert Böckl (3/243–246), Rudolf Hausner (3/260) and Albert Paris Gütersloh (3/212).

History in pictures: mainly portraits of important personalities.

** Hofburg (castle)   B/C4

Location
1, Michaelerplatz 1, Burgring

Underground stations
Stephansplatz, (U1)
Mariahilferstrasse (U2)

Bus
2A

Trams
1, 2, D, J, 52, 58

The Imperial Castle in the inner city was for more than six centuries (up to 1918) the seat of the ruler of Austria, and for two and a half centuries (up to 1806) it was the seat of the German Emperor. It is now the official seat of the Austrian Head of State. The Federal President of Austria exercises his office and carries out representative functions in rooms once belonging to Maria Theresa.

The complex consists of ten major buildings, and in them may be seen a reflection of the 700-year-long architectural history of the Hofburg. Nearly every Austrian ruler since 1275 ordered additions or alterations to be made to the palace.

Accordingly in the Hofburg examples may be seen of architecture in a great variety of styles – Gothic, Renaissance, Baroque, Rococo, Classicism and the early 1870s.

Together with its squares and gardens the entire Hofburg complex occupies an area of some 59 acres (240,000m²). This "city within a city" comprises 18 ranges of buildings, 54 major staircases, 19 courtyards and 2,600 rooms. Some 5,000 people are employed here.

Castle layout

Schweizerhof or Schweizertrakt (the Swiss courtyard or range) is the name commonly given to the Alte Burg (Old Castle). There is evidence that it has been here since 1279. Ferdinand I had the buildings reconstructed in the style of a Renaissance castle between about 1547 and 1552.

Alte Burg (Old Castle)

The massive Schweizertor (Swiss Gate) dates from this period. All the emperors resided in the Burg from Ferdinand I's time until 1916.

Burgkapelle. The present castle chapel was constructed on the orders of Emperor Ferdinand III between 1447 and 1449. In the 17th and 18th c. there were alterations and additions in the Baroque style. More changes were made in the 19th c. when the interior was reconverted to the Gothic style in 1802.

Maria Theresa had the old wooden altars replaced by marble ones, and the present High Altar dates from 1802. The tabernacle contains Ferdinand II's miraculous cross; according to legend it inspired him with courage during the Wars of Religion.

Burgkapelle

The Burgkapelle is now a much-favoured and distinguished setting for weddings. The cynics say that the thirteen 500-year-old wooden statues of the "Helpers in time of need" – the 14th was removed to make space for the pulpit – are in their right place in a church used for marriages.

Conducted tours
Tues. & Thurs.
2.30–3.30 p.m. except
July–mid Sept. and mid
Dec.–mid Jan.

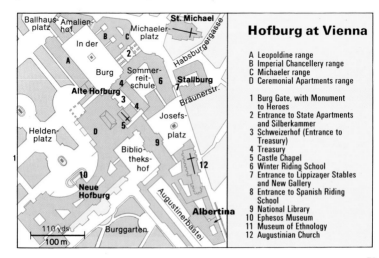

Hofburg at Vienna

A Leopoldine range
B Imperial Chancellery range
C Michaeler range
D Ceremonial Apartments range

1 Burg Gate, with Monument to Heroes
2 Entrance to State Apartments and Silberkammer
3 Schweizerhof (Entrance to Treasury)
4 Treasury
5 Castle Chapel
6 Winter Riding School
7 Entrance to Lippizaner Stables and New Gallery
8 Entrance to Spanish Riding School
9 National Library
10 Ephesos Museum
11 Museum of Ethnology
12 Augustinian Church

Hofburg

The boys' choir was originally founded to sing in the Burg-kapelle used by the Imperial Court. The Vienna Boys' Choir (see entry Wiener Sängerknaben) developed from this. It now sings at Sunday Mass at 9.15 a.m. except July–mid Sept.

Innerer Burghof

Innerer Burghof. The Inner Courtyard of the castle was used by the Emperor Maximilian II as a tilt-yard as early as 1545. Later it was the site of tourneys, festivities and executions. Today it is simply a park.

In 1846 a monument was erected to the memory of Emperor Francis II. On its plinth may be read a line from his will: "My life is for my peoples."

Stallburg (Mews)

Opening times
Visits to mews
See entry: Spanish Riding
School

In 1558 Emperor Ferdinand I ordered the construction of a Renaissance palace, one of the most important Renaissance buildings in Vienna, for the particular use of his son Maximilian. When Maximilian became Emperor and moved into the Hofburg, Maximilian's palace was converted into Court mews. Since the time of Charles VI the stables for the Lipizzaner horses have occupied the ground floor.

The Neue Galerie (see entry) is on the second floor of the Stallburg.

Amalienburg

Following the example of his father, Maximilian II had a palace built for the particular use of his son. He was called Rudolf, hence the original name of Rudolfsburg. In the 18th c., how-ever, the name was changed to Amalienburg when the Empress Wilhelmina Amalie lived here during her widowhood. The rooms later used by the Empress Elisabeth and Tsar Alex-ander I were furnished as State Apartments (Apartments 1322).

Leopoldinischertrakt

The Leopoldinischertrakt is a range of buildings built at the behest of Emperor Leopold I, Maria Theresa's grandfather. This Baroque range of buildings connects the Schweizerhof and the Amalienburg; they were erected between 1660 and 1680. They were occupied by Maria Theresa and her husband Francis Stephen of Lorraine; their apartments, together with those of Joseph II opposite them, now form part of the Presidential Chancellery. The Austrian President works in what was for-merly Joseph II's study.

Reichskanzleitrakt

The Imperial Chancellery range constitutes the NE wing linking the Schweizerhof and the Amalienburg. It was designed by J. E. Fischer von Erlach who gave it its Baroque façade. The building was completed in 1730. Some of its rooms are set out as State Apartments (see entry for Schauräume 1–12).

Winterreitschule

Opening times
Displays and morning
exercises see entry: Spanish
Riding School

The Winter Riding School, where the Spanish Riding School gives its equestrian displays, was the scene of numerous glit-tering events, especially during the Congress of Vienna in 1814 and 1815. This handsome white room was designed by J. E. Fischer von Erlach at the behest of Emperor Charles VI. The coffered ceiling spans an arena in which the horses exercise and which is 175ft (55m) long and 60ft (18m) wide. The gallery is borne on 46 pillars. The arena may be visited in July and August.

Michaelertrakt

The Michaeler range was the site of the Hofburg Theatre until 1888. After its demolition Emperor Franz Joseph I went back to the old plan drawn up by J. E. Fischer von Erlach and ordered

Heldenplatz: the Prince Eugene Monument

Wall-fountain in the Michael range

Schweizertor on the Schweizerhof

the construction of a range of buildings linking the Reichskanzleitrakt and the Winterreitschule. This was done between 1889 and 1893. The grandiose Michaelertor (Michael Gate) which is flanked by figures of Hercules leads into the domed chamber. The figures in the niches symbolise the mottoes of various rulers: "Constantia et Fortitudine" (With Constance and Fortitude – Emperor Charles VI), "Justitia et Clementia" (Justice and Mercy – Maria Theresa), "Virtute et Exemplo" (By Might and Example – Joseph II) and "Viribus Unitis" (With all our Strength United – Franz Joseph I). In the hallway are the entrances to the Silver Room (see entry) and to the State Apartments (see entry).

Hoftafel und Festsaaltrakt

In 1804 Francis I ordered the reconstruction of the oldest part of the castle to provide a ceremonial suite in Classical style. The area of the chamber is 1,200 sq. yd (1,000m^2). The magnificent coffered ceiling is supported on 24 Corinthian columns. It served as throne-room and ballroom. It was here that the Habsburgs formally renounced their rights to the throne in the event of a morganatic marriage (i.e. a marriage to a partner of lower social status). Nowadays the chamber is part of the Hofburg Congress Centre. Each year it provided the fitting setting for the Imperial Ball on New Year's Eve.

Heldenplatz

The Heldenplatz (Heroes' Square) was originally the parade-ground. After the erection of the two statues, one of Prince Eugene who defeated the Turks and the other to Archduke Charles who won the Battle of Aspern, it was given the name Heldenplatz. Both statues are the work of A. Ferkorn.

Ausseres Burgtor

The Outer Gate of the palace was built exclusively by soldiers, just as in Roman times. The plans were drawn up by Peter Nobile. It was inaugurated in 1824 on the anniversary of the Battle of Leipzig at which Napoleon was at last defeated. It was converted into a memorial to heroes in 1933.

Neue Burg

Plans for a vast Imperial Forum and a gigantic New Palace were drawn up by the architects Karl Hasenauer and Gottfried Semper. Emperor Franz Joseph I, however, gave his approval only to the building of a new wing to the palace, and the over-all plan was never carried out.

Work on the interior of the Neue Burg went on until 1926. It has only once been the scene of historic events: it was here that Hitler proclaimed the annexation of Austria in 1938. Nowadays museums are housed here: Museum für Völkerkunde (see entry), Ephesos-Museum (see entry), Reading Room of the Nationalbibliothek (see entry), the Portrait Collection and Picture Archive (see Nationalbibliothek), the Sammlung alter Musikinstrumente (see entry) and the Waffensammlung (see entry).

Court Tableware and Silberkammer

Location
Entry through Domed
Chamber in Michaelertrakt
(Michaelerplatz)

The so-called "Silver Chamber" has on display in six rooms the ceremonial and everyday tableware of the Imperial Court.

Opening times
Tues.–Fri. & Sun.
9 a.m.–1 p.m.

Room 1: East Asian porcelain; most of the exhibits belong to the 18th c.

Room 2: Formal service of the time of the Emperor Franz Joseph, now used at State receptions. Silver travelling service

of the Empress Elisabeth Christine, wife of Charles VI (Par
1717/18).

Room 3: Sèvres Services. There are three particularly fin
18th c. services of tableware in Sèvres porcelain, gift of th
French Court. 18th c. cutlery (Vienna, Paris).

Room 4: Milanese table centre. It is nearly 10ft (3m) long and
made of meticulously carved and gilded bronze. Meissen se
vice (c. 1775), Viennese Empire service (early 19th c.).

Room 5: The Ruby service. This is the most important of the
services for Imperial grand occasions, with settings for 140
guests. It is decorated with silver which was given a gold hue by
heat treatment. It was made by a Parisian goldsmith in the early
19th c. Smaller glass services (c. 1850), plates decorated with
pictures and flowers (1800–30).

Room 6: 19th c. tableware. The most important exhibits are
vases decorated with historical scenes and the "English service" which Queen Victoria gave to the Emperor Franz Joseph
and a Romantic period service in Neo-Gothic style (Vienna
1821–24).

Schauräume der Hofburg (Imperial Apartments)

The State Apartments open to the public in the Hofburg comprise the Franz Joseph Apartments in the Reichskanzleitrakt,
together with Elisabeth and Alexander's apartments in the
Amalienburg. It is not possible for visitors to see the living-
quarters and ceremonial apartments of Empress Maria
Theresa and of her son Emperor Joseph II (the Leopoldinischertrakt). This is because they are the official residence of the
Austrian President. The furnishing of most rooms remains
unaltered.

Location
Entry through Domed
Chamber in Michaelertrakt

Tours
Mon.–Sat. 8.30 a.m.–
4 p.m.; Sun. 8.30 a.m.–
12.30 p.m.

Dining-room: Here the Emperor used to take his meals with his
Staff officers. The cartoons for the Gobelins tapestries from

Franz Joseph's Apartments

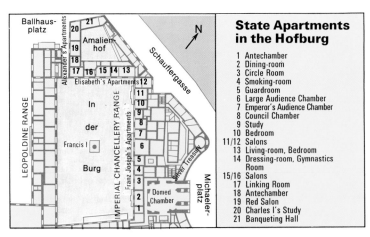

State Apartments in the Hofburg

1 Antechamber
2 Dining-room
3 Circle Room
4 Smoking-room
5 Guardroom
6 Large Audience Chamber
7 Emperor's Audience Chamber
8 Council Chamber
9 Study
10 Bedroom
11/12 Salons
13 Living-room, Bedroom
14 Dressing-room, Gymnastics Room
15/16 Salons
17 Linking Room
18 Antechamber
19 Red Salon
20 Charles I's Study
21 Banqueting Hall

Oudenarde in Belgium were probably the work of the Flemish painter Peter Paul Rubens.

Circle Room: This was where the Court used to meet for conversation after meals. Rococo ceramic stove which was fuelled from the corridor. 17th c. Flemish tapestries with scenes from the life of the Emperor Augustus.

Smoking-room: The tapestries represent themes from Graeco-Roman history.

Guardroom: In the guardroom of the Imperial Life Guards the most interesting exhibit is the model of the old Hofburg.

Large Audience Chamber: This was the waiting-room for the audiences which took place twice a week. The Bohemian crystal candelabrum with 80 candles is especially fine.

The Emperor's Audience Chamber: On a lectern lies a list of people coming to an audience on 10 January 1910. It is said that audiences were conducted with everybody standing. Even the Emperor stood by his desk when he received those who came to an audience.

Council Chamber: It was in this room that the Emperor discussed matters with the Privy Councillors and his Ministers. It is furnished in Empire style.

Study: The rose-wood furniture is in the Louis XV style. The study contains the bust and sabre of Field-Marshal Radetzky who was one of the small select band permitted to appear unannounced before the Emperor.

Bedroom: Franz Joseph I lived simply. He slept in a modest iron bed and took his bath in a wooden tub which was placed in the bedroom. (He died at Schönbrunn; see entry.)

Large Salon: This room has rose-wood furniture with bronze fittings. Francis Xavier Winterhalter's famous picture shows the Empress Elisabeth in a fine gown with jewelled stars in her hair.

Small Salon: In the former breakfast-room may be seen one of the few portraits of Maximilian of Mexico, the Emperor's brother, and a bust of Admiral Tegetthof who brought back from Mexico the body of this unfortunate Prince.

Elisabeth's Apartments

Living-room: This is one of the prettiest rooms in the Hofburg. It served as living-room and bedroom, with its bureau, reading-desk, Neo-Gothic altar of Carrara marble and bed. The Spartan iron bed was pushed away during daytime.

Gymnastics Room: Elisabeth was fanatical about keeping slim and was a superb horsewoman. She, therefore, had gymnastic equipment fitted in her dressing-room which, moreover, she used regularly, much to the disgust of the Court.

Large Salon: Everything here is splendid. There is Louis XIV furniture, large Sèvres porcelain vases, Romantic landscape-paintings and Antonio Canova's marble statue of Napoleon's sister.

Small Salon: The showcases contain mementoes of the Empress who was assassinated in Geneva in 1898. There is a photograph of the gown she was wearing on the day she met her death.

Antechamber: The pictures are by Martin van Meytens, Maria Theresa's Court Painter (or from his studio); they portray her children. There is also a life-size statue of the 15-year-old Empress Elisabeth.

These take their name from Tsar Alexander I who occupied the rooms during the Congress of Vienna.

Alexander's Apartments

Linking Room: The busts are of the last Austrian emperor, Emperor Charles I, and of his consort, Empress Zita.

Red Salon: It is also called the "Boucher Salon" because the tapestries were worked to designs by François Boucher. They were presented to Emperor Joseph II by Marie-Antoinette. After 1916 it became Emperor Charles I's Audience Chamber.

Study: Charles I used to work beneath these 18th c. Brussels tapestries. It was at this desk that he drafted his abdication proclamation. The picture near the desk shows the Emperor in the uniform of an Imperial and Royal Field-Marshal.

Banqueting Hall. A special feature of the canopied "Highest Table" which is bedecked with gold and silver is the placing of all the cutlery on the right-hand side of the plate, in accordance with Spanish Court etiquette.

Secular and Sacred Treasury

The Treasuries – reopened in 1987 after four years of restoration – contain in 21 rooms the Imperial regalia and relics of the Holy Roman Empire of the German Nation, coronation and chivalric insignia, badges of rank, secular and sacred treasures, and ornaments and mementoes formerly owned by the Habsburgs. It is all of incalculable artistic, historic and material value.

Opening times
Mon., Wed.–Fri. 10 a.m.–6 p.m. Sat., Sun 9 a.m.–5.30 p.m.

The origins of the Treasury go back to Ferdinand I's "Kunstkammer" (art chamber). From the 16th c. onwards all the emperors brought their treasures here and kept them in various rooms in the Hofburg. During Charles VI's reign the Treasury was moved to the ground floor of the palace. The iron door at the entrance bears the date 1712 and the Emperor's monogram. Secular and Sacred Treasuries are described together in the text. After leaving Room 8 of the Secular Treasury the visitor passes through the Robes Corridor into the 5 rooms housing the Sacred exhibits. Then, beginning with Room 9, the visitor returns to the Secular Treasury.

The Secular Treasury is housed in 16 rooms, with the collections organised on a thematic basis.

Secular Treasury

Room 1: Insignia of hereditary fealty. This applied to the Habsburg monarchs who as rulers of Austria had the rank of Archduke until 1804, whereas in the Holy Roman Empire they ruled as Emperors and Kings. The Imperial orb (second half of the

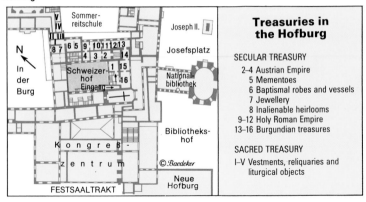

Treasuries in the Hofburg

SECULAR TREASURY

2–4 Austrian Empire
5 Mementoes
6 Baptismal robes and vessels
7 Jewellery
8 Inalienable heirlooms
9–12 Holy Roman Empire
13–16 Burgundian treasures

SACRED TREASURY

I–V Vestments, reliquaries and liturgical objects

15th c.) was borne by the Emperor Matthias. The sceptre (mid 14th c.) belonged to Charles IV, and the sword of investiture, used at fealty ceremonies, belonged to Maximilian I.

Room 2: The Habsburgs, who remained Holy Roman Emperors until 1806, had their own private insignia made, since the insignia of the Empire were kept in Nuremberg from 1424. On view are the Imperial Crown ("Kaiserliche Hauskrone") of Rudolf II, made by the Court Jeweller Jan Vermeyen (1598–1602) together with the orb and sceptre made in Prague (1612–15).

Room 3: In 1804, with the rise of Napoleon, the Holy Roman Empire came to an end and Francis II proclaimed the hereditary Austrian Empire. Exhibited is his gold-embroidered mantel with an ermine collar which he wore in 1830 when his son was crowned King of Hungary. Also on view are civil orders; the Hungarian Order of St Stephen (1764), the Austrian Order of Leopold (1808) and the Order of the Iron Crown (1815).

Room 4: The Congress of Vienna awarded Austria the Lombardo-Venetian kingdom. The coronation regalia and sword are exhibited, together with a herald's tabard of this kingdom.

Room 5: Mementoes of Marie Louise, daughter of Emperor Francis I and consort of Napoleon I. These include a silver jewel box, a silver-gilt trivet presented by the City of Milan on the birth of her son (King of Rome, Duke of Reichsstadt), a silver-gilt cradle given by the City of Paris on the same occasion. There are also mementoes of the Emperor Maximilian of Mexico.

Room 6: Baptismal robes and vessels. Among the exhibits are the baptismal robes given by Maria Theresa. It is said that the Empress herself undertook some of the embroidery. There is also a gold christening flagon and spoon (1571) and a little gold jug from the Prague Court workshop.

Room 7: Jewellery. Only very little of the Imperial jewellery was preserved. On 1 November 1918 the Senior Chamberlain,

Count Berchtold, took the Habsburgs private jewellery out of the country at the command of Charles I. On view are the Colombian emerald (2,680 carats), hollowed out to form a salt-cellar and polished (1641) and the hyacinth "la bella" (416 carats), set as a double eagle into enamel, flanked by an opal and an amethyst. A small genealogical tree presents sixteen portraits of the Habsburgs in chalcedony cameos; there are displays of 19th c. jewellery and insignia. There is also the "Golden Rose", a Papal decoration given in 1819 to Carolina Augusta, fourth wife of Frances I, two Turkish sabres used by Charles VI and Maria Theresa at the Hungarian coronation and the crown of Stephen Bocskay who became King of Hungary in 1605.

Room 8: Inalienable heirlooms. Two items left by King Ferdinand I (1564) were considered so valuable that the Habsburgs raised them to the status of inalienable heirlooms. They are an agate dish of the 4th c., the largest of its kind that is known and which was once considered to be the vessel of the Holy Grail, and the 96in. (243cm) long narwhal's horn which in the Middle Ages was believed to be the horn of the legendary unicorn, a symbol of Christ.

Room 9: Holy Roman Empire. The presence of the regalia of the Electoral Prince of Bohemia is explained by the fact that from the 14th c. the elected king was also King of Bohemia and, therefore, the duties of the electoral office were delegated to a deputy at the coronation festivities. Also on show are pictures and documents of the coronation of Joseph II (1764).

Room 10: Holy Roman Empire. Garments which formed part of the Imperial regalia from the 13th c. came into the possession of the Hohenstaufens; they were presumably used at the coronation of Frederick II and were assigned in 1246 to the Imperial Treasury. They include the coronation mantel of King Roger II, made 1133–34, an indigo tunic of the same period, a white robe of 1181 which corresponded to the outer garment of the Byzantine emperor and which was later worn as an alb, red silk stockings of the last Norman king, William II, sumptuous shoes and gloves and a gold-woven sword belt from Sicily. Two items were added in the 14th c. – the eagle dalmatic which was worn instead of the blue tunic and a stole.

Room 11: Imperial Jewels and Coronation Insignia of the Holy Roman Empire. On view are the Imperial Crown (2nd half of 10th c.), the Sacred Lance, the Processional Cross and the Imperial Cross (1024–25), the orb (end of 12th c.), the Gothic sceptre, the Aspergillum used for sprinkling holy water on the altar and the Imperial Cross (renewed c. 1200). Also exhibited are the Imperial Gospel, a Carolingian purple codex (end of 8th c.), on which the new ruler took the oath and the sword (first half 10th c.) formerly a relic of Charles the Great with which kings were girded at their coronation.

Room 12: Here can be seen the sacred relics belonging to the Imperial Treasury.

Rooms 13–16: Treasures of the Burgundians. These comprise the treasures of the Order of the Golden Fleece and the inheritance of Maria of Burgundy who married the future Emperor Maximilian. On show are the insignia of the Order, coats

The crown of the Holy Roman Empire and the Imperial Cross

of arms and Mass vessels (between 1425 and 1475) as well as the Cross (about 1400) of the Order of the Golden Fleece on which the oath was taken and Philip the Good's Court cup (c. 1453–67).

Sacred Treasury

The five rooms of the Sacred Treasury exhibit liturgical objects, reliquaries and robes which were used at the Imperial Court. Room 1: 18th c. robes and the silver-gilt replica of the Am Hof Maria Column (see Am Hof).

Room 2: Medieval objects and the reliquary cross of the Hungarian King Ludwig the Great (between 1370 and 1382). St Stephen's purse, the oldest item in the Sacred Treasury (late 11th or early 12th c.), a Gothic goblet belonging to the Emperor Frederick III (1438). Also to be seen is a collection of reliquaries and small altars of ebony with silver or gold decoration (late 16th–early 17th c.).

Room 3: As well as cut gem stones, Augsburg silver work and rock-crystal there are valuable carvings including crucifixes (Giambologna, Guglielmo della Porta), a Crucifixion group (Geremias Geisebrunn), an ebony tempietto (Christoph Angermair).

Room 4: Among the most impressive items are the reliquary which holds the nail which is said to have pierced the right hand of Christ, two reliquary altars (1660–80) which belonged to the Emperor Leopold I and the monstrance containing the fragments of the Cross, which were preserved in a miraculous fashion in 1668 when the Hofburg caught fire.

Room 5: 18th and 19th c. works including 22 reliquary busts, some of them very large and made of silver, rosaries and a tempietto with one of St Peter's teeth.

*Hoher Markt

B4/5

The oldest square in Vienna is found on the edge of the textile district (called "Fetzenviertel" by the Viennese, meaning "the rag district"). It is rich with memories that go back to the very start of the city's history. The Romans called it the "old forum"; here stood the palace of the Commander of the Roman fortress of Vindobona, and it is here that Emperor Marcus Aurelius died. In the Middle Ages executions were carried out here. It was the Reuthof of the Babenbergers, the fish market and the trading site favoured by the cloth-sellers. After the destruction resulting from the events of 1945 nearly all the houses in the Hoher Markt had to be rebuilt. The focal point of the square is the Espousals Fountain (sometimes called Joseph's Fountain) which depicts the espousal of Joseph and Mary. The statue is by Antonio Corradini. Originally it was erected by J. B. Fischer von Erlach who used wood. In 1792 it was restored by his son J. E. Fischer who replaced the wood with white marble. It was paid for by Leopold I.

Location
1 Hoher Markt/
Rotenturmstrasse-
Wipplingerstrasse

Underground stations
Stephansplatz, Schwedenplatz
(U1, U4)

Buses
2A, 3A

Trams
1, 2 (quayside)

Ankeruhr

On the E side of the square it is impossible not to see the splendid clock of the Anker Insurance Company on the archway

The Anker clock – historical figures pass across on the hour

Roman ruins at the Hoher Markt

spanning Rotgasse. Every hour historical figures solemnly go past in order from 1 to 12 – Emperor Marcus Aurelius (1), Charlemagne (2), Duke Leopold IV and Theodora of Byzantium (3), the poet Walter von der Vogelweide (4), King Rudolf I with his consort, Anna of Hohenburg (5), Master Hans Puchsbaum (6), Emperor Maximilian I (7), Mayor A. von Liebenberg (8), Count Rüdiger von Starhemberg (9), Prince Eugene (10), Empress Maria Theresa with Emperor Francis I (11) and Joseph Haydn (12). At noon all the figures form up and process, accompanied by music.

This remarkable clock was built by the painter Franz von Matsch at the beginning of the First World War. It is dedicated to "the people of Vienna".

Roman Remains

Opening times
Daily (except Mon.)
10 a.m.–12.15 p.m.,
1–4.30 p.m.

A stairway by house No. 3 leads down to underground ruins dating from the Roman period. It is possible to see the footings of walls of houses for officers in the neighbourhood of the barracks of Vindobona (2nd and 3rd c.). There are also remains of a Germanic house (4th c.), as well as casts of reliefs, stamped tiles, remnants of a palisade and, in showcases, various remains.

*Hotel Sacher ·   C4

Location
1, Philharmonikerstrasse 1

Vienna's most famous old-world hotel still preserves its style and quality, with silk tablecloths, Biedermeier furniture from the mid 19th c. and valuable pictures.

Eduard Sacher had the hotel built in 1876. But his cigar-smoking wife Anna Sacher became more famous than he did. She used to allow unlimited credit to the scions of rich parents – the so-called "Sacher lads" – until they came into their inheritances. She also organised those discreet little "séparées" which have survived at any rate in literature in Arthur Schnitzler's "Abschiedssouper" (The Farewell Supper). Now the famous "separate rooms" have become little dining-rooms.

A hint: for genuine Sacher "Torte", the only ones that are genuine as was made clear in a long-drawn-out court case, it is necessary to go to a tiny shop round the corner in Kärntnerstrasse. They come in all sizes and all sorts of packages. The "Torte" were invented by a predecessor of Sacher during the Congress of Vienna

Underground stations
Stephansplatz (U1), Karlsplatz (U1, U2, U4)

Trams
1, 2, D, J (Ring)

*Hundertwasser Haus   B/C5/6

This fantastic residential complex is the creation of artist Friedensreich Hundertwasser (b. 1928), built between 1983 and 1985 by the local authority as part of a housing project. Most of the residents are artists, a fact which pleases Hundertwasser. The residents, on the other hand, are perhaps not as happy about the crowds of visitors who flock daily to see the controversial building, and, understandably, are no longer willing to put their homes on show.

There are 50 apartments of various sizes, outlook and structure in the complex which also contains a terrace café, doctor's surgery and health food store.

Location
3, Kegelgasse/Löwengasse

Underground and S-Bahn station
Wien-Mitte/Landstrasse (U4, S7)

Bus 75A

Tram O

The Hundertwasser House

91

Each apartment has its own colour and round the whole edifice runs a 3 mile (5km) long ceramic band, joining the apartments and at the same time separating them by an individual colour. In general Hundertwasser follows the principle of "the tolerance of irregularity", so that all corners are rounded, the windows are of different sizes; internally bathrooms are irregularly tiled, corridor floors uneven and the walls wavy (on the lowest storey the wall provides a surface on which children can scribble and paint). The façades of the complex imitate those of the aristocratic palaces and houses on the Grand Canal in Venice. In addition a piece of the old house was incorporated into the façade so that the "spirit of the old house resettles in the new one" and places it under its protection.

Note
Hundertwasser fans may like to visit the snack-bar at 43 Kegelgasse to see the toilets he designed.

Two golden "onion towers" surmount the building which, according to Hundertwasser, raises the occupier to the status of a king. Lively elements are the coloured crooked pillars, the fountain and the figural decoration, all copies of originals. Art or kitsch – the viewer must decide for himself!

*Josefsplatz   C4

Location
1, Augustinerstrasse

Underground station
Stephansplatz (U1)

Bus
2A

The Josefsplatz is deservedly called the finest square in Vienna. It is 200 years old, was built in a unified Late Baroque style and creates a fine impression. Round it stands the Österreichische National Bibliothek (see entry), the Winterreitschule (see Hofburg), the Palais Pálffy (see entry) and the Palais Pallavicini. The Palais Pallavicini (No. 5 – now a club and conference centre) is a noble Classical building with a magnificent portal supported on caryatides and figures on the metopes dating from 1786 by F. A. Zauner. The Palais itself was built by Ferdinand von Hohenberg in 1783–84.

The memorial in the middle of the square shows Maria Theresa's son, Joseph II; it is by A. Zauner and dates from 1795 to 1806. The reformer, clad in the garb of a Roman emperor, is shown blessing his people. The reliefs on the memorial celebrate Joseph's services to Austrian commerce and recall the many journeys he made abroad in order to benefit his people. The memorial became the spot where Viennese people loyal to the Imperial principle gathered in 1848 while the Revolution was in progress. It was their homage to an Emperor who had died half a century earlier.

Josefstädter Bezirksmuseum (Regional Museum)   B3

Location
8, Langegasse 34

Underground station
Lerchenfelderstrasse (U2)

Bus
13A

Opening times
Tues.–Sat. 8 a.m. to midnight,
Sun. 2 p.m. to midnight

Up until 1963 rolls, croissants and bread were baked in the Old Bakehouse. Since 1965 it has been in part an offshoot of the Josefstadt Regional Museum with displays illustrating the crafts and trades of the area and, in part, a unique gastronomical business.

All sorts of objects connected with baking are on show – dough-troughs, weights, measures and the old baking-ovens. These all date from 1701. It was at that period that a well-to-do baker built for himself one of the finest Baroque houses in Vienna.

The bakery has been restored meticulously to its original form, and a café has been installed here. The wine bar was once the flour store, and the "snug" was the coachman's room.

Josefsplatz, Vienna's finest Late Baroque square

A tip – the "Millirahmstrudel" taste best when they have just come out of the ovens at midday.

*Josephinum (anatomia plastica)   B4

The Institute of the History of Medicine and the Pharmacognostic Institute for Medicine are housed in the palatial Late Baroque building designed by Isidor Canevale.

The world-famous collection of anatomical and obstetric models (anatomia plastica) in wax was commissioned by Joseph II from Tuscan sculptors. These lifelike and for the most part coloured wax figures and models provide an unusual but fascinating collection for the study of the human body. There is an experimental apothecary's collection which is protected for its historical significance and also a great collection of drugs and remedies.

The Josephinum was founded during the reign of Joseph II for the training of doctors and surgeons for the army. The buildings were remodelled in 1822. It was elevated to the status of a military academy in 1854, which was, however, taken away again in 1872. In the Court of Honour there is a fountain with the figure of Hygeia; the lead statue is by J. M. Fischer and dates from 1787.

Location
9, Währinger Str. 25/
Van-Swieten-Gasse 3

Underground station
Schottentor (U2)

Trams
37, 38, 40, 41, 42

Opening times
Mon.–Fri. 11 a.m.–3 p.m.

Judenplatz   B4

The Judenplatz (Jews' Square) was the centre of Vienna's ghetto from 1294 to 1421. Here stood the rabbi's house, the

Location
1, Jordangasse/Drahtgasse

93

Underground station
Schwedenplatz (U1, U4)

Bus
2A

Trams
1, 2 (Quayside)

school and the synagogue. The synagogue was demolished in 1421, materials from it being used to build the Old University. One of the most remarkable houses in the square is Hans "Zum grossen Jordan". Its relief depicting the Baptism of Christ dates from the 16th c. It serves as a reminder of the burning to death of Jews on the Gänseweide in 1421.

The house was built in the 15th c. In 1560 a descendant of the original owner Jörg Jordan sold the house to the Jesuits, but it has been in private ownership since 1684.

Other remarkable houses are No. 8 (the Tailors' Guild House) and the Böhmische Hofkanzlei (see entry) in Wipplingerstrasse whose rear façade bounds the Judenplatz on one side. From the W corner of the square Drahtgasse leads through to Am Hof (see entry).

*Kahlenberg

Location
19th District

Underground station
Heiligenstadt (U4)

Bus
38A

Kahlenberg stands 1,585ft (484m) high. It is, so to speak, Vienna's own "mountain" and virtually the last part of the Vienna Woods to the E. There is a magnificent view from the terrace. Near by are the vineyards of Grinzing (see entry) and Nussdorf, and farther off, beyond the city and the Marchfeld, the Little Carpathians and the Schneeberg region.

On the summit of Kahlenberg stands a television tower and the Stephanie Observatory (125 steps to top; entrance fee). It was from up here that in 1683 the relieving army of the Polish Prince Sobieski brought aid at the 11th hour to the city of Vienna which was being besieged and almost overrun by the Turks for a

The Kahlenberg, Vienna's own mountain summit

second time. The event is commemorated by the Sobieski Chapel in the little Church of St Joseph.

Poets and composers have always had a soft spot for Kahlenberg. The fact that it was once called "Sow Hill", presumably on account of the numbers of wild boar in the dense oak woods, was forgotten long ago. Grillparzer wrote: "If you have seen the land all around from the top of Kahlenberg, you will understand what I have written and what I am."

Kapuzinerkirche   C4

The Capuchin Church dedicated to Our Lady of the Angels is, as befits a Mendicant Order vowed to poverty, modest, sober and almost totally lacking in ornamentation. Nothing visible reminds us that it was founded by an empress (Empress Anna) in 1618.

Location
1, Neuer Markt

Underground station
Stephansplatz (U1)

The most precious work of art in the church is a "Pietà" by the altar in the right-hand transept. It is by Peter von Strudel, the Founder of the Academy of Fine Arts.

On the left-hand side of the church is the entrance to the Imperial Vault

** Imperial Vault (also called Capuchin Vault)

Beneath the Church of the Capuchins is the Habsburg family vault where 138 members of the House lie buried. Since 1633 all the Austrian Emperors have been buried here, with just a few exceptions. (Ferdinand II was buried at Graz, Frederick III in St Stephen's Cathedral (see entry – Stephansdom), and Charles I, the last Emperor, at Funchal in Madeira where he had gone as an exile.) The coffins contain only the embalmed bodies without the internal organs (see entry – Stephansdom) and the hearts (see entry – Augustinerkirche).

Opening times
Daily 9.30 a.m.–4 p.m.

The nine vaults are arranged in chronological order which makes it easy to trace the evolution of taste. Unfortunately the bronze caskets dating from the 17th and 18th c. have been attacked by decay, which necessitates extremely expensive conservation work.

Founder's Vault: Emperor Matthias, who died in 1619, and Empress Anna, who died in 1618, are considered to be the

Entrance

Imperial (or Capuchin) Vault

1 FOUNDERS' VAULT (1622–33) – Emperor Matthias I
   (d. 1619), Empress Anna (d. 1618)
2 LEOPOLDINE VAULT (1657 and 1701) – 16
   sarcophagi, 12 for children
3 CAROLINE VAULT (1720) – 7 sarcophagi
4 MARIA THERESA VAULT (1754) – double
   sarcophagus for Empress Maria Theresa (d. 1780)
   and Francis of Lorraine (d. 1765)
5 FRANCIS II VAULT (1824)
6 FERDINAND VAULT (1842)
7 TUSCAN VAULT (1842)
8 NEW VAULT (1960-62) - 26 sarcophagi
9 FRANZ JOSEPH VAULT (1909) – Franz Joseph I
   d. 1916, Empress Elisabeth (d. 1898)
10 Chapel: In the chapel is a memorial tablet to
   Emperor Charles I (d. 1922)   •

95

inaugurators of the family vault. Originally they were laid to rest in the Monastery of St Dorothea, and their bodies were the first to be transferred to the Imperial Vault in 1633.

Leopoldine Vault: It is also called the Angel Vault for among the 16 bronze caskets are 12 in which children were laid to rest. Ferdinand III, who died in 1657, is also buried here. Balthasar Ferdinand Moll's casket for Elenore of Pfalz-Neuburg who died in 1720 made such a favourable impression on the Emperor that Moll, a Professor at the Academy for Fine Art, spent half the time of his remaining years working on sarcophagi.

Caroline Vault: Johann Lucas von Hildebrandt designed the sarcophagi for Leopold I (d. 1704) and for Joseph I (d. 1711). B. F. Moll designed the sarcophagus of Charles VI (d. 1740); a magnificent work of art it rests on four lions and is decorated with the coats of arms of the Holy Roman Empire, Bohemia, Hungary and Castile.

Maria Theresa Vault: Jean-Nicholas Jadot de Ville Issey designed the domed chamber dominated by Moll's masterly double sarcophagus in the Rococo style for Maria Theresa, who died in 1780, and for Francis I, who died in 1765. The sarcophagus takes the form of a bed of state; at the head of the Imperial couple an angel of fame with trumpet and a crown of stars proclaims the triumph of faith. On the sides are numerous reliefs depicting scenes from Maria Theresa's life. It is also ornamented with four mourning figures and the crowns of Austria, Hungary, Bohemia and Jerusalem.
B. F. Moll is also responsible for several Rococo sarcophagi for the children of the Imperial couple, though not for the exces-

The Capuchin Vault: the tomb of Emperor Franz Joseph

sively simple copper coffin for Emperor Joseph II who died in 1790.

In a niche in the Maria Theresa Vault is found the coffin of the Countess Karoline Fuchs-Mollart who died in 1754. She was responsible for the upbringing of Maria Theresa and is the only person buried here who was not a member of the Imperial House.

Francis II Vault: the last Emperor of the Holy Roman Empire, Francis II who died in 1835, lies here with the graves of his four consorts all round. The Classical copper coffin is the work of Peter Nobile.

Ferdinand Vault. Ferdinand I, the Kindly, who died in 1875, whose coffin stands on a pedestal, shares this chamber with 37 other members of the Habsburg family who are placed in niches in the walls.

Tuscan Vault: This vault for members of the Tuscan collateral branch of the Habsburg House is at present being altered.

New Vault: It was created between 1960 and 1962 under the direction of Professor Schwanzer. In the sarcophagi lie Emperor Maximilian of Mexico who was executed in 1867 and Marie Louise, Napoleon's wife who died in 1847. The body of their son, the Duke of Reichstadt, was transferred to Paris where it was buried in the Invalides on the orders of Adolf Hitler as a gesture intended to win the good will of the French.

Franz Joseph Vault: Emperor Franz Joseph who died in 1916 was the last Habsburg to be buried in the vault. He was predeceased by the Empress Elisabeth who was murdered in Geneva in 1898 and by his son, Crown Prince Rudolf, who committed suicide in the hunting-lodge at Mayerling in 1889.

Chapel: There is a memorial tablet to Emperor Charles I, the last Emperor of Austria. He died in exile on the Portuguese island of Madeira in 1922.

Karl Marx Hof

Karl Marx Hof is the symbol of the 398 housing complexes which were built between the wars by the social democratic city council (1919–34) and immortalised in a workers' song as the "little red brick to build a new world". There were 64,000 dwellings in total, built in mainly outlying districts and financed by taxes on luxury items such as champagne, the employment of servants and cars, and steep graduation of taxes on housing construction. The tenants, however, paid rents which were well within their means (5–8% of their wages) for the relatively small flats; gas and electricity rates were low and there was no charge for water. The scheme also offered excellent community facilities such as baths, laundries, community rooms, public houses, shops and libraries, nursery schools and paddling pools; but not least there were many green areas which made living in the "Welfare Palaces" more agreeable.

Location
19, Heiligenstädter Strasse 82–92

Underground and S-Bahn Station
Heiligenstadt (U4, G)

Tram
D

Karl Marx Hof was built with 25 million bricks between 1927 and 1930 to a design by Karl Ehn and contains some 1,600 flats and communal facilities grouped around several inner court-yard gardens (about 80% of the Karl Marx complex is made up of parks and gardens). In 1934 Karl Marx Hof was the centre of the riots between left-wing workers and right-wing extremists and was stormed by the army to suppress the uprising. Estimates are now being made of the cost of urgent repairs and modernisation required in the extensive complex.

**Karlskirche   C4

Location
1, Karlsplatz

Underground station
Karlsplatz (U1, U2, U4)

Bus
59A, 4A

Trams
1, 2, D, J

The church dedicated to St Charles Borromeo was designed by J. B. Fischer von Erlach and his son. It is Vienna's most important religious building in the Baroque style. Emperor Charles VI vowed he would build it when the plague was raging in 1713, and in 1737 the church was dedicated to St Charles Borromeo, one of the saints invoked during plagues. In 1738 it was handed over to the Knights of Malta, and in 1783 it was declared an Imperial prebend.

The vast Baroque building is some 262ft (80m) long and 200ft (60m) wide. The dome rises to a height of 235ft (72m). It cost 304,000 guilders to build. All countries owing allegiance to the Crown had to contribute to the cost, as did Hamburg which also had to contribute to the cost as a fine for the deliberate destruction of the chapel of the Austrian Embassy.

There is much to be seen in the church with its tall oval central area, two major side-chapels and four smaller chapels in the corners.

Porch

The relief on the metope over the portal portrays the plague being overcome. The Latin inscription means: "I fulfil my vow in the presence of those who fear the Lord."

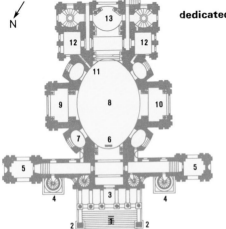

N

Karlskirche
dedicated to St Charles Borromeo

1 Stairway
2 Angel with bronze crosses
3 Porch in form of Greek portico with reliefs on the metopes
4 Triumphal pillars with spiral bands in relief
5 Campanile
6 Organ. Fresco ceiling above the organ-case by J. M. Rottmayr: it shows St Cecilia with the angels
7 Baptistery with stone dome
8 Dome with frescoes of the Apotheosis of St Charles Borromeo by J. M. Rottmayr (1725–30)
9 Reredos of the Assumption of the Virgin, by Sebastiani Ricci
10 Reredos of St Elisabeth of Thuringia by Daniel Gran (1736–37)
11 Pulpit
12 Vestries
13 High Altar by L. Mattielli

The Karlskirche, designed by the architects Fischer von Erlach father and son

The Karlskirche, looking toward the High Altar

Karlsplatz

Triumphal Pillars	These are based on Trajan's Column at Rome. Their spiralling bands in relief depict scenes from the life of St Charles Borromeo. The pillars, which are 110ft (33m) high, are surmounted by the Imperial Crown over the lanterns.
Organ	M. Rottmayr painted the fresco on the organ-case. It depicts St Cecilia with angels making music.
Dome Frescoes	The light interior is dominated by Rottmayr's frescoes in the dome. They represent the apotheosis of St Charles and the petition that plague may be averted. On the left an angel with a flaming torch sets fire to Luther's Bible which has fallen to the ground.
Noteworthy Reredoses	"Jesus and the Roman Captain" and "Healing of a man sick of the palsy" by Daniel Gran; "Raising of the Young Man" by M. Altomonte; "St Luke" by van Schuppen. The painting of the Assumption of the Virgin on the left of the High Altar is by Sebastiani Ricci, and that of St Elisabeth of Thuringia to the right of the High Altar is by Daniel Gran.
High Altar	The subject is the ascent into Heaven of St Charles Borromeo. The sculptural decoration with clouds behind the High Altar is based on designs by J. B. Fischer von Erlach.

Karlsplatz   C4

Location
1st District

Underground station
Karlsplatz (U1, U2, U4)

Buses
4A, 59A

Trams
1, 2, D, J

Karlsplatz, where important tram and underground routes converge, is one of the busiest squares in central Vienna. In 1977–78 the square was newly laid out and the striking station building of Otto Wagner was re-erected. One of Wagner's 1901 pavilions, decorated with marble and gold leaf, now serves as an entrance to the U-Bahn station and also for minor temporary exhibitions of the Historical Museum (see entry); the other one becomes a café in summer.

In the gardens in the southern part of Karlsplatz stand monuments to Johannes Brahms (1908), to Josef Ressel (1862), the inventor of the ship's screw, and to Josef Madersperger (1933), the inventor of the sewing-machine. On the N side of the square stand the Kunstlerhaus and the Musikverein building (see entries), on the S side are the Karlskirche (see entry) and the Technical University, a building erected 1816–18 with an upper storey added later. On the E side stands the Historisches Museum (see entry) and on the W the Secession Building (see entry).

---

*Kärntner Strasse   C4

Location
1, Stephansplatz
Opernkreuzung

Underground stations
Karlsplatz (U1, U2, U4),
Stephansplatz (U1)

Trams
1, 2, D, J

Vienna's most elegant shopping street leads from Stephansplatz (see entry) to Karlsplatz. Since 1973 it has been a pedestrian precinct up as far as Walfischgasse, with lime trees, and pavement cafés, with mountebanks and buskers. The modern-style street lights and idiosyncratic fountains have given rise to much debate. Between the junction of Kärntner Strasse and the Ring lies the "Operngasse", with shops, snack bars and the central Tourist Information Office at 38 Kärntner Strasse.

Kärntner Strasse is first mentioned in documents as early as 1257 under the name of "Strata Carinthianorum". Most of the

A Wagner Pavilion in Karlsplatz, now an entrance to an Underground station

houses date from the 18th c. and the most interesting façades are those of Nos 4, 16 and 17. Only the Maltese Church still has a few features dating back to 1265. Inside there are numerous coats of arms of Knights of Malta as well as the 1806 stucco monument with Turkish figures on either hand to the memory of Jean de la Valette, the Grand Master who defended Malta against the Turks in 1565.

Kirche am Steinof

The church, designed by Otto Wagner, was built between 1904 and 1907 in the grounds of the Vienna psychiatric hospital and is considered to be one of the most important buildings of the Art Nouveau style in Vienna. The church stands on the estate's highest point and its dome and flanking towers can be seen from some distance. The dome is, however, a fake structure; inside only shallow vaulting may be seen. The church interior is simple and light; the floors and walls are tiled in accordance with Wagner's aim to create "cleanliness", of light, air and function, in a church building. The glass mosaics in the windows were designed by Kolo Moser.

Location
14, Baumgartner Höhe 1

Bus
48A

Guided tours
Sat., 3 p.m.

Kleiner Bischofshof   B5

The former Small Bishop's Palace which later became the "Haus zum roten Kreuz" (House with the Red Cross) dates, in

Location
1, Domgasse 6

Klosterneuburg

Underground station
Stephansplatz (U1)

part, from the 15th c. Matthias Gerl gave it a new façade in 1761. The Madonna relief in a pretty Rococo frame with Turkish trophies on the wall is especially noteworthy.

It was here that Franz Georg Kolschitzky died in 1694. According to the history of the city, he had set up the first Viennese coffee house here.

**Klosterneuburg (monastery)

Distance
7½ miles (12km) N, on the Danube

Underground station
Heiligenstadt (U4) thence by bus

Tours
Mon.–Sat. 9 a.m.–noon and 1.30–5 p.m., Sun. and public holidays 11 a.m., 1.30–5 p.m. (according to demand).

Klosterneuburg stands on the NE edge of the Vienna Woods (see Practical Information, Excursions) and is separated from the Danube by a broad grassy island. It attracts many visitors mainly on account of its monastery which was founded by the Augustinian Canons. There is an extensive range of buildings high up above the Danube. It originated as a monastery founded by the Babenberg Margrave Leopold III ("The Pious") in the 12th c. In 1730 Emperor Charles VI embarked on a programme of large-scale new building, but this was stopped again in 1755. Work was only completed in 1842, and then on a reduced scale.

The buildings of the monastery comprise the monastery church with Romanesque features and which was refurbished in Baroque style in the 17th c., the Leopold Chapel, a Romanesque-Gothic Cloister, the Leopold Courtyard and the monastery wine-vaults.

The famous "Verdun Altar" in the Leopold Chapel is especially noteworthy. It is made up of 51 enamelled panels by the goldsmith Nikolaus of Verdun and dates from 1181. This reredos for a funerary chapel is among the finest examples of High Medieval goldsmith's and enameller's work.

Cloisters and Freisinger Chapel, and the monastery lapidarium. Entry is through the Leopold Chapel to the beautiful Gothic Cloisters, the 600-year-old Freisinger Chapel and the monastery lapidarium. In the latter is preserved, with other examples of Romanesque and Gothic sculpture, the sandstone "Klosterneuburg Madonna", a life-size figure dating from about 1310.

New Building. The new monastery building erected during Charles VI's reign in the Baroque style has two copper domes, one of which is surmounted by the German Imperial Crown, the other by the Lower Austrian Archducal Bonnet. Among the features shown by guides when a conducted tour is taken are the Baroque main staircase, the Marble Hall with frescoes by Daniel Gran, the Imperial Apartment, the Tapestry Room and the Treasury.

Monastery Museum. The Museum has a rich collection including a Habsburg genealogy, the Albrechts Altar which was given in 1438 and valuable medieval pictures.

The monastery also possesses vineyards and famous wine-vaults. In the monastery cooperage may be seen the "Thousand bucket barrel" dating from 1704. Each year on St Leopold's Day, 15 November, there is a great barrel-rolling carnival.

Kafka Memorial

In nearby Kierling, the room in the former Hofmann sanatorium in which Kafka spent the last days of his life, has been turned into a memorial to the writer.

Klosterneuburg: 12th c. monastery founded by Margrave Leopold III ▶

A Imperial Courtyard in the New Building (Collegiate Museum on 2nd floor)
B Cloisters: Freisinger Chapel; Lapidarium
C Leopold Courtyard

1 Main stairs (1723; Library above)
2 Marble Hall
3 Imperial Apartment
4 Prelate's Door
5 Leopold Chapel (Verdun Altar)

6 Collegiate Church
7 Former tower
8 Collegiate Archives
9 Fountain (1592)
10 Mosmüller Wing (1620)
11 Gothic Door
12 Gothic Chapter House

Kunstgewerbemuseum

See Österreichisches Museum für angewandte Kunst.

Kunsthistorisches Museum C4

Location
1, Maria-Theresien-Platz

Underground station
Mariahilferstrasse (U3)

Buses
2A, 3A, 57A

Trams
1, 2, D, J, 52, 58

Opening times
Apr.–Oct.:
Tues.–Fri. 10 a.m.–6 p.m.;
Sat., Sun. 9 a.m.–6 p.m.
Nov.–Mar.:
Tues.–Fri. 10 a.m.–4 p.m.;
Sat., Sun. 9 a.m.–4 p.m.
Evening illumination (parts of collection alternately) Tues, Fri. 7–9 p.m.

The Museum of Art History was founded when it was realised that Vienna had no counterpart of the great art galleries of London and Amsterdam, particularly since the Imperial collections in Prince Eugene's former summer mansion had become far too large for those premises.

Karl Hasenauer and Gottfried Semper were charged with the task of drawing up plans for two splendid museums, the Kunsthistorisches Museum and the Naturhistorisches Museum (see entry), its counterpart in the life sciences. Between 1872 and 1891 they erected the vast pair of buildings which form the left- and right-hand sides of Maria-Theresien-Platz. Though the State was close to bankruptcy, the architects were under instructions not to make economies, and they were able to use expensive materials and commission highly rated artists with the decoration of the interior.

Among those who worked on the embellishment of the Museum's interior were Viktor Tilgner, Hans Makart, Michael Munkacsy, the brothers Ernst and Gustav Klimt and Franz Matsch.

The Kunsthistorisches Museum: view of exterior

The Künsthistorisches Museum's collections are divided into 10 departments. The main building houses the following:
The Egyptian-Oriental Collection; the Collection of Antiquities; the Sculpture and Applied Arts Collection; the Collection of Paintings with the so-called "secondary galleries", and the Collection of Medals, Coins and Tokens.
The following collections belonging to the Kunsthistorisches Museum are found elsewhere:
The Neue Galerie (New Gallery) in der Stallburg (see entry).
The Treasure in the Hofburg (see entry).
The Sammlung alter Musikinstrumente (collection of old instruments; see entry).
The Waffensammlung (collection of weapons; see entry).
The Ephesos-Museum (see entry).
The Wagenburg (Mews) in Schönbrunn (see entry).

A tour of the main building of the Kunsthistorisches involves climbing four flights of stairs, walking 2½ miles (4km) of corridors and visiting 51 rooms. It is generally advisable to follow the order given here.

Note: visitors without a lot of time at their disposal should note that the Egyptian-Oriental Collection and the Picture Galleries are the most highly rated departments of the Museum.

Room I: Exhibits illustrating the cult of the dead. Large stone sarcophagi (600–100 B.C.); painted wooden coffins (1100–100 B.C.); mummies with painted wrappings, etc.

Egyptian-Oriental Collection (Raised First Floor)

Room II: Oriental Collection. Glazed tile relief with representation of a pacing lion from Ischtartor in Babylon (c. 580 B.C.); tiles and tablets, stone inscriptions, reliefs and bronzes from southern Arabia (1st c. B.C.), etc.

105

Kunsthistorisches Museum

Museum of Art History

FIRST FLOOR

Picture Gallery

East Wing

Rooms
VIII 15th–16th c. Dutch
  IX 16th c. Dutch
   X P. Brueghel the Elder
  XI 17th c. Flemish
 XII Van Dyck
XIII Rubens
XIV Rubens
 XV 17th–18th c. Dutch
Cabinets
 14 Bosch, Mor

15 Dürer
16 Altdorfer, Huber
17 Cranach
18 Holbein the Younger,
    Clouet
19 Mannerists
20 Rubens
21 Teniers the Younger
22 Hals, Van Goyen
23 Rembrandt
24 Ruysdael, Vermeer

West Wing

Rooms
  I Raphael, Correggio
 II Titian
III Veronese, Bordone
IV Tintoretto
 V Caravaggio, Ribera
VI Reni, Fetti, Giordano
VII Crespi, Tiepolo
Cabinets
 1 Mantegna, Vivarini
 2 Bellini, Titian
 3 Dossi, Savoldo

4 Bassano
5 Schiavone
6 Moretto, Marino
7 De Predis, Luini
8 Barocci, dell'Abate
9 Bronzino, Coello
10 Velázquez, Murillo
11 Poussin, Cortone
12 Fetti, Strozzi, Cavallino
13 Guardi, Canaletto

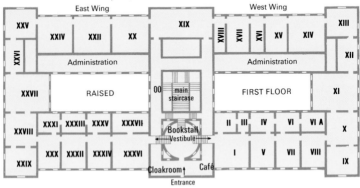

RAISED FIRST FLOOR

East Wing

Sculpture and Applied Arts Collection
Middle Ages
Rooms XXXIV–XXXVII
Renaissance
Rooms XXVIII–XXXII

Mannerism
Rooms XXIV–XXVII
Baroque and Rococo
Rooms XIX–XXII

West Wing
**Egyptian
Oriental
Collection**
Rooms I–VIII

Antiquities
Rooms IX–XVIII

Room III: Cult of animals. Mummified sacred animals; figures of animal gods; Apis stele from Sakkara, etc.

Room IV: Everyday objects including furniture, clothes, jewellery, tools for working with stone and wood representation of the development of old Egyptian writing, etc.

Room V: Ptolemaic Age. Two copies of colossal statues of rulers (2nd c. B.C.). Sphinxes, statues, reliefs, bronzes; two seated statues of the lion-headed goddess Mut, etc.

Room VI: Pre- and early history of Egypt (5000–2635 B.C.). Stone and earthenware vessels; Nubia and its connection with Egyptian culture; Hyksos as a foreign ruler in Egypt (1650–1550 B.C.); Austrian excavations in Tel el Dab'a, etc.

Room VIA: Old Kingdom. Cult chamber of Prince Kaninisut from Giza (about 2400 B.C., 2nd Dynasty).

Room VII: New Kingdom (1550–1080 B.C.). Statues of gods, kings and citizens; grave steles, memorials, reliefs and vessels. Middle Kingdom (2134–1650 B.C.). Statues and parts of statues of kings and citizens; steles, small stone vessels, etc.

Room VIII: Old Kingdom (2635–2155 B.C.). Statues, architectural relics and vessels from private tombs of the 4th–6th Dynasty (about 2500–2150 B.C.) in Giza. Of especial interest and one of the finest examples extant is the "head of a man" (about 2450 B.C.) sculpted from the finest limestone.

Room IX: Art from Cyprus. Bronze Age pottery and sepulchral reliefs from Palmyra.

Antiquities
(Raised First Floor)

Room X: Greek and Roman sculpture, including the precious bronze statue "The Youth of Helenenburg" (second half of the 5th c.) and a head of Artemis (2nd c. B.C., possibly a copy).

Room XI: Later Greek and Roman sculpture and a magnificent Roman mosaic pavement (2nd c.).

Room XII: Greek bronzes and Minoan statuettes from Crete (end of 2nd millennium B.C.).

Room XIII: Etruscan art, including the clay statue of Athena from Rocca d'Aspromonte (5th c. B.C.).

Room XIV: Pottery decorated with pictures and reliefs, Tanagara figures and an especially precious Ptolemaic cameo with the portraits of a Ptolemaic king and his consort (Showcase 14).

Room XV: Roman art, portraits of Emperors, ceremonial utensil, miniature sculptures and cameos, including the world-famous "Gemma Augustea" (1st c. B.C.).

Room XVI: Art of Late Antiquity, individual finds from Austrian excavations, including marble portrait heads from Ephesus.

Room XVII: Textiles from Egypt and Early Christian handicrafts, including the Siebenburg golden treasure from Szilagysomlyo.

Room XVIII: Byzantine and Old Bulgarian work, including silver treasures from Galicia and Bukovina. The prime exhibit is the treasure from Nagyszentmiklós with 23 gold vessels.

Kunsthistorisches Museum

Sculpture and Applied Arts
Collection
(Raised Ground Floor)

The sequence of the rooms is clear from the plan.

Room XXXVI: High and late Middle Ages. Ivory carving, rock-crystal vessels and two famous chalices, one from Wilten Abbey at Innsbruck, the other from St Peter's at Salzburg.

Rooms XXXVII and XXXV: Clocks, scientific instruments and automata of the 16th and 17th c.

Room XXXIV: Late Medieval German sculpture. Fine Nuremberg vessels, including the so-called Dürer and Maximilian cups. Gothic sculpture including the famous "Krumau Madonna".

Room XXXII: Florentine Early Renaissance. Many reliefs and busts from Donatello's and Della Robbia's workshops; Settignano's "Laughing Boy" and Laurana's "Portrait of a Young Lady".

Room XXXI: 16th and 17th c. small bronzes, ivory work, rock-crystal and carved stone vessels.

Room XXX: Upper Italian Renaissance. Busts, plaques and bronzes by Antico (Venus Felix), Moderno and Riccio.

Room XXIX: Italian vessels of rock-crystal, lapis lazuli, etc.; valuable 16th c. cameos; Spanish gold work.

Room XXVIII: German Renaissance. Wooden statuettes; inlay work and carving.

Room XXVII: 16th c. Italian bronzes. Many impressive works by Giambologna and Benvenuto Cellini's famous salt cellar.

Room XXVI: French 16th c. Mannerism with elegant vessels and Limoges display pieces.

Room XXV: German 16th c. Mannerism. Items from Archduke Ferdinand II's collection; rare Venetian jewellery; Tyrolean pottery, etc.

Room XXIV: Collection of carved stone vessels from the time of Rudolf II; fine gold and silver work, jewellery and cameoes of the 16th and 17th c.; so-called Florentine mosaic.

Room XXII: High Baroque. Mainly miniature work, ebony statuettes, bronze busts and figurative reliefs made from Kehlheim stone.

Room XX: Austrian High Baroque and Rococo. Notable are the bust of Marie-Antoinette, Marie Theresa's gold breakfast service and the toilet set of her husband, Francis II.

Room XIX: 17th c. carvings in crystal and quartz. The tapestries on the walls are frequently changed as they are sensitive to light and dust.

Picture Gallery
(First Floor)

The world-famous Picture Gallery is housed in 15 rooms and 24 cabinets. It is a good idea to go round rooms VIII to XV and rooms I to VII, turning off to see the cabinets on either side.

Room VIII: Early Netherlandish painting of the 15th and 16th c. Works by Rogier van der Weyden, Hans Memling, Joos van Cleeves and two portraits by Jan van Eyck.

Room IX: 16th c. Netherlandish painting. Genre pictures by Pieter Aertsen and a series depicting the Seasons by Lucas van Valckenborch.

Room X: A definitive collection of works by Pieter Brueghel the Elder, with about one third of the surviving works of the Master, including "The Seasons" and "The Peasant Wedding".

Room XI: 17th c. Flemish masters. Still-lifes by Frans Snyderss and Jacob Jordaens.

Room XII: Paintings by Rubens's pupil and collaborator Sir Anthony van Dyck, with his "Picture of a young general".

Rooms XIII and XIV: Peter Paul Rubens Collection. More than 30 of his works hang here, including many of his masterpieces.

Room XV: Dutch 17th and 18th c. painting, with pictures by Rembrandt and landscapes by Ruysdael.

The most important cabinets in this part of the gallery are:
Cabinet 15, with eight major works by Dürer.
Cabinet 18, with portraits by Hans Holbein the Younger.
Cabinet 20, with more paintings by Rubens.
Cabinet 23, with self-portraits by Rembrandt and landscapes by Ruysdael.
Cabinet 24, works by Vermeer.

Rooms I to VII are devoted to Italian, Spanish and French painting.

The Peter Paul Rubens Collection

Kunsthistorisches Museum

Room I: Works by Raphael, Parmigianino and Correggio.

Room II: Titian's masterpieces and later works, including "Ecce Homo" and "Danaë".

Room III: Representative works by Paolo Veronese – "Death of Lucretia", "Judith with the head of Holofernes", etc., and large pictures of Old and New Testament subjects.

Room IV: Venetian Mannerism, represented primarily by Tintoretto, including his painting "Susanna in the Bath".

Room V: 17th c. chiaroscuro paintings. The major work here is the famous "Madonna of the Rosary" by Michelangelo Caravaggio.

Room VI: Christian themes from the Counter-Reformation era. Notable is the famous "Baptism of Christ" by Guido Reni.

Room VII: 18th c. Italian Baroque masters. Giambattista Tiepolo's scenes from Roman history are outstanding.

The most important cabinets in this part of the gallery are:
Cabinet 2, with early works by Titian.
Cabinet 4, with works by Bassano.
Cabinet 10, with works by Velázquez and an altar-painting by Murillo originating in Seville and only acquired in 1987.

The Second Floor of the Museum houses the so-called "secondary galleries", where the exhibits are changed from time to time. However the famous Vienna townscape by Bernardo Belotto ("Canaletto") is permanently on display.

Numismatic Collection/
Numismatic Cabinet
(Second Floor)

The Numismatic Collection, one of the largest and most important of its type, occupies three rooms.

Room I: Development of money from natural forms of currency to modern forms of monetary transaction without cash. There is natural currency from Asia, Africa and America, stone currency from Yap Island, money in the form of bars and rings, minted currency and rare old versions of paper money.

Room II: Medals. Exhibition of the artistic and cultural history of medals from the Roman era to the present day.

Room III: Modern medals, insignia of Orders and honorific badges.

Künstlerhaus (art gallery)   C4

Location
1, Karlsplatz 5

Underground station
Karlsplatz (U1, U2, U4)

Trams
1, 2, D, J, T

The Künstlerhaus (House of the Artists) is used for art shows, cultural events and art festivals. The most famous are the "Gschnas" festivals at carnival time.
The Vienna Artists' Society had this Neo-Renaissance building put up in 1865–68. The marble standing figures by the entrance represent Diego Velázquez, Raphael Santi, Leonardo da Vinci, Michelangelo Buonarroti, Albrecht Dürer, Titian, Bramante and Peter Paul Rubens.

Kupferstichkabinett

See Akademie der Bildenden Künste

Lainzer Tiergarten (wildlife park)

The Lainzer Wildlife Park occupies some 10 sq. miles (26km²) of almost unspoiled landscape. Here the Vienna Woods have remained almost untouched, with oaks and beeches, roe-deer and red deer, wild boars, moufflons, fallow deer and aurochs. Once it was the hunting reserve of Emperor Joseph II and was fenced off with a stone wall 15½ miles (25km) long. Since 1923 it has been open to the public, and it has been a nature sanctuary since 1941. In September a Hunters' Fair is held in honour of St Eustace, patron saint of the hunt. In the park there are 50 miles (80km) of footpaths, almost half unfenced, with refreshment places and shelters, children's playgrounds and the Huburtuswarte observation tower. In July and August the Lipizzaner horses of the Spanish Riding School (see entry) spend their "summer holidays" in the Hermes Villa Park. The former hunting-lodge has been partially restored to its original condition and is now used for temporary exhibitions.

There are six other entrances apart from the Lainzer Tor, but they are not always open. A brochure is available from the City or Tourist Information offices (see Practical Information, Information) which shows access routes and a map of the park.

Location
13, Entrance Lainzer-Tor

Trams and Buses
Tram 60 or 62 to Speising then bus 60B

Opening times
April–Nov. Wed.–Mon. from 8 a.m. to dusk.
Hermes Villa Park
Wed.–Sun. 9 a.m.–4.30 p.m.

Note

Landhaus (Provincial Government)   B4

The official seat of the Lower Austrian Provincial Government is in the "Palace of the Lower Austrian Estates". The Estates acquired the former "Liechtensteinisches Freihaus" in 1513. In the 16th c. the building was completely renovated, and in the 19th c. it was restored according to historical principles.
The Renaissance rooms in which Beethoven, Liszt and Schubert performed and in which Abraham a Sancta Clara wrote his account of the plague in 1679 were restored in 1953. If a booking is made in advance it is possible to view the Hall of the Knights, the Hall of the Aldermen, the Hall of the Prelates, the great Debating Chamber and the parlours.
It was in the great Debating Chamber that the foundation of the Republic was approved in 1918.
In the courtyard of the Landhaus there is a 1571 tablet with an Imperial injunction that nobody should venture to scuffle or fight or cause a disturbance in front of or within the chartered Landhaus.
The Imperial peace was, however, broken, and in 1848 it was actually from the Landhaus that the Revolution started.

Location
1, Herrengasse 13

Underground stations
Schottentor (U2),
Stephansplatz (U1)

Bus
2A

Opening times
Tours if booked in advance
Chapel: Sun. from 9 a.m.

Laxenburg

The Court rode out to Laxenburg to seek refreshment when Vienna was hot in the summer. Three palaces stand in a

Distance
9½ miles (15km) S

Railway
from Wien-Mitte to
Laxenburg-Biedermannsdorf
(R61)

Franzensburg
Open: Easter to Oct. daily
10 a.m.–noon, 2–5 p.m.

delightful park. The Old Castle dates from the 14th c. It is historically important because it is here that Emperor Charles VI promulgated the "Pragmatic Sanction" which ensured the succession to the throne of his daughter Maria Theresa. The Franzensburg is an 18th and 19th c. copy of a Gothic castle. The New Castle (also called the Blue Castle) is a Late Baroque building which was the centre of the life of the Court in the time of Maria Theresa and during the Congress of Vienna.

The romantic Franzensburg which stands on an island in the Large Pool is now a museum. In the courtyard can be seen 37 busts of the Habsburgs.

Lehár Schlössl (Schikaneder Schlössl)

Location
19, Hackofergasse 18

Underground and S-Bahn Station
Heiligenstadt (U4/S9)

Tram D

From 1802 to 1812, the small late-Baroque palace (Schlössl) was the home of the thespian, singer and librettist of the "Magic Flute", Emanuel Schikaneder. In 1932 Franz Lehár bought the house where he wrote "Giuditta"; one of the rooms has been turned into a small Lehár museum.

Richard Tauber was married in the Schlössl chapel. Only groups may visit the Lehár Schlössl by prior appointment.

*Maria am Gestade (church)   B4

Location
1, Salvatorgasse 12

Underground station
Schwedenplatz (U1, U4)

Bus
3A

The Church of Maria am Gestade (Mary on the Strand) is popularly called the "Maria-Stiegen-Kirche" (Mary on the Steps). It is the Czech national church, and its entrancing pierced Gothic cupole is one of the characteristic sights of the N Old City.

Maria am Gestade, originally a wooden oratory dating from the 9th c., used to stand on the steep slope up from the Danube. The present building, and its Gothic stained glass, was put up in the 14th c. The tower was rebuilt in the 16th c., and restoration was undertaken in 1817, 1890, 1930, 1946 and 1973.

The W front of the church is only some 30ft (10m) wide, but nearly 105ft (33m) high. The church looms above the old narrow lanes like the prow of a ship.

Inside there are two Gothic sandstone figures (by the second pillar on the E side of the nave) dating from the 14th c., and two

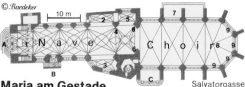

© *Baedeker*

Maria am Gestade
('Maria Stiegen')

A Main Doorway
(West front)

B Baldachin Doorway
(c. 1500)

C Choir Doorway
(reliefs of 1350)

Salvatorgasse

1 Organ gallery (c. 1515)
2 Joseph Altar (copy of 1878)
3 Clemens-Maria-Hofbauer Chapel
  with panels of the Gothic
  High Altar (1466)
4 Pulpit (c. 1820)
5 St Alphonse of Liguori
6 Column figures (c. 1370)
7 Perger Chapel (1520)
8 High Altar (c. 1846)
9 Choir window (14th/15th c.)

15th c. Gothic paintings in the chapel, dedicated to Clemens Maria Hofbauer, the Patron Saint of the city of Vienna. The organ-gallery and a stone Renaissance altar in the Johann Perger Chapel date from the 16th c. The other furnishings of the church are 19th c. work.

*Maria-Theresien-Platz and Memorial   C4

The monument to Empress Maria Theresa is one of the most impressive in all Vienna. It dominates the square of the same name but is surrounded by the Naturhistorisches Museum (see entry) and the Kunsthistorisches Museum (see entry). The square itself is laid out as a formal Baroque garden.

It was Franz Joseph who gave the commission to the sculptor Kaspar von Zumbusch, and his work was unveiled in 1887. The female monarch sits on her throne, holding the Pragmatic Sanction of 1713 in her left hand. She is surrounded by the major figures of her day: the standing figures are State Chancellor Kaunitz, Prince Liechtenstein, Count Haugwitz and her Physician, van Swieten, and Generals Daun, Laudon, Traun and Khevenhüller are on horseback.

The SW side of Maria-Theresien-Platz is formed by the Exhibition Palace. This 1,200ft (360m) long building was erected between 1723 and 1725 to plans by J. B. Fischer von Erlach and his son J. E. Fischer. Originally the Palace mews, it is now used for the Vienna International Fair.

The Tobacco Museum (entrance 2 Mariahilferstrasse) is housed in the side wing of the Exhibition Palace. Here there are

Location
1, Burgring

Underground stations
Mariahilferstrasse,
Volkstheater (U2)

Buses
3A, 48A

Trams
1, 2, D, J

Opening times
Tues. 10 a.m.–7 p.m.
Wed.–Fri. 10 a.m.–3 p.m.
Sat., Sun. 9 a.m.–1 p.m.

Maria-Theresien-Platz with the memorial to the Empress

113

2,500 exhibits concerned with tobacco and smoking world-wide. In 1900 there were in Vienna 400 workers engaged in carving Meerschaum pipes; now there are only 2. Among the more exotic exhibits are South American clay pipes, marijuana pipes from Morocco, brass pipes from Cameroon and Upper Volta, silver pipes from Thailand, Chinese heroin pipes and opium pipes from Vietnam.

*Michaelerkirche   B4

Location
1, Michaelerplatz 1

Underground station
Stephansplatz (U1)

Bus
2A

Guided Tours
Church and crypt daily
11 a.m.
Mon.–Sat. also 3 p.m.

The Redemptorist Church of St Michael, (now also a cultural centre) used to be the Imperial Court's parish church, and it was also favoured for the interment of important Austrians. It stands directly opposite the Michaeler range of the Hofburg (see entry) on the E side of Michaelerplatz.

It is not known who was the founder of the church. It may have been the Crusader Archduke Leopold VI or else perhaps Otto-kar Přemysl. The three-naved arcaded Late Romanesque basilica was built in the 13th c., in the same period as the "Alte Burg" (see Hofburg). The architects were connected with St Stephen's Cathedral. The basilica was enlarged in the 14th c. and restored in the Gothic style in the 16th c. The Baroque narthex with its portal was added in 1724–25 by A. Beduzzi. The W portal with the sculpture of the Fall of the Angels by Lorenzo Matielli dates from 1792, as does, too, the Classical façade.

Among the oldest treasures of the church are the remains of the once-famed Late Romanesque frescoes in the tower chapel, the "Man of Sorrows" (1430) in the Baptistery and the stone figures of 1350 in the Chapel of St Nicholas. Jean Baptiste

St Michael's, once the parish church of the Imperial Court

d'Avrange designed the High Altar in 1781. The Chapel of St Nicholas, to the right of the choir, was founded by a ducal cook in about 1350 as a thank-offering when he was acquitted in a poisoning case.

The crypt was a burial place: the floors and walls are covered with bones and there are some 250 wood, metal or stone coffins. Those wishing to look inside may see the corpse of a pregnant women and the outline of the unborn child.

Crypt

Near the church, at the entry to Kohlmarkt, stands the Large Michaeler House; this, with its handsome inner courtyard, was built for the Barnabites in 1720.

---

*Minoritenkirche (officially the Snow Madonna Italian National Church)   B4

The former Minorites' church has been called the Snow Madonna Italian National Church since 1786. It has been a Franciscan church since 1957.

Location
1, Minoritenplatz

The first church of the "Fratres Minores" in Vienna dates from 1230. It was a little chapel dedicated to the Holy Rood and twice burnt down. To replace it Duke Albrecht the Wise had the present Gothic aisle-less church built in the 14th c. It was altered in the 17th, 18th and 20th c.

Underground station
Schottentor (U2)

Bus
2A

The Gothic main portal is of architectural interest. It was created by Duke Albrecht's Confessor, Father Jacobus (1340–45). Inside may be seen Giacomo Raffaelli's copy in mosaic of Leonardo da Vinci's famous "Last Supper". It was commissioned by Napoleon because he wanted to take the Milan original to Paris and replace it by the Vienna copy.

Trams
1, 2, D, J (Ring)

After Napoleon's fall the Austrian Court agreed to purchase the copy at a cost of 400,000 guilders. Sight was lost of it when it was put in store at the Belvedere and only brought to the Minoritenkirche in 1845–47.

The picture above the High Altar by Chr. Unterberger is also a copy. The original "Snow Madonna" is an object of veneration in the Esquiline in Rome.

Museum Alte Backstube

See Josefstädter Bezirksmuseum

Museum des 20. Jahrhunderts (see entry: Gartenpalais Liechtenstein)   D5

The Austrian Pavilion at the 1958 Brussels World Fair was taken down and rebuilt in the Schweizergarten in Vienna. The Museum of Modern Art was housed here until it moved to the Gartenpalais Liechtenstein (see entry). Since then the pavilion

Location
3, Schweitzergarten

Museum für Völkerkunde

Museum of the 20th Century: sculpture garden

Underground station
Südtirolerplatz (U1)

Trams
18, D, O

has served as the Museum of the 20th Century ("Zwanziger-haus") as a venue for temporary exhibitions (open daily except Wed. 10 a.m.–6 p.m.). Next to it is a garden where Austrian and other sculpture is displayed, including works by Arp, Giaco-metti, Hartung, Marini, Maillol, Moore, Rodin and Wotruba.

Museum für Völkerkunde (Museum of Ethnology)　　　　C4

Location
1, Neue Burg, Heldenplatz

Underground stations
Volkstheater
Mariahilferstrasse (U2)

Bus 3A

Trams
1, 2, D, J, 52, 58

Opening times
Mon., Thur., Fri., Sat.
10 a.m.–1 p.m.;
Wed. 10 a.m.–5 p.m.;
Sun. 9 a.m.–1 p.m.
Film Shows (Oct.–May)
Sun. 9.30 a.m. and
11.30 a.m.

This museum developed from the Ethnographical Department of the Naturhistorisches Museum (see entry).
The collection is housed in the former "corps de logis" of the Neue Burg (see Hofburg). It comprises more than 150,000 objects pertaining to races that have not used writing. Because of shortage of space most of the collections can only be dis-played in temporary exhibitions.
Among the permanent exhibits are, on the ground floor, Benin bronzes with royal portrait busts going back to the 15th c. and the Mexico Collection which belonged to the Emperor Maximi-lian. It includes the famous feather head-dress and feather shield of Montezuma, the Aztec ruler. In 1987 Aztecs tried to further their aim of recovering this exhibit by repeatedly stag-ing demonstrations outside the museum, but until now these have had no effect. Here, too, are the collections made by the British seafarer James Cook which were purchased in London in 1806 at the Emperor's command. The most valued exhibits come from Polynesia.

Museum mittelalterlicher österreichischer Kunst

See Belvedere-Schlösser

*Musikvereinsgebäude (concert hall)   C4

It is in the famous "Golden Hall" of the Musikvereinsgebäude that the Vienna Philharmonic Orchestra gives its major concerts. The New Year concert is broadcast world-wide from here. The Gesellschaft der Musikfreunde (Music Lovers' Society) was founded in 1812. In 1867 it commissioned Theophil Hansen to design this building. The terracotta statues are mainly by Franz Melnizki.

The "Golden Hall" was altered in 1911 when it was given its golden coffered ceiling. It can seat an audience of nearly 2,000; it is 165ft (51·2m) long, 63ft (18·9m) wide and 55ft (17·6m) high. There is room for 400 musicians, and it is reckoned to be one of the world's best concert halls for acoustics.

The Musikfreunde possess a comprehensive collection of works on the history of music, an archive of musical scores and an excellent library (see Practical Information – Libraries).

Location
1, Dumbastrasse 3

Underground station
Karlsplatz (U1, U2, U4)

Buses
4A, 59A

Trams
1, 2, D, J (Ring)

Naschmarkt (market)   C4

The Naschmarkt is by far the largest and most interesting of the twenty or so markets of Vienna. The amount of produce on sale is enormous. At the S end of the Naschmarkt begins the Flea Market. Curios, valuables, new articles and rubbish are offered for sale.

In nearby Wienzeile there are two Jugendstil buildings by Otto Wagner. In 1973 the entire façade of No. 38 Linke Wienzeile was regilded. The medallions between the windows are the work of Kolo Moser; the doorway in the Köstlergasse was designed by Josef Plečnik. The oval stairway and decorative lift-cage are also of interest. No. 40 Linke Wienzeile has a façade entirely clad with majolica tiles decorated with plant motifs; on the frieze are sculpted lions' heads. This house too has an interesting stairway.

Location
6, Wienzeile

Underground station
Kettenbrückengasse (U4)

Opening times
Naschmarkt
Mon.–Fri. 6 a.m.–6.30 p.m.,
Sat. 6 a.m.–1 p.m.
Flea Market
Sat. 8 a.m.–6 p.m.

**Naturhistorisches Museum   C4

The Natural History Museum is the counterpart of the Kunsthistorisches Museum (see entry) which is directly opposite. It was designed, like the latter, by G. Semper and K. Hasenauer and was finished in 1881.

The objects are displayed in 39 galleries and a domed hall. The collection was founded by Francis I, the consort of Maria Theresa, who was interested in natural history. It was opened to the public by the Empress in 1765. The collections have been on show in the present buildings since 1889, and have been constantly extended and modernised.

Mineralogical and Petrographical Department (Raised Ground Floor).

Location
1, Maria-Theresien-Platz

Underground station
Volkstheater (U2)

Bus 2A

Trams
1, 2, D, J

Opening times
Daily except Tues.
9 a.m.–6 p.m.

Naturhistorisches Museum

Children's Room in the Natural History Museum

Rooms I–V: The nucleus is the collection of minerals, with many examples from Austria.

In Room IV (precious stones) are the finest pieces of the collection (posy of precious stones of Maria Theresa, graduated emeralds, giant topaz weighing 258lb (117kg).

Room V is at present under rearrangement.

Geological and Palaeontological Collections (Raised Ground Floor)
Rooms VI–X: Fossils and petrified skeletons.
Rooms VI–IX are at present closed for reorganisation.
Room X houses dinosaurs.

Prehistory Collection (Raised Ground Floor)
Rooms XI–XV: Finds from excavations in Austria are displayed, from the Stone Ages to the La Tène culture. In Room XI the world-famous chalk figure of the "Willendorf Venus" can be seen. It dates from about 22000 B.C. (casting). In Rooms XIII and XIV can be seen the Hallstatt finds.

Anthropological Department (Raised Ground Floor)
Rooms XVI and XVII: Osteological collection with a great number of human skulls and skeletons from the Neo-Palaeolithic period to the present day. Somatological collection.

Children's Room (Raised Ground Floor)
Room XVIII: Microscopes, video recorders, dioramas, library.

Dome Hall (First Floor)
Skeleton of a giant lizard (extinct), giant crab, manatee.

Botanical Exhibition Gallery (First Floor)
Room XXI: Models of fungi and forms of spores.

Zoological Department (First Floor)
Rooms XXII–XXXIX: The collection illustrates in impressive fashion the long evolution from the single-cell organism to the anthropoid apes. – Bird collection. – Mammals.
Of interest are many extinct types (Moa, Dodo).

Neue Burg

See Hofburg

Neue Galerie in the Stallburg (art gallery)   B/C 4

The New Gallery is housed above the "Silver Stallions" on the second floor of the Stallburg (see Hofburg).
It was founded by Archduke Leopold William in 1656, enlarged by Emperor Charles VI in 1720, and in 1967 was adapted to serve as the New Gallery of the Kunsthistorisches Museum (see entry).
The six rooms are devoted to 19th and 20th c. art by painters who are not of Austrian extraction. There are paintings representing all recent periods – Romanticism, Realism, Idealism, Impressionism and Expressionism.
Among the artists represented are Böcklin, Corot, Degas, Feuerbach, Van Gogh, Manet, Monet, Munch, Liebermann, Renoir, Spitzweg and Toulouse-Lautrec.
In the Stallburg's arcaded courtyard are statues, including Meunier's "The Carrier" and Renoir's "Vénus Victorieuse".

Location
1, Reitschulgasse 2

Underground station
Stephansplatz (U1)

Buses
2A, 3A

Opening times
Mon., Wed., Thur., Sat., Sun.
10 a.m.–4 p.m.

Neuer Markt   C4

This square is noisy and all bustle. In the afternoon rival gangs of youths often gather round the Fountain. From 1220 onwards the "New Viennese Market-place" served as a corn and vegetable market, as the site for tourneys, as an arena for mountebanks such as Hans Wurst, and as a place where the Court and nobility could come and skate. Today it is an important car park and feeder for the Kärntnerstrasse pedestrian zone (see entry). The oldest houses remaining here are from the 18th c. No. 14 is a Baroque bourgeois house, No. 25 was the residence of the piano virtuoso Mayseder and No. 27 is the so-called "Herrnhuter House".
Joseph Haydn lived from 1795 to 1796 in the house where No. 2 now stands. It was there he wrote the Austrian Imperial Anthem. The Kapuzinerkirche (see entry) dominates the W side of the square.

Location
1, Kärntnerstrasse

Underground station
Stephansplatz (U1)

*Donner Fountain (officially Providentia Fountain)

In 1737–39 Georg Raphael Donner was commissioned by the city to create the Providentia Fountain which is better known in Vienna as the Donner Fountain.

Donner Fountain on the Neuer Markt

The City Fathers desired that the central figure of Providentia should express the concept of the caring and wise government of the city. Donner decorated its plinth with four graceful naked putti. The figures on the edge of the fountain's basin symbolise the Rivers Enns, Traun, Ybbs and March.

Empress Maria Theresa objected to so much nakedness and had the figures removed. They were replaced only under Francis II in 1801. In 1873 the lead figures were so decayed they had to be replaced with bronze replicas. Donner's originals are on show in the Baroque Museum at the Belvedere (see entry).

Niederösterreichisches Landesmuseum   B4

Location
1, Herrengasse 9

Underground station
Schottentor (U2)

Opening times
Tues.–Fri. 9 a.m.–5 p.m.,
Sat. 9 a.m.–2 p.m.,
Sun. and public holidays
9 a.m.–noon

A former palace and its former Rococo apartments are the setting for the Niederösterreichisches Landesmuseum (the Museum of the State of Lower Austria).

On the second floor is the Department of Cultural History, the most important department of the Museum. Here a series of pictures lead the visitor into the past, from Kokoschka via Gauermann, Waldmüller, Kupelweiser, Schnorr von Carolsfeld, Röttmayr, Maulbertsch, Altomonte and Kremser-Schmidt right back to 15th and 16th c. altar-pieces and wood-carvings (e.g. the Flachau Madonna of 1500).

Oberlaa Health Centre

Location
10, Kurbadstrasse, Oberlaa

Vienna is not only renowned for its theatres, museums and as a centre for international congresses, but also for its health spa.

View of the Oberlaa Health Centre

On the S edge of the city is the "Kurzentrum Oberlaa", the Oberlaa Health Centre, part of the old wine-producing village of the same name.

The sulphurous thermal spring was originally discovered in 1934 while boring for oil and resealed. It was uncovered again in 1965: the spring is 1260ft (418m) below round, is 54°C and produces 32 litres every second. In 1969 the spa building was completed and the new health centre, with the Ludwig Boltzmann Institute, opened in 1974. The spa offers treatment for rheumatism, sciatica, slipped discs, neuralgia and circulatory disorders and aftercare for fractures and sports injuries.

There are four thermal baths, two indoor and two outdoor pools; a children's pool; a sauna; a eucalyptus treatment room for breathing disorders and the spring pavilion on the edge of the spa park. This beautiful park also offers play areas for children and sports facilities, including 25 tennis courts. It was landscaped for the International Garden Festival of 1974, though the "Filmteich" (film lake) was already used by the Austrian film industry in the 1920s for large productions.

Underground station
Reumannplatz (U1), then further with tram 67 or bus 68A

Österreichische Nationalbibliothek (library)   C4

The Austrian National Library is housed in the commanding Baroque building on Josefsplatz (see entry). It was built during the reign of Charles VI to plans by Fischer von Erlach, father and son, between 1723 and 1726.

The Baroque building was originally free-standing, but it was linked by the Redouten range to the Hofburg (see entry) in 1750–60. The huge central section is crowned by a group of

Location
1, Josefsplatz 1

Underground station
Volkstheater (U2)

Buses
3A, 48A

Österreichische Nationalbibliothek

Trams
1, 2, D, J (Ring), 46, 49

All Departments closed
1–21 Sept.

statues representing the goddess Minerva with her chariot, drawn by four steeds. It is by L. Mattielli and dates from 1725. The National Library was formerly the Court Library, and it came into the possession of the State in 1920. Its collection goes back to the 14th c. The first Imperial Library Director was appointed in the 16th c. and in the 17th c. the collections were kept in the upper storey of the Reitschule (see Hofburg). By the 18th c. there was simply not enough space available in the Burg, and it was plain a new building must be provided.

The total collection of the National Library amounts at present to some 2½ million books. There are also the following special collections: printed materials, manuscripts, maps, papyri, portraits and picture archive, music and theatrical collections and an Esperanto Museum. The "New" building became far too small long ago, and it was necessary to expand into the S wing on Josefsplatz and into the Neue Burg (see Hofburg).

Entry is from Josefsplatz: hall of honour, manuscript collection, map collection, reading room and administrative offices.

Hall of Honour

Opening times
Temporary exhibitions
From May to Oct. Mon.–Sat.
10 a.m.–4 p.m. and Sun.
10 a.m.–1 p.m.; otherwise
Mon.–Sat. 11 a.m.–noon.

The Hall of Honour is one of the most splendid of Baroque rooms. It was designed by Fischer von Erlach, father and son. It is 250ft (77·7m) long, 46ft (14·3m) wide and 65ft (19·6m) high. The paintings in the dome are by Daniel Gran, the life-size statues by Paul and Peter von Strudel. In the middle stand the 15,000 gold-stamped books from what was once Prince Eugene of Savoy's Library. The Hall of Honour is used for temporary exhibitions.

Manuscript Collection

The holdings amount to 43,000 manuscripts from the 6th c., 8,000 incunabula and some 240,000 holographs.

Austrian National Library: Hall of Honour

Among the most impressive manuscripts held are the "Vienna Dioskurides", a Byzantine herbalist's treatise, written and illustrated about 512, the 6th c. "Vienna Genesis"; St Peter's Antiphonary (1160); the Black Prayer Book of Duke Galeasso Maria Sforza, one of the most valuable examples of Flemish illuminated scripts (c. 1470); the 16th c. Ambras Book of Heroes and a 15th c. Gutenberg Bible from Mainz. In the four showcases original material is on display.

Opening times
Aug. Mon.–Fri. 9 a.m.–
1 p.m.; closed 1–21 Sept.;
from 22 Sept. Tues., Thur.
1–6.45 p.m.

The Map Collection comprises at present about 240,000 sheets of maps and 280,000 geographical views. The most valuable objects are the copy of a 4th c. Roman map for travellers, the 46-volume Atlas by Blaeu, dating from the second half of the 17th c., and a map of the world made for Charles V in 1551.

Map Collection

Opening times
Reading Room Mon., Tues.,
Wed., Fri.
9 a.m.–3.45 p.m.

Of the 150 items in the Collection of Globes (open Mon.–Wed., Fri. 11 a.m.–noon; Thur. 2–3 p.m.) the two Mercator globes (c. 1550) and the 17th c. Coronelli globes are the most impressive.

Globe Museum

The collections of the Nationalbibliothek in the Neue Burg amount to about 2½ million books which have been catalogued. There is also an open-shelf collection of about 56,000 volumes for ready reference.
The main reading-room is connected to the old buildings by teleprinter, pneumatic communication tube and telephone.

Printed Materials

Opening times
Reading Room Mon.–Fri.
9 a.m.–7.45 p.m.,
Sat. 9 a.m.–1 p.m.
(earlier closing in summer)

The Picture Archive and Collection of Portraits comprises about 1½ million articles and 120,000 volumes of specialist literature. It is the largest and most important institution for the scholarly collection of pictorial documentation in Austria and comprises negatives, graphics and photographs of every variety and produced by every kind of technique.

Picture Archive

Opening times
Mon. 9 a.m.–6.45 p.m. Tues.,
Wed., Fri. 9 a.m.–3.45 p.m.;
earlier closing in summer

The Theatrical Collection is kept in the Michaelertrakt of the Hofburg (see entry), where the entrance is to be found. The Hugo Thimig Collection forms the basis of the collection. Among the most important recent acquisitions are the Hubert Marischka and the Albin Skoda Collections. There are more than 1 million printed items, holographs, theatrical manuscripts, drawings and prints.

Theatrical Collection

Opening times
Mon.–Wed., Fri.
9 a.m.–3.45 p.m.
Closed on each 1st and 3rd
Tues. in the month

The International Esperanto Museum is also housed in the Michaelertrakt of the Hofburg (entrance Batthyanystiege). The basis of the collection consists of the printed works and stock of the International Esperanato Museum of Vienna, founded in 1927 and taken over by the National Library in 1928. Today the special collection comprises more than 17,000 volumes; 260 periodicals were authenticated and put into the archives, including gazettes from China and Korea.
As well as text books, autographs, posters and inscriptions in Esperanto the museum also exhibits translations of the Bible, Dante's "Divine Comedy", works by Goethe, Heine, Raimund and Vicki Baum.

Esperanto Museum

Opening times
Mon., Wed., Fri. 9 a.m.–
3.30 p.m.

The Papyrus Collection is housed in the buildings of the Albertina (see entry) at 1 Augustinerstrasse.
Most of the papyri (100,000) come from Egypt, and they date from the 15th c. B.C. to the 14th c. A.D., forming one of the world's finest papyrological collections. The most precious possessions are three Egyptian Books of the Dead (the oldest dating from the 15th

Papyrus Collection

Opening times
Tues.–Fri. 9 a.m.–1 p.m.
Mon. 9 a.m.–6.45 p.m.; earlier
closing in summer

c. B.C.), one of the oldest Greek papyri (4th c. B.C.) and the oldest example of Islamic writing.

Music Collection

The Music Collection, too, is housed in the Albertina (see entry) at 1 Augustinerstrasse.

Opening times
Mon., Wed., Fri. 9 a.m.–1 p.m.,
Tues. noon–3.45 p.m.,
Thurs. noon–6.45 p.m.;
earlier closing in summer

Among the holdings are precious manuscripts, including Mozart's Requiem, Beethoven's Violin Concerto, Franz Schubert autographs, some of the papers left by Anton Bruckner on his death and the score of Richard Strauss's "Rosenkavalier".

Österreichisches Museum für Angewandte Kunst   B5

Location
1, Stubenring 5

Underground and
S-Bahn stations
Wien-Mitte (U4, S1, S2, S3,
S7)

Buses
1A, 74A, 75A

Trams
1, 2

Opening times
Wed.–Mon. 11 a.m.–
6 p.m.

The museum building, designed in Italian Renaissance style by Heinrich von Ferstel, was completed by an extension in Weisskirchnerstrasse in 1909.

The present Museum of Applied Art was founded in 1864 as the Austrian Museum for Art and Industry. In 1867 a School of Applied Arts was added. The museum is the oldest and one of the most important museums of applied art on the Continent. The trade and industrial development of Austria is in great measure attributable to it. Its comprehensive and varied collection from Late Antiquity (Coptic) to the present day are an eloquent testimony of artistic inspiration, not only in Europe but also in the Near and Far East. Especially renowned is the collection of Oriental carpets and other prominent exhibits including glassware, Viennese porcelain, ceramics, textiles, goldsmiths' work and furniture.

Room I: Middle Ages (emphasis on textiles). The "Gösser Ornat" (c. 1260), the only complete altar frontal remaining from such an early date; three 15th c. tapestries with hunting scenes; folding chair (early 13th c.) from Admont Monastery; 12th c. chest.

Room II: East Asian art work (especially from China). Examples from the Neolithic Age to the present day.

Room III: Dutch tapestries and Renaissance miniatures. Enamels from Limoges and Venice. Furniture and majolica from Urbino. The portal leading into Room V was originally in the Church of St Maria Novella in Florence.

Room IV: German Renaissance work. As well as goldsmiths' work, pewterware, vessels turned from ivory, and carved stone objects an attraction is an especially idiosyncratic carved Tyrol portal dating from about 1600.

Room V: Early Baroque furniture and miniatures. Meissen porcelain including a bear by J. G. Kirchner about 1730.

Room VI: 18th c. craft (especially French, German and Austrian furniture). Notable are two large intarsia wall decorations from the celebrated Röntgen workshop in Neuwied am Rhein.

Room VII: Biedermeier period. Viennese glass and porcelain; writing-desks and chairs.

Room VIII: Oriental carpets. The Vienna collection of Oriental carpets is notable for the so-called classical carpets from Persia, Egypt and Turkey which came from the former Austrian Imperial House. A silk hunting carpet and a rare silk Mameluke carpet (both 16th c.).

Room IX: Art Nouveau (especially Vienna at the turn of the century). Furniture, gold work, glass and ceramics. The star exhibit in the adjoining room is Klimt's cartoons for the dining-room frieze in the Palais Stoclet in Brussels (1911).

First Floor

The gallery of the pillared courtyard is used for small exhibitions. From a podium on the left there is a fine view of the Oriental carpets in Room VIII. Here can be found the library and art print collection; valuable old books and the most recent literature on art are available. The art print collection and the most valuable items in the so-called Baroque library can only be examined with prior permission.

Library

Opening times
Mon., Thur., Fri., Sun.
10 a.m.–6 p.m.

The rooms in the Baumann Building (3 Weisskirchnerstrasse) are reserved for exhibitions not only from the main collection but also for loans from all over the world. Details of the exhibitions may be found in the monthly programme issued by the Austrian museums authority.

Baumann Building

Östereichisches Museum für Volkskunde

B3

The Folk Museum is housed in the former Schönborn Palais. The building was designed by J. L. von Hildebrandt, and the Classical façade was added in 1770, probably by Isidor Canevale. The Museum was founded in 1895 by the Austrian Society for Folklore.

Location
8, Laudongasse 15–19

Underground station
Rathaus (U2)

Bus
13A

Trams
5, 43, 44

Ground Floor: Models, pictures and plans illustrating types of houses and farms; interiors, country furniture and utensils; farming and craftwork; food and clothing.

Upper Floor: Life and traditions, including a collection of carved masks; popular music and dance; religious life and pilgrimages; social organisation (guilds); Christmas cribs. (Temporarily closed for rebuilding.)

Opening times
Tues.–Fri. 9 a.m.–4 p.m.,
Sat. 9 a.m.–noon,
Sun. 9 a.m.–1 p.m.

Palais Liechtenstein

B4

Counts Kaunitz and Khevenhüller were previous owners of the building before it came into the possession in 1694 (completely rebuilt) of the Princes of Liechtenstein. The monumental gate with sculpture by Giuliani and a Triton fountain (1695) in the courtyard are worth seeing. The building is architecturally curious in having walls and floors that can be lowered and strange lift machinery. The summer seat of the Princes was the Gartenpalais Liechtenstein (see entry).

Location
1, Minoritenplatz 4/
Bankgasse 9

Underground station
Schottentor (U2)

Bus
1A

Palais Pálffy   C4

Location
1, Josefsplatz 6

Underground station
Stephansplatz (U1)

Bus
2A

With its interior modernised and adapted the former Palais Pálffy is now available, under the title of "Osterreich-Haus", for cultural events. The Emperors' Austrian Chancellery stood on the site of the Palais Pálffy about 1500. It was converted into a nobleman's palace towards the end of the 16th c. The buildings were damaged by fire in the 18th c. and by bombs in the 20th c.; in each instance they were partially restored.

Mozart produced his "Marriage of Figaro" for the first time before an audience of his friends in the room now called the "Figarosaal".

Palais Schwarzenberg   C5

Location
3, Rennweg 2

Underground station
Karlsplatz (U1, U2, U4)

Bus
4A

Trams
D, 71

Palais Schwarzenberg, now a hotel, was one of the first summer residences to be constructed outside the city walls. Its interior is particularly fine.

Prince Schwarzenberg settled in his own way the rivalry between the two great Baroque architects, J. B. Fischer von Erlach and L. von Hildebrandt. The first sketches were the work of Hildebrandt. In 1720 alterations were undertaken by Fischer von Erlach, and the magnificent Baroque gardens were laid out by Fischer von Erlach's son.

After the end of the war in 1945 the damaged palace was meticulously restored. It proved, however, impossible to save the frescoes by Daniel Gran.

Palais Schwarzenberg, once a summer residence, now an hotel

*Parliament   B4

Since 1918 the meetings of the National and Federal Parliament have been held in these impressive buildings. They had been built between 1873 and 1883 by Theophil Hansen for the Imperial and Provincial delegacies which had been called into being by the 1861 Declaration and survived until 1918. It was in allusion to Greece, the land where democracy was invented, that he chose for the building Greek forms with Corinthian columns and rich decoration on the metopes and pediments. The debating chamber, which has been altered, has an area of 17,250 sq. yd (16,000m^2) and the building measures 450ft (137m) by 475ft (145m). The building was severely damaged in 1945. Restoration was not completed until 1956.

Location
1, Dr-Karl-Renner-Ring 3

Underground station
Lerchenfelderstrasse (U2)

Bus 48A

Trams
1, 2, D, J

Tours
Mon.–Fri. at 11 a.m.
July and Aug. 11 a.m.,
2 p.m. and 3 p.m.

The Pallas Athene Fountain was placed in front of the main portal in 1902. The 13ft (4m) high figure of Pallas Athene with gilded helmet and armed with a lance is the work of the sculptor Kundmann. The recumbent figures symbolise the Rivers Danube, Inn, Elbe and Moldau. Josef Lax's bronze "The Horse-tamer" keeps watch over the flight of steps. On the left are the seated marble figures of Herodotus, Polybius and Xenophon, while to the right are those of Sallust, Caesar, Tacitus and Livy. The granting by Franz Joseph I of a Constitution to the 17 peoples of Austria is represented in the triangular pediment above the portico. The attic is decorated with 76 marble statues and 66 reliefs.

Pallas Athene Fountain

On 11 November 1918 the Deputies debated the choice of a new name for their land which had undergone such great changes. Among the proposals were "Markomannien", "Teutheim", "Frie-

The Parliament Building, with its impressive architecture in Greek forms

Pasqualatihaus

Pallas Athene Fountain and the bronze "Horse-tamer" outside Parliament

dland" and "Hochdeutschland". It is recorded that finally they settled on "Deutsch-Österreich" (German-Austria). On 12 November the House of Deputies of the Austrian part of the Empire went into dissolution.

Pasqualatihaus (Beethoven and Stifter Museum)   B4

Location
1, Mölkertbastei 8

Underground station
Schottentor (U2)

Trams
1, 2, D, T

Opening times
Tues.–Sun. 10 a.m.–
12.15 p.m., and 1–4.30 p.m.

Beethoven came to live here several times in the period between 1804 and 1815. It was here he composed the Fourth, Fifth and Seventh Symphonies, the Fourth Piano Concerto, the Leonora overtures and the opera "Fidelio".

Although the memorial rooms are not actually those which Beethoven occupied they are in their close proximity. On show are furniture and articles used by Beethoven as well as drawings, lithographs and music.

The Adalbert Stifter Museum has also been housed here since 1979. On show are manuscripts and first editions by the author as well as more than half the surviving pictures which he painted.

Paulanerkirche (Church of the Holy Angels)   C4

Location
4, Wiedner Hauptstrasse 6/
Paulanergasse

Underground station
Karlsplatz (U1, U2, U4)

The Paulanites were summoned to Vienna by Emperor Ferdinand II who gave them their vineyards on the "Wieden" (meadows). The church is dedicated to the Guardian Angels and was built between 1627 and 1651. It was rebuilt after destruction in 1668 and restored in 1817. Inside the church there are some important oil-paintings: a Crucifixion (second altar) by J. M. Rottmayr, a portrait of the Founder of the Order (third altar) by J. J. Bendl and an Immaculate Virgin possibly by L. Kupelwieser (first altar). The fresco on the ceiling is ascribed to Carlo Carlone.

Trams
62, 65

Pestsäule (Plague Pillar)

See Graben

---

*Peterskirche

B4

The Collegial and Parish Church of St Peter is modelled on St Peter's, Rome.

According to tradition, the site was originally occupied by a Late Romanesque church founded by Charlemagne in 792. The first documentary evidence for a church here, however, dates from 1137. That building was restored several times, but it was replaced early in the 18th c. by the present building which was probably completed by Lucas von Hildebrandt.

Location
1, Petersplatz

Underground station
Stephansplatz (U1)

Buses
1A, 2A, 3A

The church is built on an oval plan and is roofed with a massive dome (frescoes by J. M. Rottmayr). There are many artistic treasures to be seen.

Perambulation

Left-hand side
Going round the church in a clockwise direction visitors pass through Andreas Altomonte's magnificent portal and come to the Barbara Chapel. Franz Karl Remp's "Decollation of St Barbara" is especially noteworthy. The side-altar on the left has a reredos by Anton Schoonjans depicting the Martyrdom of St Sebastian. There is a painting by Altomonte in the Chapel of the Holy Family.

Choir
The choir lies just beyond the excessively richly carved Baroque pulpit. Beneath Antonio Bibiena's false dome stands the High Altar, a work by Santino Bussi. It has a reredos by Altomonte and a picture of the Immaculate Conception by Kupelwieser. The entrance to the crypt is also in the choir. At Christmas every year the crib set up here attracts many to the church.

Right-hand side
The Johann von Nepomuk Altar is on the right-hand side, with a Madonna in Glory probably by Matthias Steinl. The Michael Chapel has a "Fall of the Angels" by Altomonte. In a glass coffin may be seen Benedict, the Saint of the catacombs. The reredos on the side-altar on the right is by Rottmayr. The Antony Chapel has works by Altomonte ("St Antony with the Virgin") and by Kupelwieser ("The Heart of the Madonna"). The Empress Elisabeth sometimes used to have herself locked in this church, so that she could pray in complete privacy.

Piaristenkirche Maria Treu

B3

The Piaristenkirche is a parish church and a church of the Order of the Piarists (Patres Scholarum Piarum).

Location
8, Jodok-Fink-Platz

Peterskirche, modelled on St Peter's, Rome ▶

Maria Treu, the church of the Patres Scholarum Piarum

When the Piarists came to Vienna in the 17th c., they first built themselves a little chapel. The present church is based on plans drawn up by Lucas von Hildebrandt in 1716. A number of changes were introduced, and the building was completed in the middle of the 18th c., probably by Kilian Ignaz Dientzenhofer. Further construction took place between 1751 and 1953. The church was consecrated in 1771, but the towers were not completed until 1858–60. The church is decorated with particularly beautiful frescoes by F. A. Maulbertsch. Dating 1752–53 they are the first major frescoes by this Master. The church has eight chapels. The oldest, the Chapel of Sorrows, is in fact the foundation-chapel, dating from 1699. The historic votive picture of "Our Lady of Malta" dates from the first half of the 15th c.

Of the other chapels, the most important by far is the Holy Cross Chapel, to the left of the choir. The picture of Christ on the Cross is by Maulbertsch and dates from 1772.

The votive picture of the Virgin over the High Altar is only a copy. The original is in Rome.

Underground station
Rathaus (U2)

Bus
13A

Porzellanmanufaktur

See Augarten

*Prater

B6

The Prater, the large natural park between the Danube and the right-hand Danube Canal, is almost a world apart. It is lively and

Location
2nd District

Prater

Underground/S-Bahn station
Praterstern (U1, S7)

Bus
80A

Trams
1, N, O

gay by day, and something of a twilight zone by night. The park covers an area of some 3,200 acres (1,287ha), stretching SE almost 6½ miles (10km) from the Prater crossroads through the former "Augebiet" to the end of the Prater. In the first section lies the so-called "Wurstel" or "Volk" Prater with eating-houses, dance-halls, shooting-galleries, roundabouts and other attractions.

Nearly every kind of sport is catered for in the Prater. There is riding in the Freudenau, trotting in the Krieau, swimming in the stadium pool, football in the large stadium, rowing from the boat-houses, tennis at the WAC courts, and there is bowling, too. The Prater was first mentioned in a document in 1403. Maximilian II had the area fenced off in the 16th c., so that he could use it as a personal hunting preserve, and it was not opened to the general public until 1766. The first Punch and Judy shows date from 1767, and the first firework displays from 1771. In 1791 Blanchard's first hot-air balloon rose into the sky; in 1840 Calafati first began to run a big roundabout here.

Planetarium and Prater
Museum

Demonstrations
Sat., Sun., public holidays
3 and 5 p.m.; for children Sun.
9.30 a.m.; closed Aug

*Ferris Wheel

The Planetarium, a gift from the Zeiss family in 1927, is situated in the main avenue. It also houses Professor Pemmer's private collection concerning the history of the Prater (open Sat., Sun. 2–6.30 p.m.; closed in Aug.). In the vicinity is the Lipburg spherical house ("Kugelmugel").

Ferris Wheel: this giant pleasure wheel is an important landmark. It was built in 1896 by the English engineer Walter B. Basset for the World Exhibition of 1896. It was destroyed during the last war, but was rebuilt and has been once again in operation since 1946. The giant wheel is 200ft (61m) in diameter. The weight supported by the 8 pylons is 160 tons (165·2t); the total weight of the entire construction is 425 tons (430·05t). It revolves at a speed of about 3ft (0·75m) per second.

Wurstelprater: the earliest shows were put on here in 1766. Basileo Calafati's famous roundabout dates from 1840; it has been guarded by "the great Chinaman" since 1854. Only 18 of the attractions on the Prater survived the war, but now there are all sorts of roundabouts, dodgem cars, race-tracks, swings and helter-skelters, shooting-galleries and electronic games. There are also stilt-walkers, mountebanks, sword-swallowers, ventriloquists and ponies.

Ziehrer Monument: this larger than life statue of the composer in Deutschmeister uniform was made by Robert Ullmann in 1960.

The Constantin Hill: this mound is man-made. It was formed from the spoil dug out when the buildings for the 1873 Vienna Exhibition were erected and was named after Franz Joseph's Chief Chamberlain, Constantin of Hohenlohe-Schillingsfürst. The miniature railway operates in the area near the main avenue. It stops at the Stadium swimming-pool.

Pleasure-House: the café-restaurant at the end of the main avenue was a pleasure-house out in the country 400 years ago. Emperor Joseph II had it rebuilt by Isidor Carnevale in 1783. Its greatest moment came in 1814 when during the Congress of Vienna the allied monarchs with their generals celebrated the anniversary of the Battle of Leipzig when Napoleon was crushingly defeated. 18,000 soldiers were given a meal on tables erected all round the building.

Prater: Wurstelprater with Ferris Wheel   *Town Hall (Rathaus)*

Maria-Grün Chapel: this little pilgrimage church stands on the site occupied once by a forest shrine. The "Maria-Grün" (Madonna in Green) picture above the High Altar is an object of veneration. A "Hubert" Mass for hunters is celebrated here in November.

E of the Wurstelprater (People's Park) lies the exhibition ground of the City of Vienna with pavilions and the 492ft (150m) high Mannesmann Tower.

Praterstrasse   B5

Praterstrasse no longer has the importance it used to have in the great days of the Prater. It lives on its memories now.
Josef Lanner used to give concerts with his band in No. 26 Zum Grünen Jäger (Green Huntsman's House). The office building at No. 3 occupies the site where once the famous Carl Theatre stood which made the figure of Kasperl immortal and had Johann Nestroy as its Manager.
No. 54, the house in which Johann Strauss wrote "The Blue Danube" in 1867, has become a museum. It is open daily, except Monday, 10 a.m.–12.15 p.m. and 1–4.30 p.m. Documents relating to the Waltz King's life are on show as well as personal mementoes.

Location
2nd District

Underground station
Praterstern,
Nestroyplatz (U1)

S-Bahn station
Praterstern (S7)

Trams
1, 5, O

*Rathaus (Town Hall)   B4

The Town Hall is scarcely a hundred years old. The impressive Neo-Gothic building is the seat of the Vienna City and Provincial

Location
1, Rathausplatz

Underground station
Rathaus (U1)

Trams
1, 2, D

Tours
Mon.–Fri. at 1 p.m. (except when Assembly is in session)

Assembly and is the administrative centre of the city. The huge building, occupying nearly 17,000 sq. yd (14,000m²) of the former Parade Ground, was erected during Franz Joseph I's reign by Friedrich von Schmidt, who was also responsible for the decoration and furnishings.

The symbol of the Town Hall is the "Rathausmann" on the top of the 320ft (98m) high tower. This banner-carrying figure is 10ft (3·40m) tall and weighs 4,000lb (1,800kg); it was the gift of the master locksmith, Wilhelm Ludwig. The arcaded courtyard in the centre of the building, the largest of the seven courtyards, was originally intended for assemblies; the popular summer concerts (see Practical Information – Festivals) take place here.

The tour of the Rathaus interior begins in the Schmidthalle, the former "Community Vestibule" into which carriages could once drive. Today it houses the Civic Information Office. Proceeding up the two Grand Staircases we reach the official rooms: the Assembly Hall (233ft (71m) long; 66ft (20m) wide; 56ft (17m) high), two Heraldic Rooms, the City Senate Chamber and the "Roter Salon", the Mayor's reception room.

The council chamber of the Vienna City and Provincial Assembly extends over two floors. Since 1922 Vienna, as the country's capital, has also had the status of a province and so the City Council is also a provincial body. Notable features are the coffered ceiling decorated with gold-leaf and the Art Nouveau candelabra, weighing 3·2 tonnes and lit by 260 lamps, also the work of Friedrich Schmidt.

Ringstrasse   B/C4/5

Location
1st District

Underground stations
Karlsplatz (U1, U2, U4),
Schottentor,
Schottenring (U2),
Schwedenplatz (U1, U4)

Trams
1, 2, D, J

The handsome Ringstrasse is a thoroughfare that runs right round the city centre of Vienna. It consists, going in a clockwise direction, of the following sections: Stubenring, Parkring, Schubertring, Kärntnerring, Opernring, Burgring, Dr-Karl-Renner-Ring, Dr-Karl-Lueger-Ring and Schottenring. The circle of the Ringstrasse is completed by the Franz-Josef-Quai along the Danube Canal.

The razing of the fortifications during Emperor Franz Joseph's reign made possible the laying-out of a tree-lined ceremonial way between 1858 and 1865. Many huge buildings were erected here in the second half of the 19th c., in the grandiose style that came to be called "Ringstrasse style".

The Ringstrasse is 2½ miles (4km) long and 185ft (57m) wide. The ceremonial inauguration took place on 1 May 1865. Its finest hour was in 1879 when the painter Hans Makart mounted a parade with 10,000 participants in honour of the Imperial couple on the occasion of their Silver Wedding.

The following buildings and parks are situated along the Ringstrasse going from Stubenring towards Schottenring: the Post Office Savings Bank by Otto Wagner; the Museum für Angewandte Kunst; the Stadtpark; the Staatsoper; the Hofburg; the Kunsthistorisches Museum and the Naturhistorisches Museum; the Volksgarten; the Parliament; the Rathaus; the Burgtheater; the University and the Votivkirche (see entries).

Rohrau

Location
30 miles (47km) E
near Carnuntum

Rohrau is Joseph Haydn's birthplace (house No. 60; mementoes; open Apr.–Oct. Tues.–Sun. 10 a.m.–5 p.m.). Here, too, is Count

von Harrach's castle. The last great Viennese private noble-man's picture collection was brought here from the family mansion at Freyung (see entry) in 1970.
The gallery possesses some 200 paintings, including works by Rubens, Brueghel, Van Dyck, Jordaens, and Ruysdael.

S-Bahn
to Petronell (S7), then by bus (1793, 1795)

Roman Ruins

See Hoher Markt

Ruprechtskirche (officially St Ruprecht's Church)   B5

St Ruprecht's Church is the oldest church in Vienna. It stands on the N edge of the former Roman military settlement. It is sup-posed to have been built by Bishop Virgil of Salzburg, on the site of the subterranean Oratory of Cunard and Gisalrich, two apostles of the Faith. The church is first mentioned in docu-ments in 1161.
There is evidence that the nave and the lower storeys of the tower were built in the 11th c. The tower was twice made higher, in the 12th and 13th c. A choir was added in the 13th c., as was a S side aisle in the 15th c. The church was thoroughly restored between 1934 and 1936 and between 1946 and 1948. Its treasures include the oldest stained glass in Vienna (13th c.) in the central window in the choir, and the Altar of Our Lady of Loretto, the so-called "Black Madonna", whose aid was in-voked when there was danger from the Turks or the plague.

Location
1, Ruprechtsplatz

Underground station
Schwedenplatz (U1, U4)

Trams
1, 2

Opening times
From Easter to Sept.
10 a.m.–1 p.m.

Salvatorkapelle   B4

The Salvator Chapel was founded in 1301 by Otto Heimo, a famous conspirator. It formed part of the house which the authorities took over after the failure of the rebellion against Frederick the Fair and converted into the Altes Rathaus (see entry).
On 10 October 1871 the church passed into the possession of the Old Catholics. After sustaining severe damage in the Second World War the building was fully restored in 1972–73. The magnificent Renaissance portal, dating from 1520 and one of the few Renaissance works in Vienna, is especially note-worthy. The statues of knights are copies; the originals are in the Vienna City Historisches Museum (see entry).

Location
1, Salvatorgasse 5
(Entrance through the Altes Rathaus)

Underground stations
Stephansplatz (U1),
Schwedenplatz (U1, U4)

Bus
3A

Sammlung alter Musikinstrumente (museum)   C4

The Collection of Old Musical Instruments is housed in the middle section of the Neue Burg (see Hofburg). To form the collection the resources of the Archduke Ferdinand of Tyrol and of the Union of Viennese Music Lovers were pooled.
The greatest feature of the collection is the exceptionally fine stock of keyboard instruments from clavichords and cemba-loes of the 16th c. down to modern pianos. The exhibits are arranged in such a way as to give a sense of general develop-ment, in the Marble Hall, the Keyboard Rooms, and in the

Location
1, Neue Burg, Heldenplatz

Underground stations
Karlsplatz (U1, U2, U4),
Mariahilferstrasse (U2)

Bus
2A

Trams
1, 2, D, J

Opening times
Mon., Wed.–Fri. 10 a.m.–
4 p.m.,
Sat. and Sun. 9 a.m.–
4 p.m.

rooms for stringed instruments, plucked instruments, for woodwind and brass. There is also a gallery.

The most valuable instruments are in the Marble Hall, together with those with the most interesting personal associations. There is a cembalo and a table piano which belonged to Joseph Haydn, a grand piano which Erard Frères of Paris presented to Beethoven, and a Viennese table piano at which Schubert composed his music.

Among the brass wind instruments are a richly ornamented trumpet made for Duke Ferdinand of Tyrol in 1581 and silver trumpets from Maria Theresa's Court Band. The woodwind collection includes the cornetti used by the City Waits. In the gallery there are wind instruments from the time of Mozart.

Sammlung Religiöser Volkskunst (museum)   C4

Location
1, Johannesgasse 8

Underground station
Stephansplatz (U1)

Opening times
Wed. 9 a.m.–4 p.m.,
Sun. 9 a.m.–1 p.m.

The Collection of Popular Religious Art is housed in the former Ursuline Convent. It is an offshoot of the Museum für Volkskunde (see entry). In its four rooms are exhibited examples of popular religious art from the 17th to the 19th c.

Room I: Adoration of Christ. Domestic altars, pictures on glass, wooden sculpture and wax figurines.

Room II: The old convent pharmacy with original furniture and equipment. A painting depicts Christ as the Apothecary.

Room III: The room is devoted to the cult of the Virgin. All the Marian pilgrimage centres are shown on maps.

Room IV: Material concerned with popular saints.

Schillerdenkmal (memorial)   C4

Location
1, Schillerplatz

Underground station
Karlsplatz (U1, U2, U4)

Bus
59A

Trams
1, 2, D, J 62, 65

The square in front of the Akademie der Bildendenkünste (see entry) used to be called the Kalkmarkt, but it was changed to Schillerplatz (Schiller Square) in 1876. At the same time the Schiller Memorial, the work of Johann Schilling from Dresden, was unveiled. The plinth is of red granite. The allegorical bronze figures represent the Four Ages of Man, and the reliefs portray Genius, Poetry, Truth and Learning.

On the monument Schiller is shown standing, with Goethe sitting to one side. It is said that the admirers of Schiller were furious about this, but Franz Joseph I is supposed to have spoken in favour of portraying Goethe as sitting: "Let the old fellow be comfortable...."

Schloss Belvedere

See Belvedere-Schlösser

**Schönbrunn (Palace and Park)   D1

Location
13, Schönbrunner
Schlossstrasse

After the glorious defeat of the Turks in 1683 Emperor Leopold I commissioned J. B. Fischer von Erlach to design an Imperial

Palace of Schönbrunn: the Gardens ▶

Schönbrunn

Underground stations
Schönbrunn,
Hietzing (U4)

Bus
15A

Trams
10, 58

Guided tours
State Apartments: Daily
8.30 a.m.–5 p.m. (July–Sept.
to 5.30 p.m.; Nov.–Mar.
9 a.m.–4 p.m.)

palace on the site of the little Palace of Katterburg which had been destroyed. For the Gloriette Hill Fischer planned a castle larger and more magnificent than the Palace of Versailles. The project was never carried out.

The more modest Baroque Palace of Schönbrunn with 1,441 rooms and apartments was built between 1696 and 1730. Nikolaus Pacassi was responsible for converting the palace into a residence for Maria Theresa. There were some alterations also between 1816 and 1819. Reconstruction of severe war damage was completed in 1952. Nowadays it is used for receptions given by the President of Austria.

After the time of Maria Theresa the most brilliant period for the palace was during the Congress of Vienna. It went into decline after the death of Franz Joseph I who was born in the palace and also died there. It was here, too, that Charles I renounced the Imperial Crown. Victors have twice resided in the palace. Napoleon I occupied Maria Theresa's favourite rooms in 1805, and in 1945 the British High Commissioner set up his office in the room where the great Corsican had given his orders, much to the disgust of the French.

Palace Grounds

Palace Yard

The wrought-iron gate to the former parade ground (25,000 sq. yd (24,000 sq. m)) a magnificent example of Baroque layout, is flanked by two obelisks. Since 1809 these have been surmounted by French Imperial eagles. Austria's emperors were opposed to removing them after Napoleon's death. Franz Joseph I settled the matter: "They don't worry me," he said, "and folk seem to like them."

Palace Theatre

The sole remaining Baroque theatre in Vienna was built in 1747 by Nikolaus Pacassi, Maria Theresa's favourite architect. Its Rococo decoration dates from 1767. Here in the "Habsburgs private theatre" concerts were given by Haydn and Mozart. Nowadays the Viennese Chamber Opera gives performances in July and August.

▼ *The Gloriette, with the Neptune Fountain in the foreground*

Historical coaches, sledges and sedan-chairs, with harness, etc. from the Imperial Palace are on show in the former Winter Riding School. The chief exhibits are the Viennese Court Imperial Coach, the black Funerary Coach to take the Hapsburgs to their final resting place in the Imperial Vault in the Kapuzinerkirche (see entry), Napoleon's coach from Paris which was used for the coronation in Milan, the baby carriage, made in Paris for the Duke of Reichstadt (son of Napoleon I and Marie Louise), the Empress Caroline's Coronation Landau, the Emperor Franz Joseph's State Coach and the simple coach in which the Empress Elisabeth drove to Geneva, never to return.

Mews

Opening times: May–Sept.: Tues.–Sun. 10 a.m.–5 p.m.; Oct.–Apr.: Tues.–Sun. 10 a.m.–4 p.m.

Palace Park

The park round the palace covers an area of about 500 acres (2km²). It is one of the most important Baroque gardens in the French style. It was laid out by Jean Trehet in 1705. In 1765 it was altered by Adrian von Steckhoven. By the paths on each side of the flower-beds stand 44 marble sculptures from the period about 1773.

Opening times
Daily from 6 a.m. until dusk

Neptune's Fountain forms the S boundary of the garden area. This fine ornamental fountain was designed by F. A. Zauner in 1780. The stone sculptures are based on themes from Greek mythology: Thetis implores Neptune's aid when her son Achilles sets out on a sea-voyage.

Neptune's Fountain

The "Kaiserbrunnl" (Emperor's Spring), the old spring from which Emperor Joseph I had his drinking-water drawn, was turned into a grotto-like pavilion in 1799; the nymph Egeria pours out the water.

Schöner Brunnen (the Beautiful Fountain)

The so-called Roman ruins are a Romantic folly with the appearance of a half-buried palace with Corinthian columns. It

Roman ruins

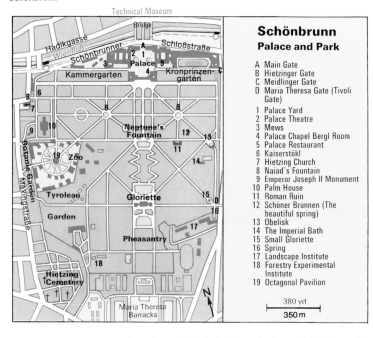

Schönbrunn
Palace and Park

A Main Gate
B Hietzinger Gate
C Meidlinger Gate
D Maria Theresa Gate (Tivoli Gate)

1 Palace Yard
2 Palace Theatre
3 Mews
4 Palace Chapel Bergl Room
5 Palace Restaurant
6 Kaiserstökl
7 Hietzing Church
8 Naiad's Fountain
9 Emperor Joseph II Monument
10 Palm House
11 Roman Ruin
12 Schöner Brunnen (The beautiful spring)
13 Obelisk
14 The Imperial Bath
15 Small Gloriette
16 Spring
17 Landscape Institute
18 Forestry Experimental Institute
19 Octagonal Pavilion

380 yd
350 m

dates from 1778. J. F. Hetzendorf von Hohenberg who designed it wanted to symbolise the fall of Greece before the might of the Roman Empire. Recent archaeological research has led to the belief that the Roman ruins may have come from the Neugebäude ("new building"), an Imperial palace which once stood in the present-day suburb of Simmering. Emperor Maximilian II (d. 1576) had the palace built for his recreation activities and court festivities, but by the time of Maria Theresia's reign, the palace had been reduced to a gunpowder store. The Empress ordered the palace to be dismantled and brought to Schönbrunn. There is a theory that the Roman architect Palladio may have submitted designs for the palace and Roman ruins, but much more research must be carried out before the origins of the Roman ruins can be established.

Obelisk

This, too, was designed by Hetzendorf von Hohenberg and dates from 1777. It used to stand on top of a gilded turtle. The carved scenes depict the family history of the Habsburgs.

Small Gloriette

Once the Empress Maria Theresa used to take her breakfast here from time to time. Nowadays this little pavilion with its wall-paintings serves as a tea-room open to all.

Gloriette

The park is crowned by the Classical Gloriette Arcade up on the top of the hill. J. F. Hetzendorf von Hohenberg built it in 1775 to close the prospect at the end of the park. The Gloriette commemorates the Battle of Kolin (1757), where Maria Theresa's troops defeated the Prussian army of Frederick the Great.

Opening times
Daily May–Oct.
8 a.m.–6 p.m.

Palace of Schönbrunn

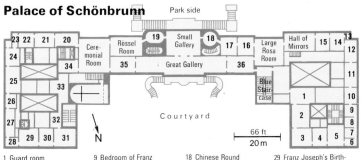

1 Guard room
2 Franz Joseph's Antechamber (Billiard Room)
3 Walnut Room
4 Franz Joseph's Writing-room
5 Franz Joseph's Bedroom
6 W Terrace Cabinet
7 Stair Cabinet
8 Dressing-room
9 Bedroom of Franz Joseph and Elisabeth
10 Empress Elisabeth's Salon
11 Marie-Antoinette Room
12 Nursery
13 Breakfast-room
14 Yellow Salon
15 Balcony Room
16 Small Rosa Room
17 Small Rosa Room
18 Chinese Round Cabinet
19 Oval Chinese Room
20 Blue Chinese Salon
21 Vieux Laque Room
22 Napoleon's Room
23 Porcelain Room
24 Million Room
25 Tapestry Room
26 Memento Room
27 Red Drawing-room
28 E Terrace Cabinet
29 Franz Joseph's Birth-room
30 Writing-room
31 Archduke Francis Charles's Drawing-room
32 Wild Boar Room
33 Passage Chamber
34 Machine Room
35 Carousel Room (Anteroom)
36 Lamp Room

Archduke Johann introduced an Alpine note into the Schönbrunn Park by having the two Tyrolean timber houses erected here an an Alpine garden laid out.

Tyrolean Garden

The origins of the Schönbrunn Zoo go back to Francis I's menagerie which he founded in 1752. It is the oldest zoo in Europe. At present some 750 species of animals live here, in special houses or running free in paddocks. In the middle of the zoo there is an octagonal pavilion which is now a café and restaurant; originally the Imperial family used to come there to watch their "pets".

Zoo

Opening times
Daily
Summer 9 a.m.–6 p.m.
Winter 9 a.m.–4.30 p.m.

This was the largest glasshouse in Europe; it was built in 1883 and fully renovated in 1990. There are three sections in which numerous exotic plants are kept at various temperatures. (Entrance at Hietzinger Tor; open: May–Sept. daily 9.30 a.m.– 6 p.m.; Oct.–Apr. daily 9.30 a.m.–5 p.m.) Opposite the Palm House stands the Sundial House with a butterfly garden (open: May–Oct. daily 10 a.m.–5 p.m.; Nov.–Apr. 10.30 a.m.– 3.30 p.m.)

Palm House

In the Palace 42 rooms are open to the public. They still have the character they had in Franz Joseph's day.
Rooms 1–15: The rooms used by the Emperor Franz Joseph and Empress Elisabeth.
Rooms 16–25: State Apartments.
Rooms 26–33: Guest Apartments.
Rooms 34–36: Suite for Grand Duke Charles with three antechambers.
Rooms 40–42: Reception Rooms.

Palace

This dates from about 1700. The painted ceiling is by Daniel Gran (1744), and the picture above the High Altar is by Paul Troger.

Palace Chapel

Schönbrunn

Fountain of the Naiads in the Palace Park

Bergl Rooms	Left of the entrance hall are the garden apartments which were furnished to Maria Theresa's taste. They were originally known as the "Indian Rooms" on account of their Romantic and exotic decoration which is the work of the Bohemian artist Johann Bergl. (Open: May–Sept. daily 9 a.m.–noon, 1–5 p.m.)
Walnut Room	The most handsome and important of the apartments: The Walnut Room: Emperor Franz Joseph's audience chamber takes its name from the walnut panelling dating from 1766. The candelabrum is carved out of wood covered with real gold.
Franz Joseph's Bedroom	It was in this simple soldier's bed that the Emperor died on 21 November 1916 after a reign of nearly 68 years.
Empress Elisabeth's Salon	On the walls of this reception-room hang pastel portraits by Jean-Etienne Liotard of Maria Theresa's children.
Marie-Antoinette's Room	On the left is F. Amerling's celebrated portrait of Francis I with the insignia of the Order of the Golden Fleece. A peculiarity of the picture is that the eyes of the Emperor seem to follow the spectator wherever he may go in the room.
Nursery	The Louis XVI cupboard in this panelled room belonged to Marie-Antoinette. There is a portrait of the future Queen of France on the left-hand side.
Breakfast-room	Maria Theresa used to take her breakfast in this room. The pictures of flowers embroidered in silks are said to be the work of the Empress's daughters.
Yellow Salon	The white marble clock which stands on the left-hand side was a gift of Napoleon III to Franz Joseph I. The salon takes its name from the yellow damask used for covering the chairs.

It was in this room the walls of which are covered with crystal mirrors in gilded Rococo frames, that Maria Theresa's Ministers used to swear their allegiance to her. Mozart performed here as a six-year-old prodigy.

Hall of Mirrors

Joseph I's private apartments take their name from the landscape paintings (1760–69) by the artist Josef Rosa.

Rosa Room

It was here that Maria Theresa set up her "conspiracy headquarters" amid the East Asian lacquered screen panels under the dome with its stucco decoration. At that time State Chancellor Kaunitz was allowed to enter by way of a secret staircase. Meals were provided by means of a food lift; this meant there was no need to be disturbed by servants.

Chinese Round Cabinet

It was in this 60ft (18m) long gallery that the Imperial Household ate its more intimate dinners. The painted ceiling is by Gregorio Guglielmi and dates from 1761. The huge windows offer a wonderful view out over the flower-beds in the park.

Small Gallery

Major weddings, baptisms and investitures (official inductions into certain high offices) took place here under the Habsburgs. The gold-framed paintings – School of van Meytens – depict the marriage of Joseph II to Isabella of Bourbon-Parma in 1760.

Ceremonial Room

Hand-painted Far Eastern wallpaper, blue and white Japanese vases and light blue silks form the setting in which the monarchy came to an end. It was in here that Charles I abdicated in 1918, and Austria became a Republic.

Blue Chinese Salon

In the private apartment of the elderly Empress Maria Theresa East Asian art is combined with Viennese Rococo.

Vieux Laque Room

Napoleon I lived in Maria Theresa's former bedroom in 1805. It was here, too, that his son, the Duke of Reichstadt, who had grown up in Schönbrunn, died in 1832. The room is furnished with valuable Brussels tapestries.

Napoleon's Room

Blue and white wooden garlands look deceptively like decorations of genuine porcelain. Some of the 213 blue Indian ink sketches are by Maria Theresa's children who were artistically gifted.

Porcelain Room

Maria Theresa's former private salon is panelled with precious rose wood, ornamented with gilt carvings. 260 precious Indian parchment miniatures have been set under glass in the panelling. Maria Theresa had them brought to Vienna from Constantinople. According to tradition the room cost "a million guilders".

Million Room

The walls and furniture are covered with Brussels tapestries depicting Netherlandish folk scenes. The tapestry in the middle, "Port and Fish Market" is 280 sq. ft (26m^2) in area.

Tapestry Room

Glittering Imperial banquets used to take place in the Great Gallery under Gregorio Guglielmi's ceiling-paintings. Now the Republic has its grandest receptions here, too. One of the most important was when the State Treaty was signed.

Great Gallery

Schönlaterngasse   B5

Schönlaterngasse, the winding lane in the oldest district of the inner city, takes its name from "The House with the fine lantern", which was built in 1680. The original "fine lantern" is

Location
1, Sonnenfelsgasse/
Postgasse, I

Underground stations
Stephansplatz (U1),
Schwedenplatz (U1, U4)

Opening times
Alte Schmiede Museum
Mon.–Fri. 9 a.m.–3 p.m.

now housed in the Historisches Museum (see entry). In 1971 a copy was placed on No. 6 Schönlaterngasse.

In Schönlaterngasse the houses of the bourgeoisie and the traders are basically medieval with Baroque façades. They have all been thoroughly restored and renovated. Robert Schumann lived in No. 7a.

The Heiligkreuzerhof and the Basilikenhaus (see entries) and the old Jesuit House (No. 11), where the painter Kupelwieser lived, are notable. The Alte Schmiede (No. 9) was, until 1974, the workshop of Meister Schmirler who created the present "Schöner Laterne" and gave it to the city. The old smithy is now a cultural centre with an art gallery, a café and a literary rendezvous where readings and lectures are given.

---

*Schottenkirche (dedicated to the Virgin)   B4

Location
1, Freyung

Underground station
Schottentor (U2)

Bus
1A

In the 12th c. Irish monks were invited to come to Vienna from Regensburg. At the time Ireland was called "New Scotland", and this is why the church dedicated to Our Lady which was built for Irish Benedictines came to be called the Scots Church. It has been in the possession of the German Benedictines since 1418.

The Scots Monastery was founded by the Babenberg Duke Heinrich Jasomirgott in 1155, and work on the construction of the buildings began in 1177. The church was reconstructed in the Gothic style in the 14th and 15th c. It was altered and given a Baroque appearance by Andrea Allio and Carlo Carlone in the 17th c., and was restored again in the 19th c.

The Scots Church, built for Irish Benedictines

In the interior there are reredoses by Tobias Pock dating 1651–85, by Joachim Sandrart 1652–54, and August Eisenmanger 1887–88. The finest is the "Apostles Departure" (near the Imperial Oratory). J. E. Fischer von Erlach designed the Baroque memorial, on the right behind the Penitents' Chapel, to Graf R. von Starhemberg who defended Vienna against the Turks.

The High Altar was the last work by Heinrich Ferstel, dating from 1883. The Lady Chapel Altar-piece has the oldest votive picture of the Virgin in Vienna. In the Crypt Chapel which was converted into vaults in 1960 lie the founder of the church, Heinrich II Jasomirgott, his consort Theodora and his daughter Agnes, Graf Rüdiger von Starhemberg who died in 1701, and the Baroque painter, Paul Troger, who died in 1762.

*Schottenstift (picture collection)   B4

The Schottenstift (Scots Foundation) on Freyung (see entry) is linked to the Schottenkirche (see entry) by the Schottenhof. It has a famous secondary school and an important picture gallery. The foundation Bull dates from 1161. The abbey was ceded to the German Benedictines in 1418.

The buildings date from the 12th c., but were extensively renovated in the 17th c. and enlarged in the 18th c. In 1832 they were rebuilt by Josef Kornhäusl in simple Classical style.

Among pupils of the school were the poet Bauernfeld, Nestroy, von Saar, Hamerling, the Waltz King Johann Strauss and the painter Moritz von Schwind. Austria's last Emperor, Charles I, also attended this school, as did the founder of Austrian Social Democracy, Viktor Adler. The collection of pictures here has been in existence for two and a half centuries. As well as works from the 16th c. to the 19th. c., there are in the chapter-house 19 pictures from the famous Late Gothic winged reredos of 1469–75. It was painted by two "Scottish Masters" and originally stood in the Schottenkirche. The oldest surviving views of Vienna may be seen in the backgrounds of these pictures.

Location
1, Freyung 6

Underground station
Schottentor (U2)

Bus
1A

Opening times
By appointment

*Schubert Museum   A3

On 31 January 1797 Franz Schubert was born in this little one-storey house – Zum roten Krebs (the red crab) in the Himmelpfort district.

The city of Vienna owns this house and has been able to preserve Schubert's birthplace virtually unaltered. A Schubert Museum has now been installed here, with manuscripts, pictures and everyday objects used by the composer. Not everything is entirely authentic, however, for when he was only four years old Schubert moved to a nearby house, No. 3 Saülengasse, where he lived for the next 17 years. (Schubert Memorial, see Practical Information – Memorial Sites.)

Location
9, Nussdorferstr. 54

S-Bahn station
Nussdorferstrasse (G, GD)

Trams
D, 8, 42

Opening times
Tues.–Sun. 10 a.m.–
12.15 p.m. and 1–4.30 p.m.

Schubertpark   A3

A few gravestones and a Late Baroque cemetery cross indicate that Schubert Park was laid out on what used to be the Währinger Cemetery. On the E wall of the park are the two original

Location
18, Währingerstrasse

Franz Schubert's birthplace, now a Schubert Museum

S-Bahn station
Wahringerstrasse–Volksoper
(G, GD)

Trams 40, 41

graves of Schubert and Beethoven. Both composers were exhumed in 1808 and reburied in the Zentralfriedhof (see entry). It was in the Währinger Cemetery that Franz Grillparzer pronounced his funeral oration over Beethoven. He said: "Beethoven withdrew from human society after he had given men all that he had and received nothing back in return."

*Secession (art gallery)   C4

Location
1, Friedrichstrasse 12

Underground station
Karlsplatz (U1, U2, U4)

Bus
59A

Trams
1, 2, D, J

Opening times
Tues.–Fri. 10 a.m.–6 p.m.,
Sat. and Sun. 10 a.m.–
4 p.m.

The exhibition gallery of the artists' union is easily recognised on account of its remarkable cupola in the form of an iron laurel bush. When the gilding was still visible the Viennese used to call it "the golden bunch". The building was designed by Josef Olbrich, a disciple of Otto Wagner's, in 1898. It was the first and epoch-making example of the Viennese Art Nouveau (called "Jugendstil" or sometimes "Secessionsstil"). It was damaged during the war and robbed of its treasures in 1945 but was restored and opened again in 1964. Reconstruction since 1986 has made it possible to put on musical and theatrical performances and video displays.

The need for the building arose after 1892 when the union of young artists under the leadership of the painter Gustav Klimt left – "seceded from" – the Künstlerhaus (see entry) group. In 1897 the still-surviving Artists' Union, called "Secession", came into being and created the artistic style that bears the same name.

The huge Mark Antony bronze group by Arthur Strasser on the E side is especially noteworthy. The Roman statesman's lion-drawn chariot was shown at the 1900 Universal Exhibition.

The Secession Building

Horses in the Spanish Riding School

Today in the Secession building can be seen Gustav Klimt's Beethoven frieze, a huge mural of some 270 sq. ft ($70m^2$) on the theme of Beethoven's Ninth Symphony. It was painted for the 14th exhibition of the Vienna Secession in 1902 and was purchased by the State in 1973, restored from 1977 and is now once more "at home".

*Servitenkirche

B4

The Servites' (or "Servants of our Lady") Church was founded by Field-Marshal Octavio Piccolomini, one of the leaders of the Wallenstein Conspiracy. Its dedication is to the Annunciation. It was built by Carlo Carnevale between 1651 and 1677. Dying in 1656, Piccolomini did not live to see the work completed.
The Servites' Church is the earliest building in Vienna based on a central oval form with its main space elliptical in shape. The traverse axis provides wide, rectangular chapels and in the diagonal corners there are small semicircular altar-niches. In the narthex there are two large 17th c. Baroque figures and a magnificent cast-iron trellis-work, dating from about 1670. There is rich stucco decoration by Giovanni Battista Barbarino (1669) and Giovanni Battista Bussi (1723–24). Near the 19th c. High Altar is a late 15th c. wooden Crucifix from the "Raven Stone", the site of executions in days gone by. The carved figures of the Four Evangelists and the Three Virtues on the pulpit of 1739 are by Balthasar Moll. Field-Marshal Octavio Piccolomini, who died in 1656, lies buried in front of the altar in the middle chapel on the left-hand side; there is no gravestone.

Location
9, Servitengasse 9

Underground station
Rosauer Lände (U4)

Tram
D

The Peregrini Chapel was built on to the middle chapel on the right; its fine Rococo ironwork and the frescoes in the dome are the work of Josef Mölk (1766).
The Tower Chapel on the right leads through to the little Chapel of the Poor; its altar-painting is attributed to Martin J. Schmidt. The left-hand Tower chapel leads to the Lourdes-Grotto.

Sigmund Freud Museum   B4

Location
9, Berggasse 19

Underground station
Rossauer Lände (U4),
Schottenring (U2)

Tram
D

Opening times
Daily, 9 a.m.–3 p.m.

Sigmund Freud lived in the house at 19 Berggasse for almost half a century, from 1891 to 1938. It was here that he wrote his theories, including "Dreams and Their Meaning" and received the official announcement that the Emperor had awarded him an honorary Professorship in 1902.
Of the fifteen rooms in the house, only Freud's "working" rooms are open to the public: the vestibule, waiting room, treatment room and study have been turned into a museum by the Sigmund Freud Society and contain some original furnishings, documents and photographs. The vestibule and waiting room have been almost exactly re-created, down to the hat and cane in the cloakroom. The house acted as meeting-place until 1908 of the Psychologische Mittwochsgesellschaft (the "Psychological Wednesday Society") the fore-runner of the Vienna Psychoanalytical Association. Among the displays in the museum are 60 items from Freud's collection of antiquities which Anna Freud donated to the Society; the majority of pieces used to be kept in the study.

**Spanish Riding School   B4

Location
1, Reitschulgasse 2

Underground station
Stephansplatz (U1),
Schottentor (U2)

Bus
2A

Performances
Mar.–Jun., Sept.–Dec.,
Sun. 10.45 a.m.
Apr.–Jun., Sept.–Oct.
also Wed. 7 p.m.
Short programme
Sat. 9 a.m.;
Morning exercise:
Mid-Feb.–Jun., Sept.–mid-
Dec. Tues.–Sat. 10 a.m.–noon
(also Mon. in Feb.)

The Spanish Riding School is an inheritance from the Baroque era. The institution dates back to the time of Emperor Maximilian II who introduced the breeding of Spanish horses in Austria in 1562. The name "Spanish Riding School" is first mentioned in 1572. The Spanish Riding School is the only place in the world where the Classical style of riding is still practised.
The horses of the Spanish Riding School are a cross of Berber and Arabian stock with Spanish and Italian horses. The foals are born any shade between brown and mouse-grey; their coats turn white later when they are between four and ten years old. The horses were bred in Lipizza until 1918 when the stud was transferred to Piber in Styria. The stud which was partly moved to Czechoslovakia during the Second World War was saved from destruction by Colonel Podhajsky, who was then head of the riding school (until 1956), as well as by the American horse-loving General Patton.
There still survive today six lines of stallions going back to their forefathers, Pluto (1765), Conversano (1767), Maestoso (1773), Neapolitano (1790), Favory (1799) and Siglavy (1810). The stallions do not begin their long training until they are four years old. At about the age of seven they learn the so-called "ground exercises", which involve high-speed changes in gait, piaffes, passages and pirouettes. Then they graduate to the "aerial exercises", with pesades, levades, courbettes and caprioles.
Since the time of Charles VI the prestigious riding displays have taken place in the Baroque Winter Riding School which was built by Joseph Emmanuel Fischer von Erlach between 1729

and 1735 in the Hofburg (see entry). This magnificent room was designed for the nobility to show their ability in riding skills and to compete together. It was later used for a variety of other purposes, but since 1894 it has been reserved exclusively for the training of the Lipizzaner horses and their displays.

The impressive displays of the Spanish Riding School have always been performed in historical costume. The riders wear white buckskin breeches with high black boots, a brown jacket and a bicorn hat trimmed with gold. Deerskin saddles lie over the gold-trimmed red and blue saddle-cloths. At the start and end of each display the riders silently salute the picture of Charles VI who commissioned the building.

*Spinnerin am Kreuz (officially Crispin's cross)   D4

The Spinnerin am Kreuz is a 52ft (16m) high Gothic stone pillar in the form of a phial-shaped tabernacle. One of the landmarks of Old Vienna, it was designed by Hans Puschbaum, the architect of St Stephen's Cathedral and erected in 1452 to replace an older one which had been donated by Leopold III. According to legend a faithful wife sat here at her spinning-wheel, awaiting the return of her husband from a Crusade.

From 1311 to 1747 and from 1804 to 1868 the "gallows by the Spinnerin" was the site of public executions. Severin von Jaroszynski was hanged here in front of 30,000 spectators in 1827. He was a Polish aristocrat who had robbed and murdered a man in order to satisfy the excessive financial demands of the popular actress Therese Krone.

Location
10, Triesterstrasse
(near No. 52)

Buses
15A, 65A

Tram
65

Spittelberg   C3/4

A densely built, but architecturally pretty community grew during the Baroque era on the Spittelberg, a hill which once belonged to a hospital. It was from this hill that Turkish cannon were directed at the city during the second siege of Vienna (1693) and Napoleon's troops also positioned their artillery here.

With time the district deteriorated and became the home of the lower classes, but it was a very lively quarter. The Spittelberg was not only the haunt of "lieber Augustin", the wandering piper, but also of many traditional artists and actors, ballad singers and the strolling players who created the "Spittelberg Songs", some of which are still known today.

The Emperor Joseph was thrown out of a local inn, the "Sonnenfels-Waberl", run by a notorious landlady, when he visited it anonymously in 1787. The event is commemorated by an inscription in the entrance of the house at 13 Gutenbergstrasse.

The charm of this district was re-discovered and the city authorities began renovation work in the 1970s.

Nowadays it is an attractive district offering many cultural and social facilities. The Spittelberg cultural centre in the Amerlinghaus at 8 Stiftgasse provides a venue for musical events, poetry readings, exhibitions, children's activities and dances for senior citizens, appealing to both old and new residents. In the "Werkhaus" on Stiftgasse young people have created a collective workshop where pottery, dressmaking, furniture restoration, ceramics, bookbinding and a goldsmith have been

Location
7, Spittelberggasse and surroundings

Underground station
Volkstheater (U2)

Bus
48A

Tram
49

brought together under one roof. There is a gallery in the centre of the building. The renovated old houses are now occupied by speciality shops, boutiques, pubs and galleries. A market for arts and handicrafts has also been opened; all of which make Spittelberg an attractive and popular district.

**Staatsoper   C4

Location
1, Opernring 2

Underground station
Karlsplatz (U1, U2, U4)

Trams
1, 2, D, J

Tours
July–Aug. daily 10 and
11 a.m., 1, 2 and 3 p.m.
Sept.–June on demand

The Vienna State Opera House is one of the world's three leading opera houses.

Operas have been performed in Vienna since 1688, first on the site of the present Nationalbibliothek (see entry), then in the Redoutensälen and in the old Burgtheater on Michaelerplatz, where Mozart's "Il seraglio" and "The Marriage of Figaro" were first performed, next in the Kärntnertor Theatre, where Weber's "Euryanthe" had its première. After that operas were performed in the Ring Theatre, which was subsequently destroyed by fire, and finally, from 1869, in the Hof Opera House. The vast Opera House with its clearly defined structure is designed in the French Early Renaissance style.

It was built between 1861 and 1869 to plans by August von Siccardsburg and Eduard van der Null. It was opened on 25 May 1869 with Mozart's "Don Giovanni" and a prologue spoken by Charlotte Wolter. Neither architect lived to see the day. The criticisms and cruel jokes of the Viennese while building was in progress drove van der Null to suicide, and Siccardsburg died just two months later, in 1868.

The Opera House was struck by bombs on 12 March 1945 and gutted by fire. Reconstruction was not completed until 1955. The second inauguration of the Opera House on the Ringstrasse took place on 5 November 1955 when Beethoven's "Fidelio" was performed.

The Opera House can accommodate an audience of 2,209, with 110 musicians. The area covered by the buildings is 8,650sq.yd (9,000m²). The main façade with its two-storey foyer opens on the Ringstrasse. The tripartite stage area covers an area of 1,450sq.yd (1,500m²); it is 175ft (53m) high and 165ft (51m) deep.

Inside a grand staircase leads up to the first floor. Immediately opposite is the "Schwind Foyer" which takes its name from the pictures by Martin Schwind of scenes from operas. The staircase, the foyer and the tea-room with its valuable tapestries were the only parts of the building left undamaged after the fire in 1945.

Opera Ball

Every year on the last Thursday of Carnival the Opera Ball takes place here. It is one of the most elegant and famous balls in the world. The stage and the rows of seats in the auditorium which is decorated in cream, red and gold, are brought to the same level by means of a specially fitted floor. Thousands of carnations are flown in from the Riviera to decorate the boxes just for one night.

Stadtpark   C5

Location
1, Parkring

The two parts of the City Park are linked by bridges over the River Wien. It covers an area of 28 acres (114,000m²).

Vienna State Opera: the Staircase ▶

The exterior of the Vienna State Opera House

Underground station
Stadtpark (U4)

Trams
1, 2, J

In 1857 Franz Joseph I instigated the creation of a garden where the old fortifications went down to the water, thinking the site "well suited to embellishment". The landscape-gardener Dr Siebeck carried through the plans drawn up by the landscape-painter Josef Szelleny. The gardens were opened in 1862, and the Pavilion in 1867.

In the part of the park nearest the city centre there are monuments to the painters Hans Canon, Emil Schindler, Hans Makart, and Friedrich von Amerling, to the composers Johann Strauss the Younger, Franz Schubert and Anton Bruckner, as well as to Anton Zelinka, the founding Mayor. The Donauweibchenbrunnen (The Spring with the Sprite of the Danube) is a copy; the original stands in the Historisches Museum (see entry).

Stanislaus-Kostka-Kapelle (church)   B4

Location
1, Steindlgasse 6/
Kurrentgasse 2

Underground station
Stephansplatz (U1)

Bus
2A

There is gold and silver decoration in this chapel in the courtyard of the Jesuit presbytery.

Until 1582 the chapel was a single room in the house called "Zur goldenen Schlange" (The Golden Snake) where the Polish Jesuit Stanislaus Kostka lived. After the occurrence of two miracles, the room was converted into a chapel and given particularly rich ornamentation. Stanislaus Kostka was canonised in 1726.

The chapel was refurbished during Maria Theresa's reign, and Charles I served at the altar here while a schoolboy at the Schottengymnasiums.

Stadtpark: the Strauss Monument

The chapel is open every Tuesday except in July and August.
Open 13–20 Nov. all day.

Stephansdom (St Stephen's Cathedral)   B4/5

St Stephen's Cathedral with its 450ft (137m) high spire is not
only the major sight in Vienna and the symbol of the city; it is
also the most important Gothic building in Vienna. It has been
the cathedral church of the archbishopric since 1722.

The cathedral has been the never-ending work of generations
since the 12th c. It is an architectural representation of eight
centuries of history. The original Romanesque church was
replaced by a Late Romanesque one in the 13th c. All that
remains of it are the massive gate and the Heiden (heathen)
Towers. Next came reconstruction in the Gothic style in the
14th c. by Duke Rudolf IV von Habsburg, known as "The
Donor".

The choir, and the Chapels of St Eligius, St Tirna and St Catherine were completed in the course of this century. The S tower,
the nave and the Chapel of St Barbara belong to the 15th c. The
N tower, which was not completed, was roofed over in the
16th c. Improvements and further construction followed in the
17th, 18th and 19th c.

The roof was destroyed by fire in the final days of the Second
World War in 1945. The vaulting of the middle choir and the
right-hand choir side of the choir collapsed, and the towers
were gutted. Reconstruction and restoration went on from
1948 to 1962. It was a communal effort, involving all Austria.
The new bell was paid for by Upper Austria, the new floor by

Location
1, Stephansplatz

Underground station
Stephansplatz (U1)

Bus
1A

Tours
Mon.–Sat. 10.30 a.m. and
3 p.m.; Sun. and holidays
3 p.m.
Evenings June–Sept.
Sat. 7 p.m.
July, Aug. also Fri. 7 p.m.

153

St Stephen's Cathedral

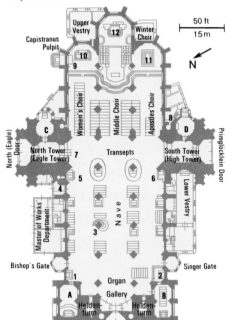

Upper Vestry · **12** · Winter Choir
Capistranus Pulpit · **10** · **9** · **11**
Women's Choir · Middle Choir · Apostles' Choir
8
North Tower (Eagle Tower) · **7** · Transepts · South Tower (High Tower)
North (Eagle) Door
C · D · Primglöcklein Door
5 · **4** · **6** · Lower Vestry
Master of Works Department · N a v e · **3**
Bishop's Gate · **1** · Organ · **2** · Singer Gate
Gallery
A · Heiden-turm · Heiden-turm · B
Giant Gateway

50 ft / 15 m
N

A Tirna Chapel (Holy Cross Chapel),
  burial-place of Prince Eugene (d. 1736);
  above it the Treasury Chapel
B Eligius Chapel
C Barbara Chapel
D Catherine Chapel

1 H. Prachatitz's altar canopy.
2 Canopy with Pötscher Madonna
3 A. Pilgram's pulpit with Peeping Tom
  on the plinth. On the pillar, the
  Servant's Madonna
4 Lift to Pummerin Bell
5 Organ-case by A. Pilgram (with
  Pilgram's self-portrait)
6 H. Puchsbaum's canopy
7 Entrance to catacombs
8 Tower stairs (313 steps)
9 Donor's gravestone
10 Wiener-Neustadt Altar (Frederick's
  reredos)
11 Emperor Frederick III's (d. 1493)
  raised sarcophagus
12 T. and J. J. Pock's High Altar

Dimensions: length, outside 350 ft
(107 m), inside 300 ft (92 m). Width
across transepts 230 ft (70 m) outside.
Width across nave, inside, 130 ft (39 m).
Height of nave, inside, 92 ft (28 m).
Height of Heiden towers 215 ft (66 m), of
N tower 200 ft (61 m), of S tower 450 ft
(137 m).
Largest Bell: Pummerin – 20 tons
(21 t); the original bell, dating from 1711,
was recast in 1945

Lower Austria, the pews by Vorarlberg, the windows by Tyrol,
the candelabra by Carinthia, the Communion rail by Burgenland, the tabernacle by Salzburg, the roof by Vienna and the
portals by Styria. Today atmospheric pollution is the danger.
The cathedral buildings cover a surface of 4,186sq.yd
(3,500m²). They are 350ft (107m) long and 128ft (39m) across.
The height of the nave amounts to 90ft (28m). The Heiden
Towers are 215ft (66m) high, the S tower 450ft (137m), and the
uncompleted N tower 200ft (61m). The roof, whose apex is
200ft (60m) above ground-level, is covered with 230,000 glazed
tiles.

Giant Gateway

The Late Romanesque Giant Gateway dates from 1230 and has
uncommonly rich ornamentation. In earlier times it was
opened only on festive occasions. In 1805 Napoleon's farewell
proclamation hung down from its frieze with its dragons, birds,
lions, monks and demons.

Heiden Towers

The Heiden Towers are part of the Romanesque church, and are
mentioned in documents as early as 1295. Their name recalls
the heathen shrine which is supposed to have occupied this site
formerly. The towers are 215ft (66m) high. From the third
storey upwards their shape alters from rectangular to
octagonal.

St Stephen's Cathedral: the symbol of Vienna ▶

Stephansdom

Tirna Chapel

Prince Eugene is buried in the Tirna Chapel, which dates from 1359. The conqueror over the Turks is commemorated in a gravestone set in the floor. The Crucifix above the altar is 15th c. work. The beard of Christ is made of genuine human hair, and according to legend it is still growing.

Stone canopy

It is likely that the pierced stone Gothic canopy dating from about 1437 is the work of Hans von Prachatiz; the picture of the Sacred Heart beneath it, however, is 18th c. work.

Bishop's Gate

The gate – a counterpart to the Singer Gate – was the entry reserved for female visitors to the cathedral. Its figurative sculptures dating from about 1370 are examples of High Gothic Art. Among coats of arms may be seen the figures of Duke Albrecht III and his consort.

Pulpit

This is the most important work of art in the nave, a masterpiece of Late Gothic sculpture in sandstone. It was carved by Master Pilgram in about 1515 and is decorated with the figures of the Four Fathers of the Church. On the plinth Master Pilgram carved a representation of himself in the pose of a Peeping Tom.

The so-called Servant's Madonna, on the pillar by the pulpit, dates from 1340. According to legend, a maid employed by a Count turned to the Virgin for help when she was under suspicion of theft. The true miscreant was discovered, and the Count's lady paid for this figure in St Stephen's to commemorate the event.

Nave

The three-nave church is divided by rows of composite pillars which support the criss-crossing network of ribs in the vaulting overhead. On the pillars there are life-size statues of donors made of stone and clay. The most precious figure is that of St Christopher on the left-hand pillar by the choir; dating from 1470 it is probably the gift of Emperor Frederich II.

Organ-case

The organ itself was removed in 1720, and only the magnificent Late Gothic organ-case by Master Pilgram remains; the monogram indicates that it was made in 1513. The man with the compass and set square, again in the pose of a Peeping Tom, is Pilgram himself. The new organ which was installed in 1960 is, with its 10,000 pipes, one of the largest and most modern in the world.

North (Eagle) Tower

Opening times
Tower and Pummerin,
daily 9 a.m.–5.30 p.m. (lift)

The reason why it remained uncompleted is according to legend as follows: Hans Puchsbaum who was in charge of construction made a pact with the Devil, but was cast down into the abyss by him because he ventured to Pronounce a holy name. The new Pummerin bell was cast in 1951, and since 1957 it has been hanging in the Tower. It weighs 20 tons (21t), and its diameter is 10ft (3·14m).

Catacombs

Tours
Daily 10–11.30 a.m.,
2–4.30 p.m.

The entrance to the catacombs is through the chamber under the N Tower. They extend from under the cathedral choir out under Stephansplatz, and the bones of thousands of Viennese citizens are piled up in tiers (but this part is not open to the public). The major attraction is the Ducal Vault which Rudolf IV

Nave of St Stephen's Cathedral with a view of the Organ ▶

had constructed for members of the House of Habsburg in 1363. After the construction of the Imperial Vault in the Kapuzinerkirche (see entry) it became the custom to place here only copper urns containing the intestines of the members of the Ruling House, while their bodies were laid to rest in the Imperial Vault and their hearts in the Augustinerkirche (see entry). Since 1953 there has also been a vault in the catacombs for the Archbishops of Vienna.

Galilee/Adlertor

Master Puchsbaum is thought to be the builder of this part of the cathedral. The upper row of figures on the canopy which was set up in the 19th c. include Frederich III, Maximilian I, Franz Joseph I, with Elisabeth and Maria of Burgundy. The iron cylinder on the pillar to the left may be a medieval sanctuary knocker.

Barbara Chapel

Its plan is similar to that of the Catherine Chapel; it was designed by Master Puchsbaum.

Donor Memorial

Among these Early Gothic stone figures dating from before 1340 there is an especially fine Angel of the Annunciation and a statue of Our Lady the Protectress. They serve as ornamentation to the so-called "Women's Choir". Among the most important graves is the Donor grave of Rudolf IV (which is, in fact, empty).

The Wiener-Neustädter Altar

Frederich III was the donor of this winged reredos in 1447. It was only in 1884 that it was brought to Vienna from Wiener-Neustadt.

High Altar

This was constructed out of black marble between 1640 and 1660 by Tobias and Johann Jakob Pock. The statues round it represent the Patron Saints of the province, Leopold and Florian, and St Roch and St Sebastian, who were invoked in time of plague. Gothic stained glass has been preserved to the left and right of the High Altar.

Frederich III's raised sepulchre

The S choir is dominated by the huge raised sepulchre of Frederich III. It is made of red marble and has a larger than life-size statue of the Emperor which is surrounded by coats of arms. The design is by the Netherlandish painter Niclas Gerhaert van Leyden (1467–1513) who himself made the top of this Gothic grave.

Catherine Chapel

The marble font dates from 1481. The reliefs on the 14-sided basin depict Christ, John the Baptist and the Twelve Apostles. The Four Evangelists are on its plinth. The carved wooden font cover is particularly fine.

South Tower

Opening times
1 Mar.–15 Nov. and
20 Dec.–7 Jan.
daily 9 a.m.–5 p.m.

The "Steffl" as the Viennese call it was begun in 1356. It is 450ft (137m) high, and is considered to rival the tower of Freiburg Minster as the most beautiful German Gothic tower.

It is possible to go up the tower as far as the watch room; that means climbing 343 stairs.

Galilee and Primglöcklein Door

The porch between the two buttresses of the tower are 14th c., as are the sitting figures of the Apostles.

Canopy

The Late Gothic canopy over the Leopold Altar is presumed to be the work of Hans Puchsbaum. It was donated in 1448.

This was the entry for male visitors to the cathedral. The donor figures, the nine Apostles and the legend of St Paul in the tympanum date from 1378.

Singer Gate

The Pötscher Madonna under its Late Gothic canopy has been an object of profound veneration in Austria and Hungary since the Battle of Zenta in 1697. According to legend, tears streamed from the eyes of the Madonna for a fortnight at the time of the battle against the Turks.

The Pötscher Madonna

It is also called the Dukes' Chapel and its statues count among the most important of the second half of the 14th c. The so-called "Hausmuttergottes" (the protective mother of god) from the former Himmelpfort Monastery was revered by the Empress Maria Theresa.

Eligius Chapel

Stephansplatz (Square)

B4

The square in front of St Stephen's Cathedral (see entry: Stephansdom) forms the centre of the inner city of Vienna and is now a bustling pedestrian precinct. After war damage and the building of an underground station, the entire open space was newly laid out. Also of interest are the houses No. 2, Zur Weltkugel (The Globe), No. 3, Das Churhaus (Election House),

Location
1, Stock-im-Eisen-Platz/
Rotenturmstrasse

Underground station
Stephansplatz (U1)

Bus 1A

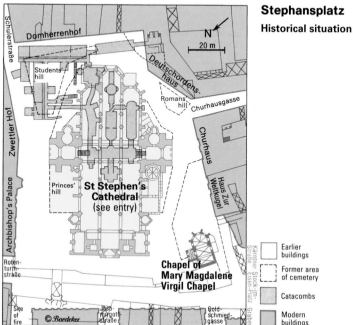

Stephansplatz
Historical situation

159

No. 5, Domherrenhof (Prebendary's Court), No. 6 Zwettlerhof (Zwettler Court) and No. 7, the Archbishop's Palace.

Until 1732 Stephansplatz was a cemetery as is indicated by the tombstones incorporated in the external walls of the cathedral and the Late Gothic column in which the eternal light burned for the dead. A copy can be seen at the W end of the S wall of the cathedral. To the right of the cathedral coloured stones mark the outline of the Chapel of Maria Magdalene which was burned down in 1781. When Stephansplatz Underground station was being constructed the Virgil Kapelle (Virgilian Chapel) was discovered beneath the crypt of Maria Magdalene.

*Virgilian Chapel

Opening times
Tues.–Sun. 10 a.m.–
12.15 p.m. and 1 p.m.–
4.30 p.m.

This extraordinary relic of Vienna's medieval past, which also houses a collection of historic Viennese ceramics, is open to the public.

A comparison of architectural features with St Stephen's Cathedral has established the date of construction of the chapel in the 13th c. The subterranean room of niches was probably planned as a mausoleum and belonged to the Chrannest family from the early 14th c. It was their family vault, in which they erected altars, the most important altar was dedicated to St Virgil. The fact that this monumental vault belonged to a family without rank is puzzling. It is possible that the Virgilian Chapel was built by Duke Friedrich the Quarrelsome (who wished to have Vienna created a bishopric) as a crypt for the bishop of the new diocese. The Duke died before his plan was realised; Vienna later became an independent diocese in 1469. The Chrannest family were then able to buy the vault. After the last of the family had died, the chapel became the seat of newly-formed religious brethren (the Gottesleichnamsbruderschaft and the Kaufmannsbruderschaft) at the beginning of the 16th c. In the 16th and 17th c. it once again became a place of burial. The subterranean vault was abandoned when the remains of the Chapel of Maria Magdalene were cleared away in 1781.

The Virgilian Chapel is rectangular, 35ft/10·5m long and 20ft/6m wide. It was c. 45ft/13 or 14m high; today its clay floor lies 40ft/12m below street level. There are niches set into the 4ft/1·5m thick walls. The entrance was probably via a trap-door in the floor of the chapel above.

Stock-im-Eisen-Platz (Square)   B4

Location
1, Stephansplatz-Graben

Underground station
Stephansplatz (U1)

Buses
1A, 2A, 3A

Stock-im-Eisen-Platz is a square next to Stephansplatz (see entry) and leading directly into Kärntner Strasse (see entry). It takes its curious name from a tree-trunk into which many nails have been hammered. It stands in a niche of house number 3/4, at the corner of Graben and Kärntner Strasse.

There is evidence the tree-trunk has been here since 1533. According to legend, every locksmith's apprentice who came to Vienna in the course of his wanderings had to hammer a nail into the tree-trunk.

On the site of No. 6 a new building by the Viennese architect Hans Hollein has been erected. It comprises an exclusive shopping centre with a "Gourmet storey" (modelled on the Ka De We in Berlin) with offices and a roof terrace from which the view of Stephansplatz, Graben and the Stephansdom (see entries) may be enjoyed.

The beautiful stairway and courtyard of the "Equitable House"   Note
at No. 3 Stock-in-Eisen-Platz are worth seeing.

*Technisches Museum für Industrie und Gewerbe   D1

The Technical Museum of Industry and Trade occupies a site on the way to Schönbrunn (see entry). Emperor Franz Joseph laid the foundation-stone of the new museum in 1908, but it was ready for opening only in 1918, after his death.

The museum's collections go back as far as the 18th c. The Imperial "physical collection" evolved into an "industrial collection", which itself later became a "production collection". Finally this gave rise to the Technical Museum. On three floors are displayed collections which show a cross-section of the development of technology, business and industry with special reference to the Austrian contribution.

Location
14, Marianhilferstr. 212

Underground station
Schönbrunn (U4)

Trams
10, 52, 58

Opening times
Tues.–Sun. 9 a.m.–4.30 p.m.

The Ground Floor houses the departments concerned with transport, machine-building, lighting, metalworking, electricity, mining, agriculture and woodworking. Among the exhibits are a Marcus car (1888), the original designs for Ressel's marine screw, an Ajax locomotive (1841), a horse-drawn railcar belonging to the Linz-Budweis Railway (also 1841), the first turbine (1919) and the first front-wheel drive car.

Ground Floor

The First Floor houses the collections concerned with the textile industries, sewing-machines and typewriters, graphic arts, construction, paper-making, measurement and surveying, aviation, physics and chemistry, the food industry, petrol and

First Floor

Technical Museum: a Lilienthal glider

Technisches Museum für Industrie und Gewerbe

SECOND FLOOR

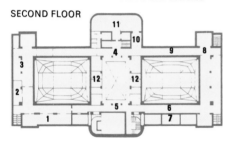

Technical Museum for Industry and Trades

SECOND FLOOR
1 Posts and Telegraphs
2 Postage Stamps
3 Telecommunications
4 Photography
5 Bridge Building and Water Supply
6 Data handling
7 Administration
8 Türmer Room
9 Fire prevention
10 Music Technology
11 Organ
12 Offices

FIRST FLOOR

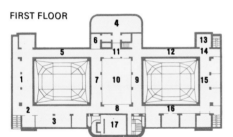

FIRST FLOOR
1 Textile Industries
2 Sewing-machines
3 Building Technology
4 Special Exhibitions
5 Printing
6 Typewriters
7 Stones and Earths
8 Weights and Measures
9 Aviation
10 Historic Aircraft
11 Paper Manufacture
12 Food Industries
13 Sugar Manufacture
14 Petrol and Natural Gas
15 Chemical Industries
16 Physics and Chemistry
17 Auditorium and Cinema

GROUND FLOOR

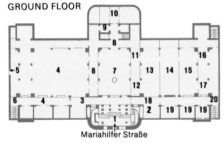

Mariahilfer Straße

GROUND FLOOR
1 Vestibule
2 Café
3 Seafaring
4 Railway Museum
5 Locomotives
6 Staircase to First Floor
7 Engine-building
8 Tram cars
9 Marcus car
10 Aviation
11 Gas Production and Distribution
12 Lighting
13 Electricity
14 Metalwork
15 Mining
16 Woodworking
17 Agriculture
18 Start of the Collections
19 Historic workshops
20 Stairway to coal-mine

industrial chemistry. Among the most interesting exhibits are the model of a flying machine by Kress (1877), a Lilienthal glider (1894), the fine clock of Philippus Imsserus (1555), the calculating machine of Antonius Braun (early 18th c.), Negrelli's own sketches of cross-sections of the Suez Canal and the model of a space capsule.

The Second Floor houses the collections of the Postal and Telegraph Museum, together with exhibits concerning bridge construction, fire prevention and the technology of music. A section devoted to physics and atomic physics is being developed.

Second Floor

The most interesting objects on show are the world's first postcard (1869), Nussbauer's first device for the transmission of music by means of wireless which dates from 1904, the workshop of a 19th c. violin-maker and the writing-machine of Knaus (1760).

Theresianum   C4

The college for diplomats and the endowed Theresian Academy are housed in the Favorita, formerly an Imperial summer palace.

Location
4, Favoritenstrasse 15

The Favorita was built between 1616 and 1625 and refurbished in the Baroque style in 1690. It was the favourite residence of Leopold I, Joseph I and Charles VI, who died here. The Empress Maria Theresa, however, preferred Schönbrunn (see entry) and handed the Favorita to the Jesuits, enjoining them with the provision of a "Collegium Theresianum" where the sons of the less well-off aristocracy could be trained as officials, as well as the Oriental Academy for the education of officials and diplomats.

Underground station
Taubstummengasse (U1)

Bus
13A

In the large park of the Theresianum (Argentinier Strasse) stands Radio House, built by Clemens Holzmeister and others between 1936 and 1938. It is a building with a simple façade and a beautiful entrance hall.

*Uhrenmuseum der Stadt Wien (Museum)   B4

The City of Vienna's Clock Museum has been housed since 1921 in the 300-year-old Obizzi Palace. It is the most important collection of clocks in the world.

Location
1, Schulhof 2

Room 1: Mainly tower clocks, among them a tower clock from St Stephen's dated 1699 (Cat. No. 3043) and the oldest item in the collection, a 15th c. tower clock.

Underground station
Stephansplatz (U1)

Bus
1A

Room 2: Hand-made, weight-driven wall clocks. The *pièce de résistance* is an astronomical wall clock of 1663 (No. 794).

Opening times
Tues.–Sun. 9 a.m.–4.30 p.m.

Room 3: Travelling, table and wall clocks. The four-poster-bed clock (No. 2472) was made in the mid 17th c.

Room 4: Pedestal clocks. One of the most valuable is a "Pendule" (No. 50) by Louis Monet of Paris; it is dated 1752.

Room 5: Part of Marie von Ebner-Eschenbach's Collection, including a Swiss gold pendant watch dated 1800 (Nos. 1490–92). Also valuable gold-enamelled clocks.

Room 6: Commode pedestal clocks and travelling clocks. The astronomical pedestal clock (No. 232) is of 1810 and comes from a Viennese workshop.

Room 7: Rare Japanese clocks, including unusual 18th c. pillar clocks (Nos. 799–802).

Room 8: Desk clocks and clocks in the form of figures. The "Rider's Clock" (No. 3064) is of Austrian manufacture and was produced about 1802.

Room 9: Empire grandfather clocks.

Following the reconstruction of the second and third floors further Empire and Biedermeier clocks are on show. On the third floor can be seen wall clocks with electric movements and compensation pendulums. The development of the wrist-watch is covered for the first time with elaborate watches from about 1850 through trench watches from the First World War, gentlemen's automatic watches from the 1930s to unusual modern creations.

Room 10: Seven clocks with pictures on them.

Room 11: Watches from the turn of the century in veneered wooden cases.

Room 12: Wall clocks, with a remarkable astronomical clock of 1863 (No. 326).

Room 13: Clocks from the turn of the century. Clock in the form of a bicycle.

Room 14: Clocks from the Black Forest and also a particularly fine Austrian carved cuckoo-clock (No. 3065).

Room 15: Novelties, such as a night-light clock (No. 250) which was probably made in Switzerland.

Room 16: About 270 pocket watches and more than 170 wrist-watches dating form 1850 to the present day.

Room 17: Toy clocks, movements for automata.

Room 18: Clocks in the form of flutes, organs and harps.

Universität (University)   B4

Location
1, Lueger-Ring, Dr-Karl 1

Underground station
Schottentor (U2)

Trams
1, 2, D

The University buildings were put up in the period when the Ringstrasse was being developed. The plans were by Heinrich Ferstel who took inspiration from the Italian Renaissance style. The buildings were opened in 1884 and renovated in 1953 and 1965.

In the arcaded central courtyard there are monuments to famous university teachers, among them Anton Bruckner, Gerhard van Swieten, Theodor von Billroth, Marie von Ebner-Eschenbach, Ludwig Boitzmann, Anton von Eiselsberg, Julius Wagner-Jauregg, I. Philipp Semmelweis, Sigmund Freud and the Nobel prize-winner Karl Landsteiner.

Vienna University: its Italian Renaissance-style buildings

*Vienna International Centre (UNO City)

The Vienna International Centre, bordering Donau Park (see entry), is also known as UNO-City. The idiosyncratic towering office-blocks were designed by Johann Staber and constructed between 1973 and 1976. They belong to the Austrian State and stand on land made available by the city of Vienna.

The entire complex is, however, leased for a peppercorn rent of 1 schilling a year to the United Nations, several of whose important organisations are housed here: The International Atomic Energy Authority (IAEA) and the United Nations Industrial Development Organisation (UNIDO). Other UNO institutions which have been transferred to Vienna from Geneva and New York include the Centre for Social Development and Humanitarian Aims (CSDHA), the United Nations Commission for Infectious Diseases and the UN organisations associated with it (INCB and UNFDAC), the Department of the UN for International Commercial Law (UNCITRAL), and, in the summer of 1978, the headquarters of the UN Aid to Palestinian Refugees in the Middle East (UNRWA) and the High Commission for Refugees (UNHCR). Since 27 August 1979 the complex has been officially extra-territorial.

The office-blocks are between 177ft (54m) and 395ft (120m) high. The city has 43 passenger lifts and 15 goods lifts.

There are 24,000 windows, 6,000 doors, 80,000 fluorescent tubes and parking spaces for 2,500 cars. The electrical installations took 185 miles (300km) of telephone wire and 155 miles (250km) of high-tension cable. Twenty-seven of Austria's most renowned artists worked on the artistic embellishment of the

Location
2, Wagramerstrasse

Underground station
Kaisermühlen Vienna
International Centre (U1)

Buses
90A, 91A, 92A

Guided tours
Apr.–Oct. Mon.–Sat. 11 a.m.
(Groups by appointment only)

165

Vienna International Centre, known as "UNO City"

interior. On UNO Plaza stands Joannis Avramidis's bronze "Polis" (The City). Inside may be seen pictures by Wolfgang Hollegha, Georg Eisler, Karl Korab, Kurt Regschek, Peter Pongratz, Friedensreich Hundertwasser as well as reliefs by Alfred Hrdlicka and Giselbert Hocke.

Austria Center Vienna

The Austria Center Vienna adjoining UNO-City was opened in 1987. It is an ultra-modern centre for events and conferences and has the latest technical facilities. Until its completion the mammoth project was strongly opposed. Nevertheless even when it is well used it still loses 600–1,000 million Austrian schillings a year.

Fourteen rooms of various sizes are available for concerts, dances, banquets, exhibitions and theatrical and TV shows, accommodating from 50 to more than 4,000 participants. The accommodation is on four floors and each has its own foyer and refreshment facilities, so that different events can be held at the same time. The floor space of the foyers totalling over a million square feet (9,390m²) can also be used for exhibitions. All the public rooms have the necessary technical provision for TV, film and slide projection, as well as for simultaneous translation in up to nine languages.

In addition there are offices and rooms for 10–70 people available for meetings. In the main centre conferences of UN size can be held (there are direct connections to the HQ of the United Nations). When laid out in parliamentary style it can accommodate 2,100 participants. In rows twice as many can be

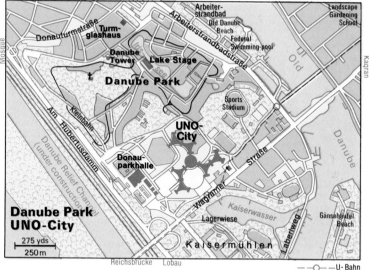

accommodated. There are, of course, in such a huge modern congress building a press centre and a radio station, a post office, bank, travel bureaux, restaurants, coffee-shops and a cocktail lounge.

Volksgarten (Park) B4

The Volksgarten lies between the Hofburg (see entry) and the Burgtheater (see entry). This, the second largest park in the City Centre, was opened in 1820 on the site of the fortifications which had been blown up by the French, and soon became a favourite place for the Viennese out for a Sunday-afternoon stroll.

In the middle of the gardens stands the Temple of Theseus which was built in 1823 for Antonio Canova's statue of Theseus. The order for this had originally been given by Napoleon I while he was in Vienna, but nothing came of it, for obvious political reasons, until Francis I sprang into the breach. Later, in 1890, the statue was removed from the Temple and placed in the staircase of the Kunsthistorisches Museum (see entry).

Notable monuments in the park include the Grillparzer Memorial with reliefs portraying scenes from six of his plays and the memorial to the Empress Elisabeth.

Location
1, Dr-Karl-Renner-Ring

Underground station
Volkstheater (U1)

Bus
48A

Trams
1, 2, D

Votivkirche B4

The prebendal church Zum Göttlichen Heiland (The Divine Saviour) was built as a votive offering after the failure of an

Location
9, Rooseveltplatz

attempt in 1853 to assassinate Emperor Franz Joseph I. Archduke Maximilian, Franz Joseph's brother, who was later to become Emperor of Mexico, led the way in providing the necessary finance.

Heinrich Ferstel chose the Neo-Gothic style, in imitation of the French Gothic cathedrals, and the chancel is one of the best examples of 19th c. historically inspired architecture. It was dedicated in 1879.

The church possesses several important works of art. There is Count Niklas Salm's Renaissance (1530–33) sepulchre with a recumbent figure of the Count surmounting it and 12 masterly reliefs on the sides in the Baptistery in the S transept; it comes from Loy Hering's Antwerp workshops. In the side-chapel in the S transept may be seen the Antwerp reredos, an important 15th c. carved altar with scenes from the Passion. In the N transept there is a copy of Our Lady of Guadelupe which recalls Emperor Maximilian of Mexico, the church's first protector. As a former garrison church, the building has many monuments to Austrian Army units.

* **Waffensammlung** (Museum)   C4

The first collectors were Archduke Ernst of Styria (15th c.) and Archduke Ferdinand of Tyrol (16th c.). It eventually became the most important collection of its type when in 1889 all the Habsburg armouries were combined. It was transferred from the Kunsthistorisches Museum (see entry) to the Neue Burg (see Hofburg) in 1935–36.

Location
1, Neue Burg, Heldenplatz

Underground station
Mariahilferstrasse (U2)

Bus
2A

Trams
1, 2, D, J, T

Opening times
Mon., Wed.–Fri.
10 a.m.–4 p.m.
Sat. and Sun 9 a.m.–
4 p.m.

Nine Rooms and 6 galleries are filled with exhibits which visitors can examine in chronological order, going round the collection in counter-clockwise direction from Room 1.

Room 1: 500–1480. Archaeological finds, helmets, armour, including the armour of Frederick I of the Palatinate and a ceremonial sword belonging to Frederich III.

Room 2: 1480–1500. Late Gothic suits of armour, boy's armour, swords and Louis XII's crossbow.

Gallery A: Tournament armour, Maximilian I's jousting equipment, mainly from the Innsbruck Court workshops.

Room 3: 1500–1530. High Renaissance armour and ceremonial arms, with two suits of boy's armour made for Charles V.

Room 4: 1530–1545. Parade armour for Charles V, Philip II, King Ferdinand I and Francis I. Important examples of Milan craftsmanship and the earliest firearms.

Room 5: 1545–1560. The "Adlergarnitur" (Eagle armour), some of the finest armour; richly ornamented weapons.

Gallery B: Numerous examples of armour of Archduke Ferdinand of Tyrol including parade suits of armour and garments of the mid 16th c.

Room 6: 1550–1560. Ceremonial weapons, including Maximilian II's golden dagger of 1551; richly ornamented shields and helmets and 16th c. Ottoman weapons.

◀ *The Votivkirche: a fine example of historically inspired architecture*

Room 7: 1560–1580. Richly decorated suits of armour, weapons for hunting and target practice, Maximilian II's "Rose Petal" armour and the "braided" armour of his sons.

Gallery C: 1560–1595. Papal gifts of Ferdinand II of Tyrol and Tyrolean armour of his sons.

Room 8: 1580–1610. Finely crafted weapons and Milanese parade armour.

Room 9: 1580–1620. Baroque armour and richly inlaid sporting weapons.

Arcaded Gallery: 17–19th. c. About a thousand weapons from the Court and hunting collections and from the armoury.

Hunt Room I: 1619–1657. Hunting weapons and equipment, including Archduke Leopold V's silver gun.

Hunt Room II: 1667–1720. Fine hunting weapons and Turkish weapons seized as booty in the time of Leopold I.

Hunt Room III: 1720–1916. Imperial hunting weapons and equipment of the 18th and 19th c.

Wallfahrtskirche Maria Grün

See Prater

Wallfahrtskirche Maria Hilf (church)   C3

Location
6, Mariahilferstrasse 65

Underground station
Mariahilferstrasse (U2)

Trams
52, 58

In the Maria Hilf pilgrimage church there are numerous sacred objects which pilgrims came to venerate. The "Gnadenbild" (Portrayal of Mercy) is a copy of the original in the Mariahilfberg at Passau.
After the destruction of the original chapel by the Turks, it was rebuilt in 1683, probably by Sebastiano Carlone. It underwent considerable alterations and was dedicated in 1730.
In a chapel built on to the church there is a monumental figure of Christ on the Cross. It comes from the "Malefizspitzbuben-haus", an ancient prison. It used to stand in Rauhensteingasse, and criminals used to be conveyed from there to the Hoher Markt (see entry) where they were executed.

Winterpalais des Prinzen Eugen (palace)   C4

Location
1, Himmelpfortgasse 3

Underground station
Stephansplatz (U1)

Prince Eugene's town mansion has been occupied by the Ministry of Finance since 1848. There was almost an architectural tragedy when the conqueror of the Turks decided to change architects while construction was in progress. J. B. Fischer von Erlach was in charge from 1695 to 1698, but he was replaced by J. L. von Hildebrandt from 1702 to 1724.
Prince Eugene died here in 1736. He did not receive the final respects to which he was entitled. Emperor Charles VI was not present at his burial. In fact he went off to Laxenburg the day

before "to pass the time". Prince Eugene's heiress, Anna Victoria of Savoy-Soissons, squandered the inheritance in a short while. In the end Maria Theresa purchased the palace for the State in 1752.

Visitors are allowed only into the vestibule with the Hercules Fountain and the famous ceremonial staircase.

Wotruba Kirche (Church of the Most Holy Trinity)

This church stands on St Georgenberg. It has no tower, no dome, no pillars and no gables; it gains its powerful effect by being constructed of 152 cast concrete cubic blocks piled one above another in an asymmetrical pattern. Designed by Fritz Wotruba (1907–75), one of the most famous Austrian sculptors, the church was dedicated in 1976. Wotruba, who was not a practising Catholic, nevertheless made a statement of faith with his church:

"The form of this church is unconventional because it acknowledges the principle of asymmetry; a style of building which has been used only rarely in the past. If this building works it will be very dynamic and dramatic. The apparent chaos of the arrangement of asymmetrical blocks is really intended to create a harmonious whole: a unit of many elements which differ in form and size. The aim is to show order – law – harmony: prerequisites for faith. A community is made up of individuals; a happy community is a harmonious community. This is not only a problem of our time, but also of the church. This building is intended to demonstrate that chaos can only be overcome by law and order. It is the law of the survival . . .

It is a fact that harmony can only be achieved by overcoming many opposing forces; this church aims to demonstrate the fact."

Holy Trinity Church is a religious centre for the local community and also acts as a State school, an institute of home education and a school for the physically handicapped.

In the basement of the building which is 50ft (15·5m) high, 98ft (30m) long and 72ft (22m) wide, are meeting-rooms, an archive, a sacristy and a room for servers. The church itself can accommodate 250 worshippers. The altar consists of a marble block with a cross which is a replica of one which Wotruba made for the castle chapel of Bruchsal

Location
23, Mauer, corner of
Georgsgasse/Rysergasse

Bus
60A (from S-/R-rail station
Liesing)

Opening times
Sat. 2–8 p.m., Sun. 9 a.m.–
5 p.m.; Apr.–Sept. Mon.–Fri.
2 p.m.–6 p.m.; Oct.–Mar.
Tue.–Fri. 2.30 p.m.–4.30 p.m.
(Guided tours on request)

Wotruba Kirche

*Zentralfriedhof (Cemetery)

Vienna's Central Cemetery was opened in 1874. It is the largest cemetery in Austria, with an area of 1 sq. mile (2·5km²). From the Main Gate (Gate Two) an avenue leads to the "graves of honour" reserved for famous personalities and the vault of the Austrian Federal President. The cemetery is open in spring and autumn from 7 a.m. to 6 p.m., in summer from 7 a.m. to 7 p.m., and in winter from 8 a.m. to 5 p.m. (entry up to 30 minutes before closing time).

The following musicians are among the many notable persons laid to rest here: Beethoven, Brahms, Gluck, Mozart (commemorative grave), Schubert, Johann Strauss (the Elder and Younger), Suppé and Wolf.

Location
11, Simmeringer Hauptstrasse
234

S-Bahn station
Zentralfriedhof (S7)

Tram
71

Zum grünen Anker (restaurant)   B/C5

Location
1, Grünangergasse 10

Underground station
Stephansplatz (U1)

An aroma of Italian specialities hangs over it, for the Grüner Anker, where the Viennese first came to enjoy a glass of wine and later on a glass of beer, has specialised in Italian cooking since 1820. It was a favourite meeting-place for Schubert and his friends, and Grillparzer was a regular customer.

Close by the Grüner Anker stands the Kipfelhaus (The Croissant House) at 8 Grünargergasse. It was here that the famous Viennese delicacy started life, for here the first croissant was baked in 1683, probably as a joke at the expense of the Turkish crescent moon symbol.

The giant Ferris Wheel in the Prater ▶

Practical Information

Note

The number preceeding a street name, etc., is the number of the district of Vienna. The number following the street name is the number of the building.

Austrian telephone dialling code will change from 222 to single digit no. 1. This may be used at the moment but will be compulsory in 1993.

Advance booking

Theatre tickets

The box-offices selling tickets in advance for the Staatsoper (State Opera), Burgtheater, Volksoper and Akademietheater are situated at 1, Hanuschof, entrance Hanuschgasse 3 and Goethegasse 1; tel. 5 14 44-29 59/60 (for information only). Open: Mon.–Fri. 8 a.m.–6 p.m., Sat. 9 a.m.–2 p.m., Sun. and public holidays 9 a.m.–noon.

Advance ticket sales always open seven days before the performance. For first nights or performances with celebrated guest artists theatre-lovers often begin to queue many hours – sometimes through the night – before tickets go on sale.

All other theatres have their own box-offices. It is advisable to check by telephone whether tickets are available. Details of all theatre and cabaret programmes (together with box-office telephone numbers) are published in the "Kurier", a daily newspaper.

Postal bookings from abroad

All postal applications for tickets must arrive at the box-office at least ten days before the performance. The address is:
Österreichischer Bundestheaterverband
Goethestrasse 1
A-1010 Wien

Holders of the major credit cards can telephone requests for tickets for the Austrian State Theatres, beginning six days before the performance:
tel. (1) 5 13 15 13.

Ticket agencies

Tickets for all performances in the theatres of Vienna can also be obtained from private agencies which normally charge a commission of up to 25% of the price of the tickets. Centrally located ticket agencies are:
Flamm, 1, Kärntner Ring 3; tel. 5 12 42 25
E. Rössler, 1, Kärntner Str. 33; tel. 5 12 38 02
Weihburg, 1, Weihburggasse 3; tel. 5 12 84 34
Österreichisches Verkehrsbüro, 1, Opernring 5; tel. 5 88 00-0

Spanish Riding School

Tickets for performances at the Spanish Riding School should be ordered well in advance (except for admission tickets for the morning training session, from the end of February to the end of June, from the beginning of August to the end of September and from the beginning of November to mid-December); tickets for these training sessions can be obtained on the actual day without prior reservation. The other performances take place from March to the beginning of July and from September to December on Sunday mornings and Wednesday evenings, with shortened performances on some Saturdays. The Spanish Riding School, Hofburg, A-1010 Wien issues tickets in advance for the performances on Wednesdays and Sundays; tickets for all other performances (including the shortened ones) must be ordered through theatre ticket and travel agencies:

American Express, 1, Kärntner Str. 21–23; tel. 5 15 40-0
Austria Reiseservice, 1, Hessgasse 7; tel. 31 78 40
Austrobus, 1, Opernpassage; tel. 56 43 12
Cosmos, 1, Kärntner Ring 15; tel. 5 15 33-0
Flamm, 1, Kärntner Ring 3; tel. 5 12 42 25
Intropa, 1, Kärntner Str. 38; tel. 5 15 14
Niederösterreichisches Landesreisebüro, 1, Heidenschuss 2; tel. 5 33 47 73
Ruefa Reisen, 1, Fleischmarkt 1; tel. 5 34 04-0
Wagon-lits Reisebüro, 1, Kärntner Ring 2; tel. 5 01 60-0

Seats for the Sunday concerts of the Vienna Boys' Choir (Wiener Sängerknaben) in the Burgkapelle at 9.15 a.m. must be booked at least eight weeks in advance at the Verwaltung der Hofmusikkapelle, Hofburg, Schweizerhof, A-1010 Wien.
Tickets may be collected on payment at the Burgkapelle on Fridays between 11 a.m. and noon or on Sundays by 9 a.m. at the latest. Tickets for any seats still available are on sale at the box-office of the Burgkapelle on Fridays from 5 p.m. Only two tickets per person are allowed. | Vienna Boys' Choir

Airlines

1, Kärntner Ring 18 (city office); tel. 5 05 57 57-0, and (reservations) 7 17 99	Austrian Airlines
10, Fontana Strasse 1; tel. 68 35 11-0	Austrian Air Services (inland flights)
1, Kärntner Ring 10, A-1010 Wien; tel. 65 76 91	British Airways
1, Kärntner Ring 5, A-1010 Wien; tel. 52 66 46	Pan Am
c/o Austrian Airlines (see above); tel 7 77 00, 56 32 00, 56 32 66	TWA
1, Opernring 1; tel. 5 87 17 98-0; reservations 56 74 74-0	Air Canada

Air travel

Schwechat, Vienna International Airport, lies 19 km/12 miles south-east of the city centre. Its facilities include banks, restaurants, a supermarket, newspaper and souvenir shops, a duty-free shop, car-rental desks and a tourist information office where hotel reservations can also be made. A "finger boarding system", permitting passengers to board and disembark along bridges is already operating at Pier East and a second is to follow at Pier West. | Airport

Schwechat, Vienna's international airport

Shuttle services	There is a bus shuttle service between the airport and the Aity Air Terminal (3, Hotel Hilton/Stadtpark) every 20–30 minutes from 6 a.m. until 7.10 p.m. and every 50–70 minutes from 7.10 until 10.10 p.m. There are also shuttle bus services between the airport and the West and South Rail Stations. Express trains run hourly between the underground station at the airport and the North and Central Rail Stations (Wien Nord and Wien Mitte).
Flight information	Tel. 7 11 10-22 31/2
Inland flights	Austrian Airlines fly several times daily from Vienna to Graz, Innsbruck, Klagenfurt and Salzburg, and once daily to Linz.

Antique dealers

Shops	Antique dealers can be found in the narrow side-streets to the west of the Graben: Bräunerstrasse, Stallburggasse, Dorotheergasse, Plankengasse, Spiegelgasse and Seilergasse. A smaller "antique quarter" has become established to the south of the cathedral: Singerstrasse, Franzplatz, Himmelpfortgasse, Annagasse, Akademiestrasse, Walfischgasse and Mahlerstrasse. Goods on sale range from individual articles of medieval art to examples of Art-Nouveau and items from the Vienna workshops. An art and antique market takes place near the Schwedenplatz from May to September (Sat. 2–7.30 p.m. and Sun. 10 a.m.–8 p.m.).
Flea market	See A–Z, Naschmarkt
Auctions	See A–Z, Dorotheum and Auctions (below)

Art galleries

Altstadt-Galerie
1, Fleischmarkt 7; tel. 5 35 43 96
Vienna's first gallery of Primitive art

Selection

Galerie Asboth
1, Spiegelgasse 19; tel. 5 12 51 37
Old Asian art, antique jewellery

Galerie at the Albertina
1, Lobkowitzplatz 1; tel. 5 13 14 16
Antiques

Galerie at the Belvedere
4, St-Elizabeth-Platz 3; tel. 5 05 07 46
Art-Nouveau interiors; contemporary art, etc.

Galerie Gabriel
1, Seilerstätte 19; tel. 5 12 78 02
Drawings, sculptures, etc.; tapestries by contemporary artists

Galerie Image
1, Ruprechtsplatz 4-5; tel. 5 35 42 84
Posters

Galerie Internationale Rumänische Kunst
4, Margaretenstr. 48; tel. 5 87 05 48
Romanian art

Galerie Keramikstudio
1, Krugerstr. 18; tel. 5 13 28 13
Ceramics

Galerie Knoll
6, Esterházygasse 29; tel. 5 87 50 52
Austrian contemporary art

Galerie La Parete
1, Tuchlauben 14; tel. 63 01 33
Art-Nouveau, Art-Déco

Galerie Otto (more than 10 branches)
1, Lobkowitzplatz 1; tel. 5 12 58 01
Paintings, graphics, picture framing

Galerie Pabst
1, Habsburgergasse 10; tel. 5 33 70 14
19th and 20th c. art

Galerie Rauhenstein
1, Rauhensteingasse 3; tel. 5 13 30 09
Old jewellery

Galerie Schönbrunn
5, Schönbrunner Str. 79; tel. 55 63 47
Sculpture

Galerie Wickenburg
8, Wickenburggasse 4; tel. 4 08 18 26
Pottery and weaving studio

Auctions

Galerie 7/45
1, Wildpretmarkt 2; tel. 63 93 72
English furniture

Galerie 10
1, Getreidemarkt 10; tel. 5 87 57 44
Originals, contemporary graphics, Austrian art

Kunstforum Wien
See Museums

Auctions

Whether out of interest or simply for the atmosphere it is worth paying a visit to an auction in one of the world's greatest salesrooms, the Dorotheum (see A–Z) at 1, Dorotheergasse 17; tel. 5 15 60-0.
Auctions are held Mon.–Fri. about 2 p.m. and Sat. about 10 a.m. Items are also on sale Mon.–Fri. 10 a.m.–6 p.m.; viewing Mon.–Fri. 10 a.m.–6 p.m. and Sat. 8.30 a.m.–noon.

Emphasis

At the auctions the emphasis is on furniture Mon., Wed., and Fri. 2 p.m.; valuables Mon.–Fri. 2 p.m.; decorative and practical items Mon.–Fri. 2 p.m. and Sat. 10 a.m.

Bicycles

Plan for cyclists

Vienna has some 300 km/190 miles of signposted cycle tracks. The Association for the Environment (ARGUS; 4, Frankenberggasse 11; tel. 65 84 35 or 5 05 84 35 has published a very good plan of Vienna for cyclists, and this can also be obtained from bookshops.

Transport

Cycles can be transported in the Underground (except U.6) on Saturdays from 2 p.m. and all day on Sundays and public holidays; from May–Sept. additionally Mon.–Fri. 9 a.m.–3 p.m. and 6.30 until the last trains; Sat. from 9 a.m.; Sun. and public holidays as above.

Bicycle rental

1, Salztorbrücke Cycle Rental (on the Old Town side of the Danube Canal promenade, near the Salztor Bridge);
tel. 4 60 60 72
2, Praterstern, near the cycle track before reaching the subway to the Prater Hauptallee; tel. 26 85 57
21, Danube Island, at the Floridsdorfer Brücke parking place; tel. 38 86 98
22, Ostbahnbrücke, Lobau Schnellbahn Station; tel. 38 86 98
22, Danaube Island, Reichsbrücke; tel. 23 65 18051/57
Open: March–Oct. daily 9 a.m.–8 p.m.
(cycle repair workshop, immediate service)

Vienna Bike

Sightseeing by bicycle
Tel. 31 12 58 and 81 23 23

Business hours

See Opening times

Camping

Five large camp sites are situated between 6 and 15 km/4 and 9 miles from the city centre.

Campingplatz Wien-West I
14, Hüttelbergstr. 40; tel. 94 14 49
Schnellbahn: S45; bus 152
Open mid-June– mid-September
1 ha; reservation not possible

Campingplatz Wien-West II
14, Hüttelbergstr. 80; tel. 94 23 14
Schnellbahn: S45; bus 152
Open all year
2 ha; reservation not possible

Campingplatz Wien-Süd
(Atzgersdorf)
23, Breitenfurter Str. 269; tel. 86 92 18
Bus: 62A
Open: end of May–mid-Sept.
2½ ha; reservation not possible

Camping Wien-Süd at Rodaun Swimming Pool
(Rodaun)
23, on A2 motorway; tel. 88 41 54
Tram: 60
Open: mid-March–mid-November
1½ ha; reservation possible

Campingplatz Schloss Laxenburg
Münchendorfer Strasse; tel. (0 22 36) 7 13 33
Bus: 566 from Wien Mitte Bus Station
Open: beginning of April until end of October
4 ha; reservation possible

Spending the night in a caravan or "motorhome" away from official camp sites is classed as "wild camping" in Vienna and offenders are liable to be fined. Outside the city three nights are permitted.

Details of camp sites in and around Vienna, including size of site and plots, facilities, opening times, directions how to get there, etc. are published in the annual AA camping guides.

Camp sites

Caravans

Camping guide

Car rental

Avis
1, Opernring 1; tel. 5 87 62 41

Budget/Rent a Car
2, Landstrasser Hauptstr. 2a; tel. 75 65 65-0

International firms

Hertz
1, Kärntner Ring 17 ; tel. 5 12 86 77

InterRent/Europcar
1, Kärntner Ring 14; tel. 5 05 41 66 and 5 05 44 81
Schwechat Airport: tel. 7 70 33 16

Chemists

Business hours	Mon.–Fri. 8 a.m.–noon, 2–6 p.m.; Sat. 8 a.m.–noon. To ascertain which chemist is on duty; tel. 15 50. Details of chemists on duty at night can also be found in the daily newspapers.
International Pharmacy	Foreign medicaments can be obtained from the International Pharmacy, 1, Kärntner Ring 17; tel. 5 12 28 25

Church services

Roman Catholic	In most of Vienna's Catholic churches some services begin at 6.30 a.m.; Saturdays at 6 p.m. (including masses in several languages; see A–Z Votivkirche). High Mass is celebrated on Sundays and on church festivals at 9 a.m. (July and Aug.) and at 10 a.m. Information: tel. 5 15 52-375).
Old Catholic	St Salvator 1, Wipplingerstr. 6; tel. 63 71 33 Service on Sun. 10 a.m. (see A–Z, Salvatorkapelle)
Protestant	Anglican church Jaurès Gasse Service on Sun. at 10.30 a.m.
	Lutheran City Church 1, Dorotheergasse 18; tel. 5 12 83 92/0 Services (except July and Aug.) on Sun. 8 and 10 a.m.
	Reformed City Church 1, Dorotheergasse 16; tel. 5 12 83 93/12 Service on Sun. at 10 a.m.
Jewish	"City Temple" synagogue 1, Seitenstettengasse 4; tel. 5 31 04 Services daily, morning and evening
Ilslamic	Islamic Centre (mosque) 21, Am Hubertusdamm 17–19; tel. 30 13 89 Prayers at 5 a.m. and at 1, 5.05, 8.10, and 10 p.m. Visits (except Fridays) only outside hours of prayer

Cinemas

Admiral, 7, Burggasse 119
Old films, cult films, screening at night

Cinemas with special
programmes

Apollo, 6, Gumperdorfer Str. 63
Super-wide screen

Bellaria, 7, Museumstr. 3
Austro nostalgia (1930–1960)

Breitenseer-Lichtspiele, 14, Breitenseer Str. 21
Old films, cult films, screening at night

Burg-Kino, 1, Opernring 19
Films in original version (English and French)

Erika-Kino (oldest cinema in the world), 7, Kaiserstr. 44–46
Films shown here since 1900

Filmcasino, 5, Margaretenstr. 78
Films in the style of the 1950s; unusual

Filmhaus Stöbergasse, 5, Stöbergasse 11–15
Documentaries and alternative programmes

Filmmuseum (see A–Z; Albertina)

Gartenbau, 1, Parkring 12
Vienna's largest film theatre with super-wide screen

Künstlerhaus-Kino, Akademiestr. 13
Discriminating

Lichtspiele Urania, 1, Uraniastr. 1
Notable political film cycles, etc.

Metro, 1, Johannesgasse 4
Former theatre (boxes); discriminating

Movie, 5, Schönbrunner Str. 12
Old films, cult films, screening at night, original versions

Rondell, 1, Riemergasse 11
Nostalgic smokers' cinema

Schikaneder, 4, Margaretenstr. 24
Old films, cult films, screening at night

Cinema programmes:
tel. 15 77

Star, 7, Burggasse 71
Old films, cult films, screening at night

Recommended films:
tel. 15 22

Stadtkino, 3, Schwarzenbergplatz 7–8
Avant-garde films (often in original version), programmes at
night; videothèque

Studio Molière, 9, Liechtensteinstr. 37
Films in original version (French)

Top Kino Center, 6, Rahlgasse 1
Cult films (sometimes in original version)

Votiv, 9, Währinger Str. 12
Programmes for film devotees

City sightseeing

Suggestions for a short stay	See Sightseeing Programme
By bus	Vienna Sightseeing Tours, 3, Stelzhammergasse 4/11; tel. 7 12 46 83-0 and 7 15 11 42-0 Central departure point: Bus station, Vienna Central (Wien Mitte), also at the Opera and other places.

Cityrama Sightseeing, 1, Börsegasse 1/Tiefer Graben 25; tel. 5 34 13-0
Departure: Kursalon Stadtpark.
Special Tours, 6, Millöckergasse 6 (booking at travel bureaux)

Participants in all the above tours can be picked up at their hotels. Booking can be made at hotel reservation desks or at travel bureaux.

Round trips "Neues Wien"
of the Press and Information
service (PID)

Four-hour round tours on a particular theme (programmes may be subject to alteration) are organised by the city from May to September. Information and booking: Round tour office in the Town Hall (entrance Friedrich-Schmidt-Platz 1; tel. 40 00-8 10 50 (Mon.–Fri. 8 a.m.–3 p.m.).

Route 1: Behind the Scenes
Rathaus – Ring – Kai – Praterstern – Lassallestrasse – Engerthstrasse – Visit to the main fire station, Leopoldstadt – Handelskai – Reichsbrücke – A22 (Danube Bank autobahn) – Praterbrücke – Visit to the workshops of the underground railway at Erdberg – Rathaus.

Route 2: Jewels of the Open Spaces
Rathaus – Ring – Kai – Praterstern – Reichsbrücke – Erzherzog-Karl-Strasse – Visit to gardens and palmhouse at Hirschstennen – Lobaustrasse to the Uferhaus – Walk through part of the river landscape area of Lobau – Rathaus.

Route 3: EXPO 1995
Rathaus – Karlsplatz – Landstrasser Hauptstrasse – Danube Canal – Visit to the Tram Museum – Stadionbrücke – Prater – Handelskai – Reichsbrücke – EXPO-Exhibition in the Austria Center Vienna – Praterstern – Rathaus.

Other round trips	Guided tours through the canal network in the Karlsplatz district (no children under 14). "City Workshops", 9, Kollingasse 6; tel. 34 33 84.
By bicycle	See Bicycles, Vienna Bike
By horse-cab	See Fiaker
By tram	May–Oct.: "Oldtimer Tramway", a 2½ hour ride through the city; every Sat. 2.30 p.m., Sun. and public holidays 10 a.m., from Otto Wagner Pavillion, 4, Karlsplatz; information and tickets: tel. 5 87 31 86.
By air	Round trips (15–20 minutes) over Vienna; operated by VIENNAIR-Polsterer Jets, Hanger 3, A-1300 Vienna-Schwechat Airport; tel. 77 70 20 77.

Boat trips on the Danube are run by the Erste Donau Dampf-schiffahrts-Gesellschaft (DDSG); tel. 2 17 50-450; landing-stage: 1, Schwedenbrücke.

By boat

Round trips Vienna – Little and Great Danube: in the high season (May–Sept.) 10.30 a.m. 1, 1.30, 2, 4, 4.30, 5, and 7.30 p.m. (different departure times from Station Hotel Scandic Crown/Prater); May–Sept. additional "Evergreen" evening trips with dancing Thur. and Fri. 8.30 p.m.; disco-evening Sat. 8.30 p.m.

A prospectus about guided tours on foot (3–25 persons) can be obtained from the Tourist Information Office (see Information). The walks take place in any weather in the morning and after-noon and are devoted to distinctive themes (e.g. Old Houses; Quiet Courtyards; Amadeus in Vienna – film and reality; Medi-eval Vienna above and below ground; The Vienna Coffee House and its Customers; Graves of Honour in the Central Cemetery; Vienna, the musical capital of the world; Art Nou-veau – its precursors and successors; Karlskirche and Karls-platz; The many nationalities in Vienna). Novel city walks are also organised by the Vienna Guides (programme, booking: tel. 93 90 88, 2 20 66 20 and 6 76 41 64), with, for example, the following themes: "On the Track of the Third Man in Vienna", "Art Nouveau and Secession", "Leopoldstadt – the Vienna of the Jews on the far side of the Danube Canal", "Photo-safari through the Old Town", "Bermuda Triangle – from the Romans to the Beisl-Scene", "Dorotheum").

On foot

Charlotte Speiser, 22, Lieblgasse 2; tel. 25 11 78
Travel Point (Sidlo), 9, Boltzmanngasse 19; tel. 31 42 43
Vienna Guide Service, 19, Sommerhaidenweg 124;
tel. 4 43 09 40
Approved guides must produce their authority and official badge.

Official guides for visitors

Coffee houses (Kaffeehäuser)

The coffee house is just as much a part of the ambience of Vienna as the cathedral, yet it was a Pole, Franz Georg Kol-schitzky, who was the founder of these establishments. It is said that he brought back coffee to Vienna from Turkey in 1683 as spoils of war and two years later was granted an Imperial licence to serve the beverage. The triumphal progress of the coffee house began and it became an institution. Newspapers and games, especially billiards, became a fundamental feature of every good coffee house and every worthy citizen became a regular customer of his favourite rendezvous where he met his acquaintances, chatted, played games, studied, brooded, wrote and observed for hours on end or even a whole day. Until 1840 the coffee house was exclusively for men, and only when some establishments introduced music in the Biedermeier pe-riod (mid 19th c.) were ladies allowed inside. At this time luxuri-ously appointed coffee houses came into being, especially the elegant ones in the Ring. The Vienna Kaffeehaus became part of Viennese culture, where literary figures, artists, scholars, politicians and journalists used to meet. When the Danubian monarchy came to an end the heyday of the coffee house was over, but there has recently been a renaissance of these estab-lishments as meeting-places and centres of communication.

Coffee houses (Kaffeehäuser)

The Coffee-House, a Viennese institution

Varieties of coffee

In a coffee house the customer does not simply order a coffee (pronounced *café* as in French) but chooses his favourite from among the many varieties. The basis of all coffee specialities is "mocca", and a glass of water is always served as well.

Einspänner: black in a glass with whipped cream
Fiaker: large black coffee in a glass
Original Fiaker: black with rum
Kaffee verkehrt ("reversed"): more milk than coffee
Kaisermelange: black with yolk of egg
Kapuziner: small bowl of black coffee with a drop of "Obers" (whipped cream), and sprinkled with cocoa or grated chocolate
Konsul: black with a small shot of whipped cream
Melange: milky coffee in a cup or a glass, and a shot of cream
Mocca gespritzt: black with a shot of brandy or rum
Nussschwarzer: mocca
Pharisäer: coffee with rum, sugar and whipped cream
Piccolo: small black coffee in a piccolo bowl, with or without whipped cream
Schale Braun or Gold: black coffee which acquires a golden hue when whipped cream is added
Eiskaffee: A glass is half filled with vanilla ice-cream, topped up with cold strong black coffee, garnished with whipped cream and served with a straw and a long spoon
Mazagran: cold mocca with rum or maraschino and ice cubes, sprinkled with grated cloves and served in a glass with a straw
Türkischer: Turkish mocca served in a copper jug

Coffee houses and
Pâtisseries (selection)

Alt Wien, 1, Bäckerstr. 9
Open: daily 10 a.m.–3 p.m.

Central im Palais Ferstel, 1, Herrengasse 14/Strauchgasse
Open: Mon.–Sat. 10 a.m.–8 p.m.

Demel (coffee prepared in the house style)
See A to Z, Demel

Diglas, 1, Wollzeile 10
Open: Mon.–Sat. 7.30 a.m.–11.30 p.m.
Sun. and public holidays 10 a.m.–11 p.m.

Dom-Café, 1, Stephansplatz 9
Open: daily 10.30 a.m.–10 p.m.

Frauenhuber, 1, Himmelpfortgasse 6
Open: Mon.–Sat. 8 a.m.–10 p.m.

Gerstner, 1, Kärntner Str. 15
Open: Mon.–Sat. 9 a.m.–7 p.m.
(former Imperial and Royal confectioner)

Haag, 1, Schottengasse 2
Open: Mon.–Fri. 7 a.m.–10 p.m.
Sat. 8 a.m.–8 p.m., Sun. 10 a.m.–8 p.m.

Hawelka, 1, Dorotheergasse 6
Open: daily (except Tue.) 8 a.m.–2 a.m.
(Traditional Viennese rendezvous)

Heiner, 1, Kärntner Str. 21–23
Open: Mon.–Sat. 8 a.m.–7.30 p.m., Sun. 10 a.m.–7.30 p.m.
(former Imperial and Royal confectioner)

Heiner, 1, Wollzeile 9
Open: Mon.–Sat. 8 a.m.–7.30 p.m., Sun. 10 a.m.–7.30 p.m.

Hotel Sacher
See A to Z, Hotel Sacher

Imperial, 1, Kärntner Ring 16
Open: daily 7 a.m.–11 p.m.

Kleines Café, 1, Franziskanerplatz 3
Open: Mon.–Sat. 1 p.m.–2 a.m.
Sun. and public holidays 2 p.m.–2 a.m.

Landtmann, 1, Dr.-Karl-Lueger-Ring 4
Open: daily 8 a.m.–midnight

Lehmann, 1, Graben 12
Open: Mon.–Sat. 8 a.m.–midnight

Mozart, 1, Albertinaplatz 2
Open: daily 9 a.m.–midnight

Museum, 1, Friedrichstr. 6
Open: daily 7 a.m.–11 p.m.
(Gallery café)

1900, 1, Fichtegasse 1
Open: daily 11.30 a.m.–2 a.m., July/Aug. 5 p.m.–2 a.m.

Coffee houses (Kaffeehäuser)

Sacher
See A to Z, Hotel Sacher

Schloss Café Schönbrunn, 13, Schloss Schönbrunn
Open: (1st Apr.–15th Oct.) 8.30 a.m.–6 p.m.

Sperl (also billiards), 6, Gumpendorfer Str. 11
Open: Mon.–Sat. 6 a.m.–11 p.m., Sun. and public holidays 3–
11 p.m.
Closed in August and September

Volksgartencafé, 1, Burgring 1
Open: daily 8 p.m.–4 a.m., Sun. 5 o'clock tea

Cafés with music (selection)

Bräunerhof, 1, Stallburggasse 2
Open: Mon.–Fri. 7.30 a.m.–8.30 p.m., Sat. until 6 p.m., Sun. and
public holidays 10 a.m.–6 p.m.

Dommayer, 13, Auhofstr. 2/Dommayergasse 1
Open: daily 7 a.m.–midnight

Imperial, 1, Kärntner Ring 16
Open: daily 7 a.m.—11 p.m.

Kursalon der Stadt Wien (Hübner), 1, Johannesgasse 33
Open: daily 2–11 p.m.

Palais Auersperg, 8, Auerspergstr. 1
Open: daily 4–6 p.m. and 8–10 p.m.
(Polka and waltz concerts, dancing and singing; Danube band)

Prückl, 1, Stubenring 24
Open: Mon., Wed. and Fri. 9 a.m.–10 p.m.

Schmid-Hansl, 18, Schulgasse 31
Open: Tue.–Sat. 9 p.m.–4 a.m.

Schwarzenberg, 1, Kärntner Ring 17
Open: Mon.–Fri., Sun. and public holidays 7 a.m.–midnight,
Sat. 8 a.m.–midnight

Walzerkonzert-Café DDS "Johann Strauss", 1, on the Danube
canal, entrance Marienbrücke; tel. 63 93 67
Open: in the summer months daily 9.30 a.m.–11.30 p.m.; early
November to early April: closed Mon., Sun. open until 6 p.m.;
(Waltz concerts Tue.–Sun. and public holidays at 8.30 and
10 p.m.)

Wortner, 3, Wiedner Hauptstr. 55
Open: Mon.–Fri. 7 a.m.–11 p.m., Sat. 10 a.m.–7 p.m., Sun. and
public holidays 2–9 p.m.

Zartl, 3, Rasumofskygasse 7
Open: Mon.–Fri. 8 a.m.–midnight, Sat. 8 a.m.–6 p.m.;
Music and literary café

Currency

The unit of currency is the Austrian schilling (ös) which is divided into 100 groschen. There are banknotes in values of 20, 50, 100, 500, 1,000 and 5,000 schillings, and coins of 10 and 50 groschen and 1, 5, 10 and 20 schillings.

Unit of currency

The exchange rates fluctuate; they can be obtained from banks and travel agents and are published in the national papers.

Exchange rates

There are no restrictions on the import or export of foreign currency. Austrian schillings can be brought into the country without limit, but not more than 100,000 schillings may be taken out.

Currency regulations

Eurocheques can be used up to a value of 2,500 schillings.

Eurocheques

Most international credit cards are accepted by banks, the larger hotels and restaurants, car-rental companies and many shops.

Credit cards

Outside normal banking hours (Mon.–Fri. 8 a.m.–12.30 p.m. and 1.30–3 p.m., Thurs. until 5.30 p.m.), exchange facilities are available at:
West Station (daily 7 a.m.–10 p.m.)
South Station (daily 6.30 a.m.–10 p.m.)
Central Station (Wien-Mitte; Mon.–Fri. 7.30 a.m.–7. p.m.; Sat. and Sun. 7.30 a.m.–1 p.m.)
Airport exchange desk (daily 6.30 a.m.–11 p.m.)
Air Terminal (daily 8 a.m.–12.30 p.m. and 2–6 p.m.)
Tourist Information, Opernpassage (daily 8 a.m.–7 p.m.)

Currency exchange

Customs regulations

Visitors to Austria over the age of 17 can take in duty-free for their own use clothing, toilet articles and jewellery, together with other personal effects, including two cameras and a portable movie camera, each with 10 films, a portable typewriter, binoculars, a portable radio, a portable television set, a tape-recorder, a record-player and 10 records, musical instruments, camping equipment and sports-gear; also 1–2 days' supply of provisions for the journey (including tea and coffee). Visitors may also take in duty-free 200 cigarettes or 50 cigars or 250 grammes of tobacco, 2 litres of wine and one litre of spirits. Goods and presents to a value of 400 ÖS as well as up to 5 litres petrol in cans can also be taken in duty-free.

On entry

See Currency

Currency regulations

Personal effects, etc., may be taken out without formality.

Exit

On return to the United Kingdom the duty-free allowances depend on where the goods were obtained. If they were acquired in a country belonging to the European Community the allowances, in addition to personal effects are 300 cigarettes or 150 cigarillos or 75 cigars or 400 gr. tobacco; 3 litres wine and 1½ litres spirits over 22° Gay-Lussac (38.8° proof) or 3 litres fortified or sparkling wine up to 22° proof; 90 cc of perfume and 375 cc of toilet water.

Return to Great Britain

If any of the above goods have been bought in a country outside the EC or in a duty-free shop the permitted amounts are approximately one third less. Some of the reduced concessions also apply to visitors from other countries including the United States and Canada.

Valued added tax	See shopping

Diplomatic representation

Great Britain	Embassy: 3 Jauresgasse 12; tel. (02 22) 7 13 15 75
	Consular section 1, Wallnerstrasse 8; tel. (02 22) 63 75 02
United States	Embassy: 9, Boltzmanngasse 16; tel. (02 22) 31 55 11
Canada	Embassy: 1, Dr. Karl-Lueger-Ring 10; tel. (02 22) 5 33 36 91

Emergencies

Doctor on call	Doctors' radio-telephone service (24 hours a day); tel. 141
Mobile emergency doctor	Tel. 144 (in case of accident)
Fire brigade	Tel. 122
Police	Tel. 133
Motoring breakdown	Tel. 120 (ÖAMTC); tel. 123 (ARBÖ)

Events (Mozart Year 1991)

January	Jan. 1st: New Year concerts by the Vienna Philharmonic, the Vienna Symphony and the Vienna Hofburg orchestras
February	Last Thursday in "Fasching": Opera Ball
March	Spring International Trade Fair Haydn Festival Viennale Film Festival (events in the Urania)
April	Spring Marathon Waltz and operetta concerts (until November)
May/June	Vienna Festival (until June; see Festivals) Danube Island Festival
June	Art auction in the Dorotheum Summer Concerts ("Musical Summer"; see Festivals) Theatre in the Park (Stadtpark; until end of July) Flower parade in the Prater
July	Summer productions in Schönbrunn Palace Theatre (until August)

International Youth Music Festival ("Jugend und Musik in Wien)
Festival of Viennese classical music and literature (until beginning of Sept.)
International Summer Dance Festival (until end of August)
Spectaculum in the University Church (see Festivals)

Various events on Danube Island and on the "Old Danube"   August

Vienna Autumn Trade Fairs   September
Opening of the opera season
Austrian Film Festival
Regattas on the Danube

Theatre premières   October
Viennale Film Festival in the Künstlerhaus Cinema

Art and Antiques Fair   November
Schubert festival

Christ Child market on the Rathausplatz   December
Nativity cribs in St Peter's Church
Art auction in the Dorotheum
Christmas Exhibition in the Künstlerhaus
Dec. 31st: Imperial Ball in the Hofburg

See also Programme of Events

Excursions

Regional tickets, available on rail and bus and covering popular areas such as the Semmering, the Vienna Woods, etc. can be obtained from Austrian Railways (ÖBB).   Note

The Wienerwald (Vienna Woods), extending over 80sq.km/80 sq. miles, is the most popular local recreational district of Vienna. It lies in the extreme north-eastern part of the Eastern Alps, and, to the west of Vienna, falls in several terraces down to the Danube. In the north the scenery is charming, with broad hillocks and beech-woods; in the east it is sunny with stands of black pines; in the south-east rugged with gorge-like valleys. In the A–Z section some of the most beautiful and interesting places are described: in the south the Cistercian Monastery (see Heiligenkreuz), which was the impetus for settlement in this area; Gumpoldskirchen (see entry), where vines grow on the slopes of the Wienerwald; Laxenburg and Baden (see entries) where the Court used to pass the summer; in the north-west the vintners' village of Grinzing (see entry) and the vantage-point of Kahlenberg (see entry); in the north Klosterneuburg (see entry).   Wienerwald
Below, as an example, the route (37km/23 miles) over the Hohenstrasse to Klosterneuburg is described. Although it is some 25km/15 miles longer than the direct route via Kahlenbergerdorf, with which it can be combined in a very pleasant round trip (50km/31 miles), it is nevertheless full of delightful scenery.
By taking the roads from Vienna leading to Neuwaldegg, Neustift am Walde, Sievering or Grinzing many other round trips can be put together.

Excursions

Leave Vienna on the road to the west, passing near Schönbrunn and follow the Wien valley upstream. At Wien-Hacking (11km/7 miles) turn right and cross the River Wien. In 500m we reach Wien-Hütteldorf. Now follow the winding and scenically beautiful Wiener Höhenstrasse above the Wienerwald to the Kahlenberg (large car park). 1km beyond the car park the road to Klosterneuburg bears off to the left, but it is better to continue to the end of the Höhenstrasse at the Leopoldsberg (423m/1,388ft), the most easterly promontory of the Wienerwald, high above the Danube. Here there is an inn and a Baroque church on the site of the former Babenburg castle, and from here the view is as fine if not finer than that from the Kahlenberg. We return to the Klosterneuburg turning and descend the winding road on the northern slope of the Kahlenberg to the monastery, some 5km/3 miles distant. Visitors who would like to walk in the Wienerwald are recommended to use routes 1 and 4 of the brochure published by the Stadtinformationsamt (see details at the end of this entry).

March-Danauland

Fields and meadows, vines and woodland are the distinctive features of the March-Danauland to the east of Vienna. In the A–Z section of this guide two of the places in this area most deserving of a visit are described: these are Carnuntum (see entry), worth seeing for its Roman excavations, and Rohrau (see entry), Hadyn's birthplace.

The visitor who follows the 110km/68 mile-long route through the Marchfeld described here will be on historic ground. It was here that the Quadi fought against the Romans (1st–4th c.); it was here that battles were fought against the Hungarians in the Middle Ages, against the Turks in the 17th c. and against Napoleon at Aspern and Deutsch-Wagram in the 19th c.

We leave Vienna across the Praterstern and the Reichsbrücke. In 6km/4 miles the Kagran Bridge crosses the Old Danube, the former main course of the river. In Aspern (5km/3 miles) a stone lion outside the parish church is a memorial of the Battle of Aspern (1809), when Archduke Charles inflicted a defeat on Napoleon; the latter, however, succeeded a little later in crossing the Danube at Wagram. South of Aspern extends the Lobau Nature Reserve, a delightful scenic area of grassland, watered by the Old Danube. The route continues through Gross-Enzersdorf (5.5km/3 miles), Orth (14km/9 miles), which has a castle with four towers, and Eckartsau (9km/5½ miles), with a former imperial hunting lodge, to Stopfenreuth (7km/4 miles) where we turn north to the River March which here flows into the Danube. The route now passes through Engelhartstetten (4km/2½ miles) to Schlosshof Castle, built in 1725–1729 by Johann Lukas von Hildebrandt for Prince Eugene and later enlarged for Maria Theresa, and finally reaches Marchegg (8.5km/5 miles) on the March which forms the boundary with Czechoslovakia and where the meadows are a nature reserve. The former hunting lodge houses the Hunting Museum of Lower Austria. From here we turn west and return to Vienna via Obersiedenbrunn (15km/9 miles) with a Baroque church and a castle, which was rebuilt for Prince Eugene in 1730, and through Markgrafneusiedl (6km/4 miles) on the Russbach.

Wine producing region

The largest wine-producing area of Austria is bounded in the north and east by Czechoslovakia and in the south by the Marchfeld. Mistelbach is the chief town in the eastern part, and Retz, on the slopes of the Manhartsgebirge, in the western quarter. The principal varieties of wine produced in this region are Grüner Veltliner, Blauer Portugieser, Neuburger, Rheinriesling, Müller-Thurgau and Blaufränkische. In the charming little villages many inns and Heurige cater for the refreshment needs of visitors.

The Österreich Werbung (see Information) has brochures of popular excursions in the area.

Situated at an altitude of 1,000m/3,280ft, Semmering, on the boundary between Lower Austria and Styria, 90km/56 miles south of Vienna, is a mountain resort with a long tradition. A track over the pass existed as long ago as the 12th c. The present pass (modernised 1956–1958) was developed from a road which Charles VI had laid out in 1728 and which was extended and enlarged in 1839–1842. A trip on the Semmering railway is also very agreeable; this the first large-scale mountain railway in Europe, was constructed in 1848–1854 by Karl von Ghega. It passes through fifteen tunnels and crosses deep gorges on sixteen arched viaducts, some of them consisting of several storeys. The maximum gradient is 1 in 40.

Chairlifts go up from the top of the pass to the Hirschenkogel (1,324m/4,345ft) and from Maria Schutz to the Sonnwendstein (1,523m/4,998ft). A toll-road leads from the pass to the Sonnwendstein from which there is a wonderful view of Rax and Schneeberg, the Alpine foreland and the Semmering railway far below.

Semmering

A trip on the Danube on one of the ships of the Erste Donau-Dampschiffsfahrts-Gesellschaft is another excellent excursion; for example to Budapest or to Bratislava (Pressburg). A nostalgic trip can be made on the "MS Passau", the last paddle-wheel steamer, which operates to and from Passau, or on a modern hovercraft or a traditional Danube ship. The trips last from two to four days. In the up-stream direction there are trips to the Wachau or via Melk (visit to the Abbey or to Arstetten Castle) and Grein (sightseeing) to Passau and return through the Wachau (guided tour through Durnstein and wine tasting) to Vienna (single journey four days). It is also possible to book for part of the route Vienna–Passau or to return from Passau to Vienna by rail (in this case three days).

These trips are operated from May to September (information from Este Donau-Dampfschiffahrts-Gesellschaft; Handelskai 265, A-1021 Wien; tel. 2 17 10-0.

Boat trips on the Danube

There are also excellent walks to be enjoyed from Vienna. The Stadtinformationsamt (see Information) has put together ten walks in the brochure "Stadtwanderwege", in which not only are the individual walks indicated on corresponding small maps, but also included are the starting points (with details of suitable public transport), duration and length of walk, and places of refreshment on the route. The walks lead to the following venues:

Walks from Vienna

Walk 1: Kahlenberg
Walk 2: Hermannskogel
Walk 3: Hameau
Walk 4: Jubiläumswarte
Walk 5: Bisamberg
Walk 6: Zuberg – Maurer Wald; this route also includes the Wotruba church (see A to Z, Wotruba Kirche)
Walk 7: Laaer Berg

Festivals

Vienna Festival Weeks	The Vienna Festival Weeks are in May and June. Information and tickets can be obtained from: Direktion der Wiener Festwochen, Lehárgasse 11, A-1060 Wien; tel. 5 86 16 76-0.
Music in summer in Vienna	In July, August and September musical events include arcade concerts (Arcade-courtyard of the New Town Hall), concerts in Schönbrunn Palace, in the Town Hall Square, in churches and town houses (with special emphasis on the music of Schubert and Haydn), as well as promenade and park concerts. Tickets are obtainable from: Wiener-Musik-Sommer, Friedrich-Schmidt-Platz 5, A-1082 Wien; tel. 40 00-84 00.
Spectaculum	At the "Spectaculum" festival which takes place annually in the University Church, works by famous Baroque composers are presented. Details and tickets can be obtained from: Gesellschaft für Musiktheater, Türkenstrasse 19, A-1090 Wien; tel. 34 06 99.
Viennale Film Festival	Details from: Viennale Wiener Filmfestwochen, Uraniastrasse 1, A-1010 Wien; tel. 75 32 84/5.

Fiaker

Ranks	There are about three dozen horse-drawn "fiaker" plying for hire in Vienna. They can be found at Stephansplatz, on the Augustinerstrasse outside the Albertina and at the Heldenplatz.
Fiaker Museum	See A to Z

Food and drink

Meal times	The main meal of the day, generally of three substantial courses – soup, a meat dish and a sweet – is normally eaten between noon and 2 p.m. In the evening the Viennese tend to have their meal between 6 and 9 p.m.; many restaurants do not serve hot meals after 10 p.m.
Cuisine	The key to the success of the Viennese cuisine lies in its variety. The recipes owe a great deal to Bohemian, Hungarian, Croatian, Slovene and Italian influences. Neither light in texture nor low in calories, it nevertheless makes use of many natural ingredients. It includes an astonishing range of freshwater fish, and during the October/November season game dishes are exceedingly good. The "New Viennese Cuisine" is modelled on the French *nouvelle cuisine* but is only to be found in a small number of restaurants.
Soup	Beef broth (Rindsuppe) garnished with various types of pastry (Frittaten, Schörbell, Backerbsen); dumplings and noodles

(Markknödel, Griessnockerl, Lungenstrudel, Milzschnitten) and pea or vegetable soup with fish roe (Fischbeutschelsuppe).

Carp in garlic butter (Wurzelkarpfen); fillet of pike-perch (Zander) fried in bacon fat or grilled, with paprika sauce; steamed catfish (Wels) and fish pie (Zwiebelfisch). | Fish

Schnitzel-style chicken (Backhendel); chicken with paprika (Paprikahendel); stuffed breast of goose (Ganselbrust); capon (Kapaun) in anchovy sauce; pheasant (Faisan) roasted "in a bacon shirt"; woodcock (Schnepfen). | Poultry, game-birds

Wild boar (Wildschwein) in cream sauce with dumplings; ragout of venison (Hirschragout) with bacon; saddle of venison (Rehrücken) in a herb sauce; jugged hare (Hasenrücken) in a wine sauce. | Game

Wiener Schnitzel (i.e. veal cutlet coated with breadcrumbs and fried); cuts of beef: (Tafelspitz) with horseradish, (Beinfleisch) with chive sauce, roasted (Esterhazy-Rostbraten); larded veal (Kalbsvogerln); Viennese roast pork (Wiener Schweinebraten); stewed pork with horseradish (Krenfleisch); salted meat (Selchfleisch); roasted sucking pig (Spanferkel); braised kidneys (Nierenbraten) and goulash (Gulasch). | Meat

Dishes made from kidneys, liver, sweetbreads, etc. (Salonbeuschel, Kavaliersbries). | Offal

Pancakes (Palatschinken); stuffed pancakes (Topfenpalatschinken, Kaiserschmarren); yeast dumplings with plums (Topfenknödel mit Zwetschkenröster), with poppyseed (Germknöderl), with apricots (Marillenknödel), with jam (Buchteln); millefeuille (Millrahmstrudel) with vanilla sauce, plum purée (Powideltascherln/tatschkerln), and apple strudel (Apfelstrudel). | Hot sweets

Sachertorte, Dobostorte | Cakes

Apart from good beer (1 seidel = 0.6 pint, 1 krugel = 0.9 pint) the most popular beverage is wine. This comes mostly from Lower Austria and Burgenland and is often drunk "g'spritzt", that is mixed with soda water. | Drinks
The wines on offer include green Veltliner, Rhine Riesling, White Burgundy, Traminer, Welschriesling, Neuburger, Müller Thurgau, Zierfandler, Rotgipfler, Gumpoldskirchner, Blaufränkischer, Blue Portuguese and Blue Burgundy.
An evening of wine-drinking is best spent at the "Heurige" or cellar bars (see A to Z, Heurige and Practical Information, Restaurants).

See entry | Restaurants

Culinary terms

Frittaten	strips of pancake
Schöberl	sponge fingers
Nockerl	small elongated flour dumplings
Backerbsen	small balls of choux pastry fried in fat
Fleischlaberl	rissoles,
Fogosch, Schill	pike-perch

Gabelroller	rollmop herrings
Beuschel	braised calf's lung, spleen or heart
Beinfleisch	loin of beef
Tafelspitz	boiled loin of beef
Gulyás	goulash
Faschiertes	mince, meat loaf
Selchfleisch	smoked pork
Lungenbraten	loin of beef in a thick sauce
Lüngerl	strips of calf's lungs (and often also heart) boiled in vinegar
Kaiserfleisch	lightly cured pork spare rib
Kalbsvogel	small beef olives
Backhendl	roast chicken portions
Fisolen	green beans
Karfiol	cauliflower
Sprossenkohl	brussels sprouts
Stelze	knuckle of pork
Paradeiser	tomatoes
Häuptelsalat	lettuce
Kukuruz	maize
Kren	horseradish
Schwammerl	mushrooms
Topfen	curd cheese
Schlagobers/Schlag	whipped cream
Palatschinken	sweet filled pancakes
Strudel	thin pastry cases with all kinds of filling
Kaiserschmarrn	strips of pancake with raisins, fried in butter and sugar
Dobostorte	flan filled with chocolate cream
Sachertorte	chocolate cake filled with apricot jam
Buchteln	baked or steamed yeast-dough noodles (sometimes filled)
Powidl	thick plum purée without sugar
Germknödel	yeast dumplings filled with Powidl (see above)
Marillen	apricots
Ribisel	blackcurrants
Zwetschkenröster	stewed plums

Getting to Vienna

By air

Vienna's Schwechat Airport (see Airport) is served by flights from most major European cities. There are daily services between London and Vienna and less frequently between Manchester and Vienna (British Airways and Austrian Airlines). During the winter months flights can be delayed by fog, so it is advisable during that period to book on late morning or early afternoon services.

By rail

There are two main routes available from London; the most direct is from Victoria via Dover–Ostend which takes about 24 hours, the other from Liverpool Street via the Hook of Holland involves changes at Cologne and Wurzburg or Munich and takes longer.
The privately run Orient Express runs from London to Vienna on certain dates, but tickets are very expensive.

By road

Vienna is about 1,290km/800 miles from the channel coast. Most visitors taking their own car travel on the motorways via

Cologne, Frankfurt, Passau and Linz. In view of the long distance it is advisable to make one – or possibly two – overnight stops. There are motorail services from 's-Hertogenbosch in Holland to Salzburg and from Düsseldorf to Munich.

There are numerous package tours by coach, either going direct to Vienna or including the Austrian capital in a longer circuit. For information apply to any travel agent.

From May to September the Donau-Dampfschiffahrts-Gesellschaft (DDSG – Danube Shipping Company) operates a fast service between Passau and Vienna. The journey takes 15 hours downstream and about 22 hours upstream (with overnight stay in Linz). · By boat

Rail passengers with international tickets can opt to travel by DDSG vessels if their rail ticket covers the stretches to Vienna from Passau, Linz and Melk. Vouchers, on which a supplement is payable, for the transfer from rail to river can only be obtained from the DDSG offices at points of embarkation.

Help for the disabled

Details from Vienna Tourist Board (see Information)   Hotel list/city plan

Heuriger

The term "Heuriger" has two meanings; on the one hand it describes the wine and on the other the place where it is sold. First the wine: Heuriger must not be confused with "Federweissem" (feather-white) or "Suser" wines. These are also sold in the year in which they are produced, but under the designation "Sturm". Heuriger is the newest wine which is drawn from the barrel in spring and is on sale until the following year when the next vintage is ready. From St Martin's Day (11th November) the current Heuriger is sold under the name "alter" (old).   Wine

"Heurige" also denotes the inns where the vintner sells the wine which he has produced. In 1784 the Emperor Joseph II granted to vintners the privilege of selling their own wine for 300 days in a year in a "Buschenschank" (bush inn). The term refers to the bunch of spruce branches which is placed over the entrance to the establishment.   Inns

Nowadays many of these restaurants are franchised businesses open throughout the year; others are open only for a few months, generally early in the summer. In these inns food is served (generally self-service) and zither or "Schrammel" (guitar, accordion, violin) music provided. In an authentic Heurige music is rarely heard and when it is, it is not loud and cheerful but quiet and sad. In summer many Heurige provide shady gardens for their customers.

The best-known heurige district of Vienna is Grinzing (see A to Z) but the characteristic bush sign can also be found in Sievering, Nussdorf, Neustift, Heiligenstadt, Stammersdorf, Strebersdorf, Jedlersdorf, Mauer and Oberlaa. A brochure entitled   Heurige districts

Heriger

A "Heurige" inn

"Heurige in Wien", obtainable from the Vienna Tourist Office (see Information) gives times of opening and facilities offered (garden, music, etc.).

Heurige and Wine Cellars (selection: G = Garden)

Altes Presshaus, 19, Cobenzlgasse 15; tel. 32 23 93 (G)
Das "Alte Haus", 19, Himmelstr. 35; tel. 32 23 21 (G)
Bach-Hengl, 19, Sandgasse 7–9; tel. 32 30 84 (G)
Diem's Buschenschenke, 19, Kahlenberger Str. 1; tel. 37 49 59 (G)
Figlmüller, 19, Grinzinger Str. 55; tel. 32 42 57 (G)
Fuhrgassl-Huber, 19, Neustift am Walde 68; tel. 44 14 05
Grinzinger Hauermandl, 19, Cobenzlgasse 20; tel. 3 20 04 44
Grinzinger Weinbottich, 19, Cobenzlgasse 28; tel. 32 42 37 (G)
Kalke's Gwölb, 23, Ketzergasse 465; tel. 88 75 08
Kerlinger, 19, Kahlenberger Str. 20; tel. 37 22 64 (G)
Landstrasse Stadtheuriger, 3, Landstrasser Hauptstr. 28; tel. 75 55 75-513
Mandahaus, 19, Greinergasse 29; tel. 37 47 87 (G)
Mayer am Pfarrplatz, 19, Heiligenstädter Pfarrplatz 2; tel. 37 33 61 (G)
Piaristenkeller, 8, Piaristengasse 45; tel. 42 91 52
Reinprechts "Weinmuseum", 19 Cobenzlgasse 22; tel. 32 14 71 and 32 13 89 (G)
Schübel-Auer, 19, Kahlenberger Str. 22; tel. 37 22 22 (G)
Seitz, 21, Strebersdorf, Anton-Böck-G 5; tel. 39 57 68 (G)
Sirbu, 19, Kahlenberger Str. 210; tel. 37 13 19 (G)
Urbanikeller, 1, Am Hof 12; tel. 63 91 02
Zum Fuhrwerkerhaus, 14, Linzer Str. 169; tel. 94 61 38 (G)
Zum Weihrauch, 19, Kaasgrabengasse 77; tel. 32 58 18 (G)
Zwolf-Apostel-Keller, 1, Sonnenfelsgasse 3; tel. 5 12 67 77

Hotels

Visitors are recommended to make and confirm reservations before departure.

Visitors wishing to stay outside the city should apply to Niederösterreich-Information, Heidenschuss 2, A-1010 Wien; tel. 5 33 31 14.

For hotels suitable for the disabled see Help for the Disabled.

Hotels are officially classified in five categories: 5 star = Luxury, 4 star = first-class, 3 star = good middle-class, 2 star = simple, 1 star = modest. The list below follows this classification. b. = number of beds.

The prices given below in Austrian schillings are for accommodation (including breakfast, service and taxes). They are average prices, intended as a guide to price levels.

Category	Double room	Single room
*****	1650–5100	800–3900
****	800–2500	520–2450
***	660–1400	280–1150
**	400–1380	210– 660
*	400– 850	200– 440

Ambassador, 1010, Neuer Markt 6, 176 b.; tel. 5 14 66
Bristol, 1010, Kärntner Ring 1, 270 b.; tel. 51 51 60
Clima Villenhotel, 1190, Nussberggasse 2c, 60 b.; tel. 37 15 16
De France, 1010, Schottenring 3, 411 b.; tel. 34 35 40
Hilton Wien, 1030, Am Stadtpark, 1200 b.; tel. 7 17 00
Im Palais Schwarzenberg, 1030, Schwarzenbergplatz 9, 75 b.; tel. 78 45 15
Imperial, 1015, Kärntner Ring 16, 275 b.; tel. 5 01 10
Inter-Continental Vienna, 1030, Johannesgasse 28, 996 b.; tel. 7 11 22-0
Parkhotel Schönbrunn, 1130, Hietzinger Hauptstr. 10-14, 798 b.; tel. 8 78 04
Penta Hotel Wien, 1030, Ungargasse 60, 684 b.; tel. 7 11 75-0
Ramada, 1150, Ullmannstr. 71, 520 b.; tel. 85 04-0
Sacher, 1015, Philharmonikerstr. 4, 213 b.; tel. 5 14 56
SAS Palais Hotel, 1010, Weihburggasse 32, 310 b.; tel. 51 51 70
Vienna Marriott, 1010, Parkring 12a, 608 b.; tel. 51 51 80

*****

Alba Hotel Palace, 1050, Margaretenstr. 92, 228 b.; tel. 55 46 86
Alba Hotel Wien, 1050, Margaretenstr. 53, 93 b.; tel. 5 88 50
Albatros, 1090, Liechtensteinstr. 89, 140 b.; tel. 34 35 08
Am Parkring, 1010, Parkring 12, 106 b.; tel. 5 14 80
Am Schubertring, 1010, Schubertring 11, 73 b.; tel. 7 17 02-0
Astoria, 1010, Führichgasse 1, 180 b.; tel. 5 15 77-0
Bellevue, 1091, Althanstr. 5, 320 b.; tel. 34 56 31-0
Biedermeier im Sünnhof, 1030, Landstrasser Hauptstr. 28, 420 b.; tel. 75 55 75
Bohemia, 1150, Turnergasse 9, 203 b.; tel. 83 66 48

****

Hotels

Capricorno, 1010, Schwedenplatz 3-4, 81 b.; tel. 5 33 31 04-0
City-Central, 1020, Taborstr. 8, 114 b.; tel. 2 11 05-0
Europa, 1015, Neuer Markt 3, 152 b.; tel. 5 15 94-0
Graben, 1010, Dorotheergasse 3, 86 b.; tel. 5 12 15 31
Hungaria, 1030, Rennweg 51, 310 b.; tel. 7 13 25 21
Kaiserin Elisabeth, 1010, Weihburggasse 3, 119 b.; tel. 5 15 26-0
König von Ungarn, 1010, Schulerstr. 10, 70 b.; tel. 5 15 84-0
Kummer, 1060, Mariahilfer Str. 71a, 182 b.; tel. 5 88 95
K & K Hotel Maria Theresia, 1070, Kirchberggasse 6, 246 b.; tel. 93 56 16
K & K Palais Hotel, 1010, Rudolfsplatz 11, 126 b.; tel. 5 33 13 53
Mailberger Hof, 1010, Annagasse 7, 70 b.; tel. 5 12 06 41
Maté, 1170, Ottakringer Str. 34-36, 230 b.; tel. 43 61 33
Modul, 1190, Peter-Jordan-Str. 78, 82 b.; tel. 47 15 84-0
Opernringhof, 1010, Opernring 11, 70 b.; tel. 5 87 55 18
President, 1060, Wallgasse 23, 160 b.; tel. 5 99 90
Prinz Eugen, 1040, Wiedner Gürtel 14, 165 b.; tel. 5 05 17 41
Regina, 1090, Rooseveltplatz 15, 232 b.; tel. 42 76 81-0
Römischer Kaiser, 1010, Annagasse 16, 48 b.; tel. 5 12 77 51
Royal, 1010, Singerstr. 3, 161 b.; tel. 5 15 68
Scandic Crown, 1020, Handelskai 269, 800 b.; tel. 2 17 77
Stafanie, 1020, Taborstr. 12, 230 b.; tel. 2 11 50-0
Strudlhof, 1090, Pasteurgasse 1, 101 b.; tel. 31 25 22
Tyrol, 1060, Mariahilfer Str. 15, 68 b.; tel. 5 87 54 15

***   Alexander, 1090, Augasse 15, 114 b.; tel. 34 15 08
Arabella Hotel Jagdschloss, 1130, Jagdschlossgasse 79, 89 b.; tel. 8 04 35 08
Austria, 1010, Wolfengasse 3, 90 b.; tel. 5 15 23-0
Capri, 1020, Praterstr. 44-46, 80b.; tel. 24 84 04/05
Ekazent, 1130, Hietzinger Hauptstr. 22, 64 b.; tel. 82 74 01
Fürst Metternich, 1060, Esterházygasse 33, 112 b.; tel. 5 88 70
Kahlenberg, 1190, Josefsdorf 1, 62 b.; tel. 32 12 51-0
Mariahilf, 1060, Mariahilfer Str. 121b, 120 b.; tel. 5 97 36 05
Mozart, 1090, Julius Tandler-Platz 4, 106 b.; tel. 34 15 37
Nordbahn, 1020, Praterstr. 72, 136 b.; tel. 2 11 30-0
Post, 1010, Fleischmarkt 24, 176 b.; tel. 5 15 83-0
Tabor, 1020, Tandelmarktgasse 19/Taborstr. 25, 165 b.; tel. 3 56 51 50
Wandl, 1010, Petersplatz 9, 232 b.; tel. 5 34 55-0
Wimberger, 1070, Neubaugürtel 34-36, 174 b.; tel. 93 76 36
Zur Wiener Staatsoper, 1010, Krugerstr. 11, 40 b.; tel. 5 13 12 74/75

**   Altwienerhof, 1150, Herklotzgasse 6, 36 b.; tel. 83 71 45
Carlton-Opera, 1040, Schikanedergasse 4, 117 b.; tel. 5 87 53 02
Gabriel, 1030, Landstrasser Hauptstr. 165, 82 b.; tel. 72 67 54
Hohe Warte, 1190, Steinfeldgasse 7, 71 b.; tel. 37 31 28
Stadt Bamberg, 1150, Mariahilfer Str. 167, 50 b.; tel. 83 76 08
Steindl-Gasthof, 1100, Triester Str. 67, 40 b.; tel. 6 04 12 78
Südbahn, 1040, Weyringergasse 25, 45 b.; tel. 5 05 85 90
Wilhelmshof, 1020, Kleine Stadtgutgasse 4, 78 b.; tel. 24 55 21

*   Gloriette, 1140, Linzer Str. 105, 98 b.; tel. 92 11 46
Hospiz, 1070, Kenyongasse 15, 41 b.; tel. 93 13 04
Orient, 1010, Tiefer Graben 30-32, 51 b.; tel. 63 73 07

Pensions are generally fairly small establishments without restaurants situated in residential or office buildings. Because of
their family-like atmosphere they are popular for fairly long
visits.

Alla Lenz, 1070, Halpgasse 3-5, 26 b.; tel. 93 46 76
Arenberg, 1010, Stubenring 2, 42 b.; tel. 5 12 52 91
Barich, 1030, Barichgasse 3, 25 b.; tel. 7 12 12 73
Marc Aurel, 1010, Marc-Aurel-Str. 8, 28 b.; tel. 5 33 36 40
Mariahilf, 1060, Mariahilfer Str. 49, 24 b.; tel. 5 86 17 81
Museum, 1070, Museumstr. 3, 28 b.; tel. 93 44 26
Neuer Markt, 1010, Seilergasse 9, 97 b.; tel. 5 12 23 16
Meustift Appartement-Pension, 1190, Neustift am Walde 89,
40 b.; tel. 44 20 16 and 32 34 61
Pertschy, 1010, Habsburgergasse 5, 81 b.; tel. 5 33 70 94-97
Pharmador, Schottenfeldgasse 39, 31 b.; tel. 93 53 17
Riemergasse Appartement-Pension, 1010, Riemergasse 8,
40 b.; tel. 5 12 72 20-0
Wiener, 1010, Seilergasse 16, 19 b.; tel. 5 12 48 16-0

****

Am Operneck, 1010, Kärntner Str. 47, 14 b.; tel. 5 12 93 10
Bosch, 1030 Keilgasse 13, 20 b.; tel. 7 86 17 90
Christina, 1010, Hafnersteig 7, 60 b.; tel. 5 33 29 61
Domizil, 1010, Schulerstr. 14, 39 b.; tel. 5 13 30 93
Franz, 1090, Währinger Str. 12, 51 b.; tel. 34 36 37-39
Geissler, 1010, Postgasse 14, 58 b.; tel. 5 33 28 03
Kirschbichler, 1030, Landstrasser Hauptstr. 33, 27 b.;
tel. 7 12 10 68
Kurpension Oberlaa, 1107, Kurbadstr. 6, 62 b.; tel. 68 38 11
Lerner, 1010, Wipplingerstr. 23, 16 b.; tel. 5 33 52 19
Milanohof, 1170, Neuwaldegger Str. 44, 22 b.; tel. 46 14 97
Nossek, 1010, Graben 17, 46 b.; tel. 5 33 70 41
Residenz, 1010, Ebendorferstr. 10, 23 b.; tel. 43 47 86-0
Sankt Stephan, 1010, Spiegelgasse 1, 12 b.; tel. 5 12 29 90
Schweizer Pension Solderer, 1010, Heinrichsgasse 2, 20 b.;
tel. 63 81 56
Stadtpark, 1030, Landstrasser Hauptstr. 7, 34 b.;
tel. 7 13 31 23
Suzanne, 1010, Walfischgasse 4, 34 b.; tel. 5 13 25 07

***

Acion, 1010, Dorotheergasse 6–8, 43 b.; tel. 5 12 79 40
Kolpingswerk Wien, 1100, Sonnwendgasse 22, 177 b.;
tel. 6 04 24 51

**

Seasonal hotels are students accommodation run as hotels
from 1st July to 30th September. Service is generally in the
charge of students.

Academia, 1080, Pfeilgasse 3a, 672 b.; tel. 43 16 61/55
Atlas, 1070, Lerchenfelder Str. 1-3, 304 b.; tel. 43 16 61/55
Haus Margareten, 1040, Margaretenstr. 30, 88 b.; tel. 58 81 50
Rosenhotel Burgenland 1, 1090, Wilhelm-Exner-Gasse 4,
145 b.; tel. 4 39 12 20
Rosenhotel Burgenland 2, 1060, Mittelgasse 18, 275 b.;
tel. 59 61 24 70
Rosenhotel Burgenland 3, 1060, Bürgerspitalgasse 19, 240 b.;
tel. 59 79 47 50
Rosenhotel Niederösterreich, 1020, Untere Augartenstr. 31,
204 b.; tel. 3 53 52 60

***

Information

**

Alsergrund, 1080, Alser Str. 33, 127 b.; tel. 4 33 23 17,
5 12 74 93
Aquila, 1080, Pfeilgasse 1a, 130 b.; tel. 43 16 61/55
Auersperg, 1080, Auerspergstr. 9, 132 b.; tel. 4 32 54 90 and
5 12 74 93
Avis, 1080, Pfeilgasse 4, 117 b.; tel. 43 16 61/55
Don Bosco, 1030, Hagenmüllergasse 33, 98 b.;
tel. 7 11 84/555
Haus Döbling, 1190, Gymnasiumstr. 85, 550 b.; tel. 34 76 31
Haus Technik, 1040, Schäfflergasse 2, 198 b.;
tel. 5 87 65 69/22 and 5 12 74 93
Josefstadt, 1080, Buchfeldgasse 16, 70 b.; tel. 43 52 11/22
Kolpingshaus Währing, 1180, Gentzgasse 27, 98 b.;
tel. 31 65 15

*

Auge Gottes, 1090, Nussdorfer Str. 75, 157 b.; tel. 34 25 85
Rosenhotel Europahaus, 1140, Linzer Str. 429, 74 b.;
tel. 97 25 38

Information

Great Britain

Austrian National Tourist Office
30 St George Street
London W1R 0AL
Tel. (071) 629 0461

United States

500 Fifth Avenue
New York NY 10110
Tel. (212) 994 6880

11601 Wilshire Boulevard
Suite 2480
Los Angeles CA 90025
Tel. (213) 477 3332

1007 NW 24th Avenue
Portland, OR 97210
Tel. (503) 224 6000

500 North Michigan Avenue
Suite 1950
Chicago, IL 60611
Tel. (312) 644 8029

1300 Post Oak Boulevard
Suite 960
Houston, Texas 77056
Tel. (713) 850 9999

Canada

2 Bloor Street East
Suite 3330
Toronto, Ontario M4W 1A8
Tel. (416) 967 3381

1010 Sherbrooke Street West
Suite 1410
Montreal P.Q. H3A 2R7
Tel. (514) 849 3709

Suite 1220–1223 Vancouver Block
736 Granville Street
Vancouver B.C. V6Z 1J2
Tel. (604) 683 5808-09

Austrian National Tourist Office (Österreich Werbung)   Vienna
Margaretenstrasse 1 (corner Wiedner Hauptstrasse)
A-1040 Wien
Tel. 5 88 66-0
(Open: Mon.–Fri. 9 a.m.–5.30 p.m.)

Vienna Tourist Office (Wiener Fremdenverkehrsamt)
Kärntner Strasse 38
A-1010 Wien
Tel. 5 13 88 92 and 5 13 40 15
(Open: Mon.–Sat. 9 a.m.–7 p.m.)

Kinderspitalgasse 5
A-1095 Wien
Tel. 53 59 74 and 43 16 08-1

Stadtinformation (in Town Hall)
Friedrich-Schmidt Platz 1
A-1010 Wien
Tel. 43 89 89 and 40 00 84 10
(Open: Mon.–Fri. 10 a.m.–noon and 1–6 p.m.)

Official Tourist Information (also room reservations: tel. 97 12   For motorists
71/2) at the west motorway access road (A.1), motorway station
Wien–Auhof
(Open: in Nov. 9 a.m.–7 p.m.; Dec.–Mar. daily 10 a.m.–6 p.m.;
Apr.–Oct. daily 8 a.m.–10 p.m.)

Official Tourist Information (also room reservations: tel. 67 41
51 and 67 71 00) at the south motorway access road (A.2); turn
off to centre, Triester Strasse
(Open: Apr., May, June, Oct. daily 9 a.m.–7 p.m.; July–Sept.
daily 8 a.m.–10 p.m.)

There are tourist offices in both West and South stations, where   For rail travellers
rooms can also be booked.
West Station: tel. 58 00-3 10 60 (open: daily 6. 15 a.m.–11 p.m.)
South Station: tel. 58 00-3 10 50 (open: daily 6.15 a.m.–10 p.m.)

Official Tourist Information (also room reservations):   For air travellers
Arrival hall of airport
(Open: from July–Sept. daily 8.30 a.m.–11.30 p.m.; Oct.–May
daily 9 a.m.–10 p.m.)

Information kiosk of the DDSG (also room reservations):   For boat passengers
Reichsbrücke landing-stage;
(Open: May–Sept. daily 7.30 a.m.–8 p.m.)

Insurance

Visitors are strongly advised to ensure that they have adequate   General
holiday insurance, especially medical cover, and including loss
or damage to luggage, loss of currency and jewellery.

For nationals of the United Kingdom in-patient treatment in hospitals in Vienna is usually free (with a small charge for dependants) but other medical services must be paid for.

You are advised to apply to your local Social Security office, well before the date of departure, for a certifictae of entitlement (Form E111).

Vehicles

Visitors travelling by car should ensure that their insurance is comprehensive and covers use of the vehicle in Europe. A "Green Card" is strongly recommended.

See also Travel Documents.

Language

General

German, like English, is a Germanic language, and the pronunciation usually comes more easily to English-speakers than does a Romance language such as French. Much of the basic vocabulary, too, will be familiar to English speakers.

Standard German ("Hochdeutsch") is spoken in business and commercial circles throughout the country but many people in Vienna speak a strong local dialect.

Pronunciation

The consonants are for the most part pronounced broadly as in English, but the following points should be noted: *b, d* and *g* at the end of a syllable are pronounced like *p, t* and *k; c* (rare) and *z* are pronounced *ts; j* is pronounced like consonantal *y; qu* is somewhere between the English *qu* and *kv; s* at the beginning of a syllable is pronounced *z; v* is pronounced *f*, and *w* is pronounced v. The double letter *ch* is pronounced like the Scottish *ch* in "loch" after *a, o* and *u*; after *ä, e, i* and *ü* it is pronounced somewhere between that sound and *sh. Sch* is pronounced *sh*, and *th* (rare) *t*.

The vowels are pronounced without the diphthongisation normal in standard English; before a single consonant they are normally long, before a double consonant short. Note the following: short *a* is like the flat *a* of northern English; *e* may be either closed (roughly as in "pay"), open (roughly as in "pen" or a short unaccented sound like the *e* in "begin" or in "the"; *ä* is like an open *e; u* is like *oo* in "good" (short) or "food" (long); *ö* is like the French *eu*, a little like the vowel in "fur"; *ü*, like the French *u*, can be approximated by pronouncing *ee* with rounded lips.

Diphthongs: *ai* and *ei* similar to *i* in "high"; *au* as in "how"; *eu* and *äu* like *oy; ie* like *ee*.

Numbers

0	null
1	eins
2	zwei
3	drei
4	vier
5	fünf
6	sechs
7	sieben
8	acht
9	neun
10	zehn

11	elf	
12	zwölf	
13	dreizehn	
14	vierzehn	
15	fünfzehn	
16	sechzehn	
17	siebzehn	
18	achtzehn	
19	neunzehn	
20	zwanzig	
21	einundzwanzig	
22	zweiundzwanzig	
30	dreissig	
40	vierzig	
50	fünfzig	
60	sechzig	
70	siebzig	
80	achtzig	
90	neunzig	
100	hundert	
101	hundert eins	
153	hundertdreiundfünfzig	
200	zweihundert	
300	dreihundert	
1000	tausend	
1001	tausend und eins	
1021	tausand einundzwanzig	
2000	zweitausend	
1,000,000	eine Million	
1st	erste	Ordinals
2nd	zweite	
3rd	dritte	
4th	vierte	
5th	fünfte	
6th	sechste	
7th	siebte	
8th	achte	
9th	neunte	
10th	zehnte	
11th	elfte	
20th	zwanzigste	
100th	hundertste	
Sunday	Sonntag	Days of the week
Monday	Montag	
Tuesday	Dienstag	
Wednesday	Mittwoch	
Thursday	Donnerstag	
Friday	Freitag	
Saturday	Samstag, Sonnabend	
Day	Tag	
Public holiday	Feiertag	
Good morning	Guten Morgen	Useful words and phrases
Good day	Guten Tag	
Good evening	Guten Abend	
Good night	Gute Nacht	
Goodbye	Auf Wiedersehen	

Language

Do you speak English?	Sprechen Sie English?
I do not understand	Ich verstehe nicht
Yes	Ja
No	Nein
Pardon	Entschuldigen
May I?	Darf ich?
Please	Bitte
Thank you (very much)	Danke (sehr)
How much?	Wieviel?
What is that?	Was ist das?
When?	Wann?
Where is?	Wo ist?
I need a doctor	Ich brauche einen Arzt

Arrival	Ankunft
Baggage/Luggage	Gepäck
Bill/Check	Rechnung
Departure	Abfahrt, Abflug (aircraft)
Hospital	Krankenhaus
Letter	Brief
Main post office	Hauptpost
Non-smoking	Nichtraucher
Railway station	Bahnhof
Room	Zimmer
Smoking	Raucher
Stamp	Briefmarke
Ticket	Fahrkarte
Today	Heute
Tomorrow	Morgen
Yesterday	Gestern

Glossary

Abfahrt, Abflug (aircraft)	departure
Ankunft	arrival
Bad	bath, spa
Bibliothek	library
Brücke	bridge
Brunnen	fountain
Burg	castle
Denkmal	monument, memorial
Dom	cathedral
Fremdenverkehrs-verband	tourist information office
Gasse	street, lane
Hof	court courtyard
Kirche	church
Kloster	convent, monastery
Platz	square
Rathaus	town hall
Schloss (pl. Schlösser)	castle, palace, country house
Stadt	town, city
Strasse	street, road
Strassenbahn	tram
Vorsicht!	look out
Weinstube	wine-house, wine-bar

Libraries, archives

Archives of the Vienna Philharmonic
1, Bösendorferstrasse 12
Visits only by prior appointment; tel. 6 55 09 72

Library of the Academy of Fine Art
See A to Z
Open: Mon., Wed., Fri. 9 a.m.–4 p.m.; Tue., Thur. 9 a.m.–6 p.m.
For times of opening in July and August tel. 5 88 16-166

Library of the Albertina
See A to Z

Library of the Geologische Bundesanstalt (Federal Geological
Institute)
3, Rasumofskygasse 23
Visits only by prior arrangement; tel. 7 12 56 74-0

Library of the Austrian Federal Railways (Österreichische
Bundesbahnen)
2, Praterstern 3
Open: Mon.–Thur. 9 a.m.–3 p.m., Fri. 9 a.m.–noon

Library of the Armenian Monastery
7, Mechitaristengasse 4
Visits only by prior appointment; tel. 93 64 17-0

Library of the Museum of Art History
See A to Z, Kunsthistorisches Museum

Library of the Literaturhaus
7, Seidengasse 11
(tel. at present 5 86 12 49; opening spring 1991)

Library of the Austrian Museum of Applied Art
See A to Z, Österreichisches Museum für Angewandte Kunst
Open: Mon., Thur., Fri., Sun. 11 a.m.–6 p.m.

Library of the Austrian Folk Museum
See A to Z, Österreichisches Museum für Volkskunde

Library of Parliament
See A to Z

Library of the Technical Museum of Industry and Trade
See A to Z, Technisches Museum für Industrie und Gewerbe

Austrian National Library
See A to Z, Österreichische Nationalbibliothek

Austrian State Archives (Haus- Hof- und Staatsarchiv)
1, Minoritenplatz 1
For visits; tel. 5 31 15-25 16
War archives (Kriegsarchiv): 7, Stiftgasse 2; tel. 93 27 40-0
Transport archives (Verkehrsarchiv): 3, Nottendorfergasse 2;
tel. 78 66 41-0
Central archives (Zentralarchiv): address and telephone as for
Transport Archives

Fruit on sale in the Naschmarkt . . .

University Library (Universitätsbibliothek), 1, Dr. Karl-Lueger-Ring 1
For information on opening times of the reading rooms
tel. 4 30 00

Vienna City and State Archives and Library
(Wiener Stadt- und Landesarchiv bzw. Bibliothek)
1, Lichtenfelsgasse 2 (staircase 6 or 4)
Archives and Library (including the Hans Moser bequest)
Open: Mon.–Thur. 8 a.m.–6 p.m., Fri. 8 a.m.–4 p.m.; closed public holidays

Journal reading room of the Austrian National Library
Basement between the Hofburg and the Burggarten
Open: Mon. and Thur. 9 a.m.–7.45 p.m.; Tue., Wed., Fri.
9 a.m.–3.45 p.m., Sat. 9 a.m.–1 p.m.

Lost property

Central Lost Property Office

9, Wasagasse 22; tel. 3 13 44-0
Underground station (U-Bahn) Schottentor (U 2)
Open: Mon.–Fri. 8 a.m.–1 p.m.

Lost property office
of the railway and the City
Department of Works

Property found on the railway is sent to the central collection point at Vienna West Station of Austrian Railways at Langauerstr. 2; (tel. 58 00-0) S-Bahn Station. Articles left in trams or buses are collected by the Vienna Department of Works (tel. 5 01 30-0) and after three days are transferred to the Central Lost Property Office.

. . . and curios and heirlooms, bric-à-brac and objets d'art

Markets

Markets are open Mon.–Fri. 6 a.m.–6.30 p.m. and Sat. 6 a.m.–1 p.m. Morning is the liveliest time in the Vienna markets with the greatest choice of goods.

Opening times

Augustinermarkt
3, Landstrasser Hauptstr./Erdbergstr.
Buses 74A, 75A from Dr.-Karl-Lueger-Platz

Provision markets

Brunnenmarkt
16, Brunnengasse
Tram J from Karlsplatz

Naschmarkt
See A to Z

Schwendermarkt
15, Schwendergasse/Reichsapfelgasse
Trams 52, 58

Naschmarkt
See A to Z

Flea market

See A to Z, Dorotheum and Practical Information, Antiques

Antiques

207

Medical assistance

Before arrival	Visitors should enquire of the DSS as to the most recent regulations concerning medical assistance in Austria. (See also Insurance.)
Doctor on call	Radio-telephone service (24 hours a day); tel. 141
Consultations	Tel. 1771 (Mon.–Fri. 7 a.m.–7 p.m.)
Emergency dental treatment	Tel. 5 12 20 78 for addresses of dentists on duty

Memorial locations

Gustinus Ambrosi Museum
(Austrian Gallery)
2, Augarten/Scherzergasse 1a
Open: Fri. and Sun. 10 a.m.–4 p.m.
Life and work of the sculptor Gustinus Ambrosi (1893–1957)

Hermann Bahr Memorial Room (at present closed for rearrangement)
1, Hanuschgasse 3
(visit possible by prior arrangement; tel. 5 12 24 27)
Mementoes of the poet Hermann Bahr (1863–1934) and of his wife, the singer Anna Bahr-Mildenburg

Eduard von Bauernfeld Memorial Room
(Döbling local museum in the Villa Wertheimstein
19, Döblinger Hauptstr. 96
Open: Sat. 3.30–6 p.m.; Sun. 10 a.m.–noon
Mementoes of the comic playwright Eduard von Bauernfeld (1802–1890)

Beethoven Memorials
See A to Z, Pasqualatihaus, Heiligenstadt, Beethoven Monument
Other memorial locations:
6, Laimgrubengasse 22
Visits by prior arrangement; tel. 3 71 40 85
Beethoven resided in this house in Laimgrubengasse from 1822–23
"Eroica House": 19, Döblinger Hauptstr. 92
Open: Tue.–Sun. 10 a.m.–12.15 p.m. and 1–4.30 p.m.
Beethoven worked here in 1803–04, especially on his third symphony, the "Eroica". Among the exhibits is the first impression of this work.

Johann Brahms Memorial Room
See A to Z, Haydn Museum

Heimito von Doderer Memorial Room
(Alsergrund local museum)
9, Währinger Str. 43
Open: Wed. 9–11 a.m. and Sun. 10 a.m.–noon
Life and work of the author Heimito von Doderer (1896–1966).

Sigmund Freud Museum
See A to Z

Memorial for the sacrifice of Austrian freedom fighters
See A to Z, Altes Rathaus

Franz Grillparzer Memorial Room
See A to Z, Historisches Museum der Stadt Wien and in the
Hofkammer archives
1, Johannesgasse 6
Open: daily (except Mon.) 9 a.m.–4 30 p.m.
The furniture in Grillparzer's study is original

Haydn Museum
See A to Z

Franz Kafka Memorial
See A to Z, Klosterneuburg

Josef Kainz Memorial Room
1, Hanuschgasse 3
(at present closed for rearrangement)
Visits possible by prior arrangement; tel. 5 12 24 27
Mementoes of the actor Josef Kainz (1858–1910)

Emmerich Kálmán Memorial Room
1, Hanuschgasse 3
(at present closed for rearrangement)
Visits possible by prior arrangement; tel. 5 12 24 27
Mementoes of the composer of operettas Emmerich Kálmán
(1882–1953)

Lehár Museum
See A to Z, Lehár-Schikaneder Castle
Adolf Loos Room
See A to Z Historisches Museum der Stadt Wien

Mozart Memorial Rooms
See A to Z, Figaro House

Caspar Neher Memorial Room
1, Hanuschgasse 3
(at present closed for rearrangement)
Visits possible by prior arrangement; tel. 5 12 24 27
Mementoes of the stage designer Caspar Neher (1897–1962)

Max Reinhardt Memorial Room
1, Hanuschgasse 3
(at present closed for rearrangement)
Visits possible by prior arrangement; tel. 5 12 24 27
Mementoes of the actor Max Reinhardt (1873–1943)

Ferdinand-von-Saar Memorial Room
In the Villa Wertheimstein
(Döbling local museum)
19, Döblinger Hauptstr. 96
Open: Sat. 3.30–6 p.m., Sun. 10 a.m.–noon
Mememtoes of the writer Ferdinand von Saar (1833–1906)

Schubert Museum
See A to Z

Schubert's death chamber
4, Kettenbrückengasse 6
Open: Tue.–Sun. 10 a.m.–12.15 p.m. and 1–4.30 p.m.
The Vienna History Museum has furnished the rooms in which
Franz Schubert spent his last days as a memorial for him and
his brother Ferdinand who was also a composer.

Adalbert Stifter Museum
See A to Z, Pasqualatihaus

Johann Strauss House
See A to Z, Praterstrasse

Richard Teschner Memorial Room
Move planned from Hanuschgasse 3 to the Palais Lobkowitz, 1,
Lobkowitzplatz 2. Information: tel 5 12 24 27
Mementoes (c. 200 exhibits) of the painter, graphic artist and
puppeteer Richard Teschner (1879–1948)

Hugo Thimig Memorial Room
1, Hanuschgasse 3 (at present closed for rearrangement)
Visits possible by prior arrangement; tel. 5 12 24 27
Mementoes of the actor Hugo Thimig (1854–1944)

Otto Wagner House
7, Döblergasse 4
Open: Mon.–Fri. 9 a.m.–noon
(From July–Sept. by arrangement only; tel. 93 22 33)
Otto Wagner (1841–1918) was one of the most celebrated Aus-
trian architects.

Carl Michael Ziehrer Memorial Room
1, Hanuschgasse 3 (at present closed for rearrangement)
Visits possible by prior arrangement; tel. 5 12 24 27
Mementoes of the operetta composer Carl Michael Ziehrer
(1843–1922)

Motoring

Automobile clubs	ÖAMTC (Österreichischer Automobil-, Motorrad- und Touring-Club)
	Schubertring 1–3, A-1010 Wien
	Tel. 7 11 99-0; Breakdown: tel. 120
	ARBÖ (Auto-, Motor- und Radfahrerbund Österreichs)
	Mariahilferstr. 180, A-1150 Wien
	Tel. 85 35 35-0; Breakdown: tel. 123
Road conditions report	ÖAMT traffic news service (daily): tel. 15 90
	Brief information is broadcast at weekends on Austrian radio (Ö3) and daily update on road conditions in the radio programme "Autofahrer unterwegs" (Ö2) from 11.30/12 until 12.45/1 p.m. Information about obstructions and road closures is broadcast during normal programmes.
Traffic Regulations	Generally traffic regulations in Austria are similar to those in other countries in western Europe where vehicles travel on the

right. Information about toll-roads and additional tolls for caravans and trailers can be obtained from the motoring organisations (see above).

On motorways the speed limit for cars is 130km.p.h./80m.p.h., but 70km.p.h./43m.p.h. if towing. On all other main roads the maximum permitted speed is 100km.p.h./62m.p.h. for cars and motorcycles, but only 60km.p.h./37m.p.h. if towing a weight above 3.5 tonnes. In built-up areas the speed limit for all vehicles is 50km.p.h./31m.p.h. and the use of the horn is not permitted.

Speed limits

Lead-free normal (91 octane), lead-free super (Euro-Super 95 octane; not available everywhere), leaded super (98 octane) and diesel are available.

Petrol (gasoline) and diesel oil

The maximum permitted blood alcohol level is 0.8 pro mille

Drinking and driving

Seat-belts must be worn by drivers and front-seat passengers, and, when fitted in the vehicle, also by passengers in the rear seats. Failure to observe this regulation may lead to a fine. Children under twelve years of age may not travel in the front seat.

Seat-belts

A red triangle must be carried in the vehicle in case of breakdown.

Warning triangle

Motorcyclists and moped riders must wear a helmet and they must also carry a small first-aid kit and use dipped headlights at all times.

Helmets

Studded tyres and sometimes snow-chains are required for journeys in winter.

Winter equipment

From 15th December until 31st March parking in Vienna is prohibited from 8 p.m. to 5 a.m. on all streets where there are tram-lines, in order to facilitate clearing when there has been a heavy snowfall. Parking in designated short-stay zones (city centre, Mariahilfer Strasse, squares outside the Town Hall (Rathaus), stations and airport) is limited to 1½ hours from 8 a.m. until 6 p.m.; vehicles parked in these places must bear a parking disc. Parking tickets for 30, 60 and 90 minutes can be obtained from the ticket offices of the Vienna transport authority, from filling stations, tobacconists and from some branches of banks. Cancellation of parking tickets is effected by an indication of date and hour when the vehicles is parked (control is strict).

Parking

Parked vehicles causing serious obstruction to traffic are liable to be towed away. A visitor who discovers that the vehicle is no longer in the place where it has been parked will probably find it in the 10th district at Elbesbrunnengasse 9, where it can be recovered Mon.–Fri. 7 a.m.–3 p.m. Outside these times application should be made to the Magistratsabteilung (magistrates' department) 48, 5, Einsiedlergasse 2.

Vehicles towed away

Museums

Note	Admission to the municipal museums (marked (M) in the list below) is free on Friday mornings; to the state museums (marked (S)) it is free on the first Sunday in the month.
Museum pass	By purchasing a museum pass (14 coupons valid at any time and transferable; obtainable in the museums) the admission fee is reduced by almost 30% for all these museums.
Project	Reorganisation of the former trade fair exhibition hall will eventually provide the opportunity to present modern or contemporary art in an appropriate setting, for example in anticipation of the world exhibition in 1995 in Vienna.
Academy of Fine Arts	See A to Z, Akademie der Bildenden Künste
"Adler" Collection	See A to Z, Haarhof Heraldic and Genealogical exhibits
Adalbert-Stifter Museum (M)	See A to Z, Pasqualatihaus
Albertina Graphic Collection (S)	See A to Z, Albertina
Anatomia Plastica Collection	See A to Z, Josephinum
Armenian Monastic Museum of the Mechitharists	Armenisches Klostermuseum der Mechitharisten 7, Mechitharistengasse 4 (Neustiftgasse/Lerchenfelder Str.) Visits by prior arrangement; tel. 93 64 17-0
Art Gallery in the Stallburg	See A to Z, Neue Galerie in der Stallburg
Austrian Baroque Museum (S)	See A to Z, Belvedere-Schlösser, Österreichisches Barockmuseum
Austrian Film Museum (S)	See A to Z, Albertina
Austrian Folk Museum	See A to Z, Österreichisches Museum für Volkskunde
Austrian Museum of Applied Art (S)	See A to Z, Österreichisches Museum für Angewandte Kunst
Austrian Railway Museum (S)	See A to Z, Technisches Museum für Industrie und Gewerbe
Austrian Theatre Museum (at present closed)	Move planned to the Palais Lobkowitz, 1, Lopkowitzplatz 2
Beethoven Museum	See A to Z, Pasqualatihaus
Carnuntum Open-air Museum	See A to Z, Carnuntum
Cathedral and Diocesan Museum	See A to Z, Dom- und Diözesanmuseum
Clock Museum (M)	See A to Z, Uhrenmuseum der Stadt Wien
Collection of Old Musical Instruments (at present closed)	See A to Z, Sammlung alter Musikinstrumente
Collection of Popular Religious Art	See A to Z, Sammlung religiöser Volkskunst
Collection of Wagons	See A to Z, Schönbrunn

See A to Z, Waffensammlung	Collection of Weapons
See entry	Commemorative locations
See A to Z, Hofburg	Court Tableware and Silver Collection
Döblinger Bezirksmuseum 98 Döblinger Hauptstr. 96 Open: Sat. 3.30–6 p.m., Sun 10 a.m.–noon Biedermeier villa with commemorative rooms for Bauernfeld, the comic poet, and Ferdinand von Saar, the lyric poet. Also wine museum.	Döblinger Regional Museum
Puppen- und Spielzeugmuseum (Vaclav Sladky/D. B. Polzer) 1, Schulhof 4/first floor Open: Tue.–Sun. 10 a.m.–6 p.m. Private collection of dolls-houses and over 600 dolls from 1830–1930.	Doll and Toy Museum
See A to Z, Ephesos-Museum	Ephesus Museum (S)
See A to Z, Österreichische Nationalbibliothek	Esperanto Museum
See A to Z, Bundessammlung Alter Stilmöbel	Federal Collection of Period Furniture (S)
9, Spitalgasse 2 (in "Narrenturm" General Hospsital) Conducted tours Thur. 8–11 a.m. (closed public holidays and August)	Federal Pathological Anatomical Museum
See A to Z, Fiakermuseum	Fiaker Museum
See A to Z, Figarohaus	Figaro House
See A to Z, Albertina	Film Museum (S)
See A to Z, Am Hof	Fire Brigade Museum
In the Prater Stadium, 2, Meiereistr.; tel. 597-15 36 45 Open: Mon. and Fri. 10 a.m.–1 p.m., Tue. and Thur. 2–6 p.m.	Football Museum
See A to Z, Sigmund-Freud-Museum	Freud Museum
14, Hüttelbergstr. 26 Open: Mar.–Oct. by prior arrangement; tel. 94 85 75 The extraordinary realist Ernst Fuchs (b. 1930) restored in its original form the first Art Nouveau villa built by Otto Wagner and exhibited in it his own works.	Fuchs Private Museum
Bestattungsmuseum, 4, Goldeggasse 19 By prior appointment only: tel. 5 01 95–227; Mon.–Fri. noon– 3 p.m.	Funeral Museum
See A to Z, Belvedere-Schlösser	Gallery of Austrian Art of the 19th and 20th c. (S)
See A to Z, Neue Galerie in the Stallburg	Gallery of the 19th and 20th c. in the Stallburg
See A to Z, Österreichische Nationalbibliothek	Globe Museum
See A to Z	Haydn Museum

Museums

Hermes Villa   See A to Z, Lainzer Tiergarten (zoo)

Hernalser Regional   Hernalser Bizirkmuseum, 17, Hernalser Hauptstr. 72–74
Museum   Open: Mon. 4–8 p.m. (closed July and Aug.)
                                       History of the Hernal District.

House of the Sea   Haus des Meeres (Vivarium Wien)
                                       6 Esterházypark
                                       Open: daily 9 a.m.–6 p.m.
                                       About 3,000 living animals; particularly impressive are the
                                       tropical and Mediterranean aquariums.

Josefstadt Regional   See A to Z, Josefstädter Bizirksmuseum
Museum

Jewish Museum   1, Seitenstettengasse 4; tel. 5 31 04-0
                                       Open: Sun.–Thur. 10 a.m.–5 p.m.

Lehár Museum   See A to Z, Lehár-Schlössl

Leopoldstädter Regional   2, Karmelitergasse 9; tel. 33 16 11-229
Museum   Cultural history of the region.

Mozart Museum (M)   See A to Z, Figarohaus

Museum of Army History   See A to Z, Heeregeschichtliches Museum

Museum of Art History   See A to Z, Kunsthistorisches Museum

Museum of Austrian Art of   See A to Z, Belvedere Schlösser
the Middle Ages (S)

Museum of the Austrian   See A to Z, Altes Rathaus
Freedom Struggle

Museum of the Austrian   Österreichisches Sprachinselmuseum
Linguistic Enclave   18, Semperstr. 29
                                       Open: only by appointment; tel. 3 10 19 85
                                       History of the language and culture of Austria and of the old
                                       Austrian linguistic enclave.

Museum of Clowns and   Zirkus- und Clownmuseum
Circuses   2, Karmelitergasse 9
                                       Open: Wed. 5.30–7 p.m., Sat. 2.30–5 p.m., Sun. 10 a.m.–noon

Museum of Ethnology (S)   See A to Z, Museum für Völkerkundez

Museum of Farriery and   Museum für Hufbeschlag, Beschirrung and Besattlung
Saddlery   3, Linke Bahngasse 11
                                       Open: Mon.–Thur. 1.30–3.30 p.m.
                                       Educational collection and workshop.

Museum of the Institute of   See A to Z, Josephinum
Medical History

Museum of Modern Art (S)   See A to Z, Gartenpalais, Liechtenstein

Museum of the State of   See A to Z, Niederösterreichisches Landesmuseum
Lower Austria

Museum of the 20th c.   See A to Z, Museum des 20. Jahrhunderts (temporary
                                       exhibitions)

Natural History Museum (S)   See A to Z, Naturhistorisches Museum

See A to Z, Graben	Neidhart Frescoes (M)
See A to Z, Josefstädter Bezirksmuseum	Old Bakehouse
See A to Z, Schönlaterngasse	Old Smithy
Glockenmuseum (Glockensammlung Pfundner) 10, Troststr. 38 Open: Wed. 2–5 p.m. Old church bells	Pfundner Bell Collection
See A to Z, Schottenstift	Picture Gallery of the Schottenstift
See A to Z, Prater	Planetarium
See A to Z, Technisches Museum für Industrie and Gewerbe	Post and Telegraphic Museum (S)
See A to Z, Prater	Prater Museum (S)
See A to Z, Am Hof	Pfundner Bell Collection
See A to Z, Hohermarkt	Roman Ruins (M)
See A to Z, Schubert Museum See Practical Information, Commemorative Locations	Schubert Museum
See A to Z, Secession	Secession (S)
See A to Z, Hofburg	Secular and Sacred Treasury
See A to Z, Gaymüller-Schlössl	Sobek Collection of Old Viennese Clocks (S)
See A to Z, Pasqualatihaus	Stifter Musueum
See A to Z, Technisches Museum für Industrie and Gewerbe	Technical Museum of Industry and Trade (S)
See A to Z, Maria-Theresien-Platz	Tobacco Museum
See A to Z, Deutschordenshaus	Treasury of the German Order
1, Uranis-Str. a Conducted tours on clear nights: Wed., Fri. and Sat. 8 p.m. (Apr.–Sept. 9 p.m.), Sun. 11 a.m. (closed in Aug.).	Urania Observatory
See A to Z, Historisches Museum der Stadt Wien	Vienna City Historical Museum (M)
The Erdberg Depot of the Vienna Transport Undertaking 3, Erdbergstr. 109 Open: May–Oct. Sat., Sun., public holidays, 9 a.m.–4 p.m. Trips by "Oldtimer Tram" (May–Sept.) from Karlsplatz, Sat. 2.30 p.m., Sun. and public holidays 10 a.m. The oldest exhibit in the museum is a horse-drawn tram of 1871.	Vienna Tram Museum
Kunstforum Wien der Österreichischen Länderbank 1, Freyung 8; tel. 5 31 24-47 45 Open: daily 10 a.m.–6 p.m., Wed. until 9 p.m. Notable temporary exhibitions	Viennese Art Forum of the Austrian Provincial Bank
Wiener Glasmuseum (Lobmeyr) 1, Kärntner Str. 26; tel. 5 12 05 08 Open: Mon.–Fri. 1–6 p.m., Sat. 9 a.m.–1 p.m.	Viennese Glass Museum

Music

Virgilian Chapel (M)	See A to Z, Stephansplatz, Virgilkapelle (collection of historical Viennese porcelain).
Wine Museum	See Döblinger Regional Museum (above)
Commemorative Locations	See entry

Music

Forthcoming programme — The Vienna Tourist Board (Wiener Fremdenverkehrsverband; see Information) publishes monthly a free survey of musical events (see Events).

Tickets — See Advance Booking, except where otherwise stated.

Opera/Ballet —
State Opera
See A to Z, Staatsoper

Theater im Künstlerhaus
1, Karlsplatz 5

Volksoper
9, Währinger Str. 78

Wiener Kammeroper
1, Fleischmarkt 24
Tickets direct from the theatre; tel. 5 12 01 00

Operetta/Musicals —
Theater an der Wien
6, Linke Wienzeile 6
Computerised ticket sales (Vienna Events Service; WVS) for productions in this theatre:
Wiener Stadthalle, Vogelweidplatz 14
A-1150 Wien; tel. 95 49-0
Tickets for the same day from bank branches signed with WVS, such as the Zentralsparkasse, Die Erste and Creditanstalt (1, Kärntner Ring 1, Schottengasse 6-8).

Raimundtheater: 6, Wallgasse 18–20
Ronacher: 1, Seilerstätte/Himmelpfortgasse 9
Advance booking for both these theatres from:
Vienna Tickets Service, Box 160,
Linke Wienzeile 4/1/3
A-1060 Wien; tel. 5 87 98 43

Concert Halls —
Funkhaus des Österreichischen Rundfunks (studios of Austrian Radio)
(Concerts, broadcasts with an audience)
Argentinierstr. 30a
A-1040 Wien
Tickets: in advance from the above address or by telephone 5 01 01-881 (Mon.–Fri. 4–7 p.m.)

Konzerthaus, 3, Lothringer Str. 20
Great Hall, Mozart Hall, Schubert Hall; orchestral music, solo-
ists and chamber music.
Tickets: in advance by telephone 7 12 12 11 (Mon.–Fri. 9 a.m.–
6 p.m., Sat. 9 a.m.–noon)

Musikverein
See A to Z, Musikvereinsgebäude

Bösendorfer Saal
4, Graf-Starhemberg-Gasse 14; tel. 65 66 51

Engelmayer, Bechstein-Saal
4, Schönburgstr. 27; tel. 65 74 32

Haydn-Haus
6, Haydngasse 19

Urania
1, Uraniastrasse; tel. 72 61 91

Augustinerkirche   Church Music
1, Augustinerstr. 3; tel. 5 33 70 99 and 5 33 80 00
Sun. 11 a.m.: High Mass; in July and Aug. with organ;
from end June to middle September, Fri. 6.30 p.m.: International Organ Festival

Burgkapelle
See A to Z, Hofburg

Karlskirche
4, Karlsplatz; tel. 65 61 87
From beginning May to end Sept. Sun. 7.30 p.m.: organ/church
music

Michaelerkirche (St Michael)
See A to Z, Michaelerkirche
Tickets: tel. 5 33 70 50 and 5 33 80 00

Stephansdom (St Stephen's Cathedral)
1, Stephansplatz (tel. 5 15 52-530)
See A to Z, Stephansdom
Sun. and public holidays (except in July and Aug.) 10 a.m. High
Mass

St Barbara (Ukrainian-Greek Orthodox Parish Church)
1, Postgasse 8; tel. 5 12 21 33
Sun. and public holidays 10 a.m. (July/Aug. 9 a.m.) High Mass

Collegiate Church of Heiligenkreuz (tel. 0 22 58/22 82)
See A to Z, Heiligenkreuz
Sun. 9.45 a.m. Latin Mass with choir of monks

Collegiate Church of Klosterneuburg (tel. 0 22 43/62 10)
See A to Z, Klosterneuburg
Telephone for information about High Masses

Universitätskirche
1, Dr.-Ignaz-Seipel-Platz 1
Tel. 5 12 52 32-0 and 5 12 13 35-0
Major festival days: 10 a.m. Mass with orchestra with "Con-
sortium Musicum Alte Universität"

Votivkirche
9, Rooseveltplatz 8
Tel. 43 11 92. From mid-May to mid-Sept., Fri., Sat. 7.30 p.m.
synthesiser concerts, also church concerts

Jazz/Live music   See Nightlife

Festivals   See Festivals, see Events

Nightlife

Bermuda Triangle   This is the name which the Viennese have given to the nightlife
                        district between the Cathedral and the Danube, in the area of
                        Schönlaterngasse and Bäckerstrasse (see A to Z) and extend-
                        ing to St Ruprecht's Church. Anyone who "dives" into a night-
                        club here will disappear and not remember anything of his
                        experiences when he finally emerges into the daylight!

Popular night-spots   Alt-Wien, 1, Bäckerstr. 9
                        Amadeus, 15, Märzstr. 4
                        Apropos, 1, Rufolfsplatz 12
                        Bora-Bora, 1, Johannesgasse 12
                        Bräunerhof (gallery café with music and literature),
                        1, Stallburggasse 2
                        Café Bar in the Wiener Secession, 1, Friedrichstr. 12
                        Düsenberg, 1, Stubenring 4
                        Freihaus, 4, Margaretenstr. 11/Schleifmühlgasse 7
                        Hawelka, 1, Dorotheergasse 6
                        Kleines Café, 1, Franziskanerplatz 3
                        Krah Krah, 1, Rabensteig 8
                        Landtmann, 1, Dr.-Karl-Lueger-Ring 4
                        Mozart & Meisl, 19, Gymnasiumstr. 62
                        New Yorker, 1, Biberstr. 9
                        Oswald & Kalb, 1, Bäckerstr. 14
                        Pastaron Nudelwerkstätte, 1, Jasomirgottstr. 3
                        Pronto – Beisolo Italiano, 1, Spiegelgasse 2
                        Vincent, 2, Grosse Pfarrgasse 7
                        Wiener Stamperl, 1, Sterngasse 1
                        Zum Bettlestudent, 1, Johannesgasse 12

Jazz and Live Music   Blue Tomatoe, 15, Wurmser Gasse 21
                        Casablanca, 11, Goldschlagstr. 2
                        Chelsea, 8, Piaristengasse 1
                        Jazzland, 1, Franz-Josefs-Kai 29
                        Jazz Leitl, 16, Habichergasse 15
                        Jazz-Spelunke, 6, Dürergasse 3
                        Miles Smiles, 8, Lange Gasse 51
                        Opus One, 1, Mahlerstr. 11
                        Papa's Tapas, 4, Schwarzenbergplatz 10
                        Queen Anne, 1, Johannesgasse 12
                        Wortner, 4, Wiedner Hauptstr. 55

Folk   Nashville, 5, Siebenbrunnengasse 5a

Latin-American Music   Arauco, 3, Krummgasse 1a
                        Club America Latina, 6, Mollardgasse 17
                        Rincon Andino, 6, Münzwardeingasse 2

Blackpot, 1, Bartensteingasse 4   Reggae

Atoll (summer disco), Copa Cagrana (Danube Island)   Discos and Dancing
Atrium, 4, Schwindgasse 1
Can-Can, 9, Währinger Gürtel 96
Celentano, 1, Seilerstätte 1
Chattanooga, 1, Graben 29
Club Take Five, 1, Annagasse 3a
Crazy Cats (show disco), 1, Kärntner Str. 61
Gerard, 8, Lederergasse 11
Golden Gate, 3, Beatrixgasse 6
Jack Daniels, 1, Krugerstr. 6
Kistl, 8, Langegasse 61
Lord's Club, 1, Karlsplatz 1
Montevideo, 1, Annagasse 3a
Move, 8, Daungasse 1
Na Nou, 13, Testarellogasse 37
Pago Pago, 22, Steinspornbrücke/Am Damm
Pallas, 2, Taborstr. 36
P1, 1, Rotgasse 3
Piano Express, Handelskai 127
Queen Anne, 1, Johannesgasse 12
Safari Lodge (summer disco), at the Steinspornbrücke
Santana, 15, Avedikstr. 1
Savanna, 4, Mayerhofgasse 2
Schickeria-Treff (Evergreens/Oldies), 7 Burggasse 101
Starlight, 22, Rafineriestr./Lobgrundstr.
Tanzcafé Volksgarten, 1, Volksgarten (May–September in the open air)
Tenne, 1, Annagasse 3
Terrassencafé, 19, Cobenzlgasse 11
Triangel, 1, Wiessingerstr. 8
U4, 12, Schönbrunner Str. 222
Wake up, 1, Seilerstätte 5
Why not, 1, Tiefer Graben 22
Wurlitzer Jukebox Dancing, 4, Schwarzenbergplatz 4

Alcazar, 1, Bösendorferstr. 2   Bars
Alexander-Girardi-Bar (Hotel Ananas), 5, Rechte Wienzeile
Atrium Bar (Hotel de France), 1, Schottenring 3
Bellini-Bar, 1, Makartgasse 1
Biedermeier-Bar, 3, Landstrasser Hauptstr. 28 and Ungargasse 13
Bijou-Bar (Parkhotel Schönbrunn), 13 Hietzinger Hauptstr. 10–20
Bora-Bora, 1, Johannesgasse 12
Bristol Bar, 1, Kärntner Ring 1
Chamäleon Cocktail-Bar, 1, Blutgasse 3
Cascade Bar (Marriott), 1, Parkring 12a
Eden-Bar, 1, Lillengasse 2
Fledermaus, 1, Spiegelgasse 2
Hannes Bar (Hotel König von Ungarn), 1, Schulerstr. 10
Himmelpforte, 1, Himmelpfortgasse 24
Intermezzo-Bar (Inter-Continental, Wien), 3, Johannesgasse 28
Klimt-Bar (Hilton), 3, in the Stadtpark
La tou tou Bar (Trend-Hotel), 10, Kurbadstr. 8
Makart-Bar (SAS), 1, Weihburggasse 32
Maria Theresia (Imperial), 1, Kärntner Ring 16
Martini-Bar (Hotel Europa), 1, Neuer Markt 3

	Porta, 1, Schulerstr. 6 Reiss-Champagner-Treff, 1, Marco-d'Aviano-Gasse 1 Salle de la Fontaine (Barockbar), 15, Schweglerstr. 37
Night spots	Casanova-Revue-Bar-Theater, 1, Dorotheergasse 6–8 Chez Nous, 1, Kärntner Durchgang/Kärntner Str. 10 Eve-Bar-Cabaret, 1, Führichgasse 3 Moulin Rouge, 1, Walfischgasse 11 Renz, 2, Zirkusgasse 50 Variété Maxim, 1, Opernring 11
Casino	Cercle, 1, Kärntner Str. 41 (Palais Esterházy) Open: daily from 3 p.m.

Opening times

Banks	Mon.–Fri. 8 a.m.–12.30 p.m. and 1.30–3 p.m. (Thur. until 5.30 p.m.); for further information see Currency
Chemists	See entry
Museums, etc.	Since there are no common opening hours for museums (see entry) or other places of interest (see Vienna A–Z under the appropriate heading) it is advisable to telephone for information before setting out to visit a particular place. Opening times for Sundays generally also apply to public holidays (see entry). Most museums and collections, however, are closed on 1st Jan., Good Friday, Easter Sunday, 1st May, Whitsunday, Corpus Christi, 1st/2nd November and on 24th/25th December.
Post	Post-office counters are open Mon.–Fri. 8 a.m.–noon and 2–6 p.m. The main post office (Hauptpostamt) at 1 Fleischmarkt 19 and all post offices at railway stations are open daily day and night.
Shops	Mon.–Fri. 8.30 or 9 a.m.–6 p.m., Sat. 9 a.m.–noon (Outside the inner city shops are closed between noon and 2 or 3 p.m.) Food shops often open before 8 a.m. and close at 6.30 p.m., but close for lunch between 12.30 and 3 p.m.
Extended opening hours for shops	Thur. until 8 p.m. or on 1st Sat. in month until 5 p.m.
Shopping in the evening and on Sun.	See Shopping

Police

	Federal Police Headquarters of Vienna (Bundespolizeidirektion Wien 1, Schottenring 7-9 Tel. 3 13 10-0
	District Police Headquarters (Bezirkspolizeikommissariat) Inner City 1, Deutschmeisterplatz 3 Tel. 31 76 01
Emergencies	Tel. 133 (24 hours a day)

Postal services

See Opening times   Post offices

As well as from post offices stamps are obtainable from   Stamps
machines outside most post offices and from tobacconists.

Letters up to 20 grammes within Austria: 4 ÖS   Postal rates
To the United Kingdom: 7 ÖS
To the United States and Canada: 9 ÖS (plus 1.50 ÖS per 5
grammes for airmail)
Postcards within Austria: 2.50 ÖS
To the United Kingdom: 5 ÖS
To the United States and Canada: 7.50 ÖS

On Saturdays only newspapers are delivered, so that delays in   Deliveries
receiving mail at weekends must be expected.

Telegrams can be sent by telephone (190) or from the central   Telegrams
telegram office at 1, Börseplatz 1.

Programme of events

The Press and Information Service of Vienna and the Vienna
Tourist Board issue a comprehensive programme every month
of events at the theatres, galleries, museums, etc. The monthly
programme is also printed in the "Guide Book – sag Servus in
Wien". The cultural magazine "Falter" contains a prospectus
covering two weeks of exhibitions, festivals, etc. The Austrian
Airlines brochures "Winter Szene Wien" and "Sommer Szene
Wien", and the magazine "Rendezvous Wien" published quar-
terly by the Vienna Tourist Board also give advance
information.

Public holidays

1st January (New Year), 6th January (Epiphany), Easter Monday, 1st May (Labour Day), Ascension Day, Whit Monday, Corpus Christi, 15th August (Assumption), 26th October (National
Holiday), 1st November (All Saints), 8th December (Annunciation), 25th and 26th December (Christmas).

Public transport

All local means of transport run by the Vienna Transport Au-   Local transport
thority, the regional trains of Austrian Railways and the trains

of the Wiener Lokalbahnen (WLB, Badner Bahn – Vienna local railways) as well as the federal buses and private buses are incorporated in the Verkehrsverbund Ost Region (VOR; 7, Neubaugasse 1; tel. 5 26 60 48). On every section of this 1,600km/ 994 mile-long network the same tickets can be used. The central zone (Zone 100) covers the City of Vienna.

Information offices

Customer service office of the Vienna Transport Authority:
Favoritenstr. 9–11, A-1040 Wien
Tel. 5 01 30-23 57 and 23 59 (Mon.–Fri. 8 a.m.–3 p.m.;, also
U-Bahn Station Karlsplatz; tel. 5 87 31 86 (Mon.–Fri. 7 a.m.–
6 p.m.; Sat., Sun. and public holidays 8.30 a.m.–4 p.m.
U-Bahn Station Stephansplatz; tel. 5 12 42 27, (Mon.–Fri.
8 a.m.–6 p.m.; Sat., Sun. and public holidays 8.30 a.m.–4 p.m.
U-Bahn Station Praterstern; tel. 24 93 02, (Mon.–Fri. 8 a.m.–
6 p.m.)
U-Bahn Station Philadelphiabrücke; tel. 8 13 84 01 (Mon.–Fri.
8 a.m.–6 p.m.)

Buses

From the Wien-Mitte bus station (3, Landstrasser Hauptstrasse 1b) regular bus routes serve all the regions around Vienna. (For information tel. 7501.)

City buses

City buses operate on weekdays in the Inner City on four routes:
1 A: Schottentor–Landstrasse (Wien Mitte)–Schottentor
2 A: Dr.-Karl-Renner-Ring–Schwedenplatz–Dr.-Karl-Renner-Ring
3 A: Schottenring–Schwarzenbergplatz–Schottenring
4 A: Karlsplatz–Rasumofskygasse–Karlsplatz

Night buses

In the nights of Fri.–Sat., Sat.–Sun. and the nights preceding public holidays night buses operate between 12.30 and 4 a.m. The central departure point is Schwedenplatz. Tickets can only be obtained from the machines in the night buses and passengers are allowed to change on to other routes.
Line N 1: Kagran–Leopoldau
Line N 2: Floridsdorf–Grossjedlersdorf
Line N 3: Währing–Döbling
Line N 4: Penzing–Ottakring – Hernals
Line N 5: Meidling–Hietzing
Line N 6: Meidling–Erlaa
Line N 7: Favoriten–Wienerfeld
Line N 8: Simmering–Kaiserebersdorf

Trams

The most important routes for visitors are:
1: Circular Ring-Kai; Schwedenplatz–Julius Raab Platz
2: Circular Ring-Kai; Schottentor – Dr.-Karl-Lueger-Platz–Schwarzenbergplatz–Schottentor–Karlsplatz–Oper

31: Schottenring–Stammersdorf
38: Schottenring–Grinzing
46: Dr.-Karl-Renner-Ring–Joachimsthalerplatz
58: Burgring–Unter-St-Veit, Hummelgasse
62: Karlsplatz–Lainz, Wolkersbergenstrasse
67: Otto-Probst-Platz–Kurzentrum Oberlaa

D: Nussdoorf–Schottenring–Südbahnhof
J: Ottakring (Erdbrustgasse)–Karlsplatz
N: Floridsdorfer Brücke–Prater
O: Praterstern–Raxstrasse

At present the following lines are in operation :

U-Bahn (Underground)
Plan on page 248

U1: Zentrum Kagran–Reumannplatz
U2: Karlsplatz–Schottenring
U4: Heiligenstadt–Hütteldorf
U6: Meidling–Heiligenstadt/Friedensbrücke

Otto Wagner's Stadtbahn is now incorporated in the Vienna Underground network

Stadtbahn (City Railway)

Route: Oper–Vösendorf-Siebenhirten–Josefsplatz in Baden bei Wien

Badener Bahn

S1: Gänserndorf–Floridsdorf–Meidling–Baden–Wiener Neustadt
S2: Mistelbach–Gerasdorf–Leopoldau–Südbahnhof–Mödling
S3: Holabrunn–Floridsdorf–Meidling–West Bahnhof/Hütteldorf
S7: Praterstern–Wolfsthal
S40/R40: Franz-Josefs-Bahnhof–Tulln Stadt
S45: Hütteldorf–Penzing–Heiligenstadt
S50/R50: Westbahnhof–Neulengbach
S60/R60/R61: Südbahnhof–Neusiedl am See
S80/R80/R20: Südbahnhof–Hausfeldstrasse

Schnellbahn (S) – Express railway
and the most important connections
with the regional railway (R)

The "Vorortelinie" (suburban line) between the districts of Hütteldorf and Döbling, which was reopened only in 1987 for passenger traffic, can almost be called a "sight". Its bridges and tunnels and especially its stations were designed by Otto Wagner as an architectural unity in pure Art Nouveau style.

"Vorortelinie"
Hütteldorf–Döbling

For the local transport detailed above there is a single tariff (changing of trains permitted; for children's fares see below). It is advisable to purchase tickets in advance (advance ticket offices of the Vienna Transport Authority and tobacconists), since in the vehicles and at ticket machines only single tickets with a supplement are obtainable.
For tourists the following types of ticket should be mentioned: Single tickets (cheaper if bought in advance in blocks of five); network tickets "24 Stunden Wien" and "72 Stunden Wien" which are valid from the time of the first journey for 24 or 72 hours in the central tariff zone (Zone 100); the "8-day environmental ticket" which permits the holder to travel anywhere within the central zone on 8 freely chosen days. Weekly, monthly and annual season tickets are also obtainable.

Tariff

For short journeys without changing there are short-journey tickets at half price (HP); they are valid only within the central zone in trams, on the Baden line, in buses marked with an "A" as well as the regional bus routes mentioned in the VOR timetables.

On the U-Bahn, the Stadtbahn and railways (except the Süd-bahnhof–Meidling line) within the city boundaries a passenger can travel for two stations with one strip of the HP card.
A blue sign indicates that a tram or bus has no conductor. Passengers must purchase their tickets from the driver (entrance at front) or beforehand and must personally cancel them at the machine in the vehicle.
All tickets of the common tariff are valid on buses marked "B" but no tickets are sold in the vehicle. There are no short journey tickets. Tickets may be bought for journeys not involving a change.
All trams and buses stop at stops marked in red; those marked in blue are request stops. In vehicles without a conductor pas-sengers wishing to alight must press the stop signal.

Children's fares

Children under 7 are carried free; those between 7 and 16 may travel free on all Sundays and public holidays and during the school holidays. At other times they can obtain strip-tickets in advance at half-price for 4 or 8 journeys (proof of age may be demanded).

Radio and television

ORF (Austrian radio/television) currently broadcast on two tele-vision and four radio stations.

Radio

Ö1: 514 m, 92 MHz
Ö2: 89.9 MHz
Ö3: 99.9 and 103.8 MHz
The fourth programme is "Radio Österreich International" broadcasting on short-wave (44 m, 6155 MHz) throughout the 24 hours.
Vienna City Radio broadcasts information about the town daily from 2.05–4 p.m.

Information on BBC overseas radio transmissions in English may be obtained from BBC External Services, PO Box 76, Bush House, London WC2B 4PH.

Television

The two television channels, FS1 and FS2, transmit the main news programme "Zeit im Bild" at 7.30 p.m.
There is also a satellite programme 3sat which is a common production of all the major transmitting companies.

Railways

West Station

The Westbahnhof is the terminus of the lines serving the west of Austria, Germany, Switzerland, France, Belgium and the Netherlands. The U6 Underground runs from the West Station to Meidling or Heiligenstadt, the U4 from Längenfeldgasse to the Ring. An airport bus service runs to and from the West Station.

South/East Station

The Südbahnhof/Ostbahnhof is the terminus of lines serving the south of Austria, Italy, Yugoslavia, Greece and Hungary. The U1 runs from the South Station to Karlsplatz and Stephans-platz; the Express line (Schnellbahn) runs to Meidling and

Wien-Mitte; tram 18 goes to Stadionbrücke and Wien-Mitte. There is a bus service from the station to the airport.

This station is the terminus for trains to and from northern Austria, Czechoslovakia and Berlin. U4 runs from the station (Friedensbrücke) to Schottenring and Heiligenstadt; tram D serves the inner city and the Ring.

Franz-Josefs Station

Central Information Office (open throughout the 24 hours); tel. 17 17
Services using the West Station; tel. 15 52
Services using the South Station; tel. 15 53

Train information

The "Städteschnellzüge" (city expresses) provide an excellent service ("Austro-Takt") to the principal towns in the country. For example trains leave every hour for Salzburg and Graz, and every two hours for Villach and Innsbruck. For information about "nostalgic trips" tel. 58 00-3 22 00.

Rail services within Austria

With a network season ticket (valid for a month or a year) the holder may use any train or bus of Austrian Railways or private railways as often as desired at favourable rates (50% reduction on DDSG ships). Young people up to the age of 26 who purchase a "Rabbit Card Junior" can make any journey on four days freely chosen from an availability of ten. There are other reduced fares, including the "Nahverkehrs-Rückfahrkarte" (local return ticket), regional network tickets (for example to the wine producing areas), "Kilometerbank" and tickets for small groups.

Reduced-fare tickets

Recreational areas

Böhmischer Prater (Bohemian prater)
Tram 67, bus 15A
A corner of old Vienna in an extensive recreational area on the Laaerberg (see A to Z, Oberlaa Health Centre). Numerous bars among the allotments invite the visitor to relax.

Danube Meadows
The "Alte Donau" (Old Danube), a region of meadows and cut-off arms of the river, with many bathing beaches (see Swimming Baths). A short way downstream is the Lobau, with pools and lakes.

Danube Island
See A to Z

Lainzer Tiergarten (Zoo)
See A to Z

Prater
See A to Z

Vienna Woods (Wienerwald)
See Excursions: Vienna Woods

Restaurants

Hotel restaurants See Hotels

Austrian cuisine

Luxury restaurants

Altwienerhof, 15, Herklotzgasse 6; tel. 83 71 45 and 8 12 00 22
Belvedere-Stöckl, 3, Prinz-Eugen-Str. 25; tel. 78 41 98 (garden)
Die Savoyengemächer, 15, Plunkergasse 3-5; tel. 9 82 13 81
Kervansaray Hummerbar, 1, Mahlerstr. 9; tel. 5 12 88 43
Korso bei der Oper, 1, Mahlerstr. 2; tel. 5 15 16/546
Kupferdachl, 1, Schottengasse 7; tel. 63 93 81
Palais Schwarzenberg, 3, Schwarzenberg Platz 9;
tel. 78 45 15-600 (garden)
Schubertstüberl'n, 1, Schreyvogelgasse 4-6; tel. 63 71 87
Steirereck, 3, Rasumofskygasse 2; tel. 7 13 31 68

Restaurants and
Beisln (inns)

Alter Rathauskeller, 1, Wipplingerstr. 8; tel. 5 35 33 36
Alt Nussdorf, 19, Nussdorfer Platz 4; tel. 37 12 77
Alt Sievering, 19, Sieveringer Str. 63; tel. 32 58 88
Amon, 3, Schlachthausgasse 13; tel. 78 81 66 (garden)
Beim Novak, 7, Richtergasse 12; tel. 93 32 44
Bierhof, 1, Naglergasse 13 (entrance Haarhof 3); tel. 5 33 44 28
Bockkeller, 19, Nussberggasse 2c; tel. 37 15 16
Butterfass, 2, Prater Hauptallee 122; tel. 2 18 03 80 (garden)
Donauturm (2 revolving restaurants at 160m/525ft and
170m/558ft), 22, Donauturmstr. 4; tel. 23 53 68/9
D'Rauchkuchl, 15, Schweglerstr. 37; tel. 92 13 81
Eckel, 19, Sieveringer Str. 46; tel. 32 32 18 (garden)
Figlmüller, 1, Wollzeile 5; tel. 5 12 61 77
Fischer-Bräu, 19, Billrothstr. 17; tel. 31 62 64
Frackerl, 6, Brückengasse 11; tel. 5 97 38 40 (garden)
Glacisbeisl, 7, Messepalast; tel. 96 16 58
(reservations 9 30 73 74)
Gösser Bierklinik, 1, Steindlgasse 4; tel. 5 35 68 97
Griechenbeisl, 1, Fleischmarkt 11; tel. 5 33 19 77
Gulaschmuseum, 1, Schulerstr. 20; tel. 5 12 10 17
Himmelpforte, 1, Himmelpfortgasse 24 ; tel. 5 13 19 67
Kaiserwalzer, 6, Esterházygasse 9; tel. 5 87 04 94
Kummer, 6, Mariahilfer Str. 71a; tel. 5 88 95
K & K "Kuche und Keller", 7, Zollergasse 14; tel. 93 24 80
Leupold – Zum Schottentor, 1, Schottengasse 7; tel. 63 93 81
Ma Pitom, 1, Seitenstettengasse 5; tel. 5 35 43 13 (garden)
Marienhof, 8, Josefstädterstr. 9; tel. 48 89 05
Melker Stiftskeller, 1, Schottengasse 3; tel. 5 33 55 30
Motto, 5, Schönbrunner Str. 30; tel. 5 87 06 72 (garden)
Ofenloch, 1, Kurrentgasse 8; tel. 5 33 88 44
Oswald & Kalb, 1, Bäckerstr. 14; tel. 5 12 69 92
Petris-und-Paulus-Stuben, 3, Paulusgasse 2; tel. 7 12 10 48
Pfudl, 1, Bäckerstr. 22; tel. 5 12 67 05
Piaristenkeller, 8, Piaristengasse 45; tel. 42 91 52 (garden)
Regina Stüberl, 9, Währinger Str. 1; tel. 42 76 81-0 (garden)
Römischer Kaiser, 19, Neustift a. W. 2; tel. 44 11 04 (garden)
Sailer, 18, Gersthofer Str. 14; tel. 4 72 12 12
Salzamt, 1, Ruprechtsplatz 1; tel. 5 33 53 32 (garden
rendezvous)

Serviette, 4, Wiedner Hauptstr. 27–29; tel. 5 01 11/325
Sirk – Rôtisserie, 1, Kärntner Str. 53; tel. 5 15 16/552
Steinerne Eule, 7, Halbgasse 30; tel. 93 22 50 (garden)
Steirer Stüberl, 5, Wiedner Hauptstr. 111; tel. 55 43 49
Vincent, 2, Grosse Pfarrgasse 7; tel. 2 14 47 46
Wein-Comptoir, 1, Bäckerstr. 6; tel. 5 12 17 60
Zauberlehrling, 18, Lazaristengasse 2; tel. 34 51 35
Zum alten Heller, 3, Ungargasse 34; tel. 7 12 64 52
Zum Donnerbrunnen, 1, Kärntner Str. 18; tel. 5 13 12 23
Zum Hirschen, 6, Hirschengasse 6; tel. 5 75 00 25
Zur goldenen Glocke, 5, Kettenbrückengasse 9; tel. 5 87 57 67
Zur Schönen Aussicht, 19, Pfarrplatz 5; tel. 37 50 00 (garden)
Zur Stadt Krems, 7, Zieglergasse 37; tel. 93 72 00 (garden)

Landhaus Winter, 11, Alberner Hafenzufahrtsstr. 262;   Fish restaurants
tel. 76 23 17
Scampi, 1, Mahlerstr. 11; tel. 5 13 22 97 and 5 13 49 30

Estakost, 9, Währinger Str. 7; tel. 4 25 06 54   Vegetarian restaurants
Siddharta, 1, Fleischmarkt 16; tel. 5 13 11 97

Do & Co. 1, Akademiestr. 3; tel. 5 12 64 74-0   Snack bars
Trześniewski, 1, Dorotheergasse 1; tel. 5 12 32 91

See Heuriger   Heuriger, Wine cellars

See entry   Coffee houses/Cafés

Foreign Cuisine

Balkan-Grill, 16, Brunnengasse 13; tel. 92 14 94 (garden)   Balkan

Ming Court, 1, Kärntner Str. 32; tel. 5 12 17 75   Chinese
Turandot, 17 Dornbacher Str. 116; tel. 46 15 35

Chez Robert, 18 Gertrudplatz 4; tel. 43 35 44   French
La Baguette, 1, Rotenturmstr. 12; tel. 5 12 21 92
Salut, 1, Wildpretmarkt 3; tel. 5 33 13 22

Der Grieche, 6, Barnabitengasse 5; tel. 5 87 74 66   Greek
Jannys, 4, Prinz-Eugen-Str. 56; tel. 5 05 18 21
Schwarze Katze, 6, Giradigasse 6; tel. 5 87 06 25
Orpheus, 1, Spiegelgasse 10; tel. 5 12 38 53

Demi Tasse, 4, Prinz-Eugen-Str. 28; tel. 6 50 90 25   Indian

Firenze Enoteca, 1, Singerstr. 3; tel. 52 46 31   Italian
Grotta Azzura, 1, Babenbergerstr. 5; tel. 5 86 10 44
Pulcinella, 8, Alser Str. 29, Kochgasse 36; tel. 42 91 76
Rimini, 5, Hauslabgasse 23; tel. 55 43 56

Mitsukoshi, 1, Albertinaplatz 2 ; tel. 5 12 27 07   Japanese

Ko-Riyo Chung, 1, Schellinggasse 3; tel. 5 12 10 68   Korean
Senara, 1, Schwarzenbergstr. 4; tel. 5 12 99 83

Feuervogel, 9, Alserbachstr. 21; tel. 3 41 03 92   Russian

Kervansaray, 1, Mahlerstr. 9; tel. 5 12 88 43   Turkish

Shopping

Shopping streets	There are elegant and exclusive shops of all kinds in the inner city and in the area around the cathedral: Kärntner Strasse, Graben, Kohlmarkt, Tuchlauben, Wollzeile, Spiegelgasse and Neuer Markt. Another less expensive shopping area is Mariahilfer Strasse where large stores are also situated.
Antiques	See entry
Children's clothes	Bimba, 1, Bräunerstr. 10 Jacadi, 1, Trattnerhof 2 Le Petit Chou, 1, Brandstätte 10
Confectionery	Altmann & Kühne, 1, Graben 30 Demel, 1, Kohlmarkt 14 Gerstner, 1, Kärntner Str. 15 Godiva Chocolatier, 1, Graben 17
Costume hire	Elite, 7, Neustiftgasse 137, door 7 Lambert Hofer, 4, Margaretenstr. 19 and 25
Design	Michaela Frey Team, 6, Gumpendorferstr. 81 Passini, 1, Franziskanerplatz 6
Galleries	See entry
Glass, porcelain	Albin Denk, 1, Graben 13 E. Lackinger Glas, 1, Weihburggasse 21 Lobmeyer, 1, Kärntner Str. 26 Porzellanmanufaktur (Augarten-Porzellan), 1, Stock-im-Eisen Platz 3–4; 6, Mariahilfer Str. 99; at the airport, etc. Rasper & Söhne, 1, Graben 15 "tabletop", 1, Freyung 2 Wahliss, 1, Kärntner Str. 17
Jewellery	A. E. Köchert, 1, Neuer Markt 15 Cartier-Boutique, 1, Kohlmarkt 4 Haban, 1, Kärntner Str. 2 Schullin & Söhne, 1, Kohlmarkt 7
Model railways	Modellbahnzentrum, 4, Wiedner Hauptstr. 23
Perfume	Beauty, 3, Kardinal-Nagl-Platz 12 Douglas, 1, Kärntner Str. 26; Graben 29a; Kohlmarkt 11 Douglas for Men, 1, Kärntner Str. 26 Jacqueline, 1, Schottengasse 4 J. B. Filz Sohn, 1, Graben 13 Ritz, 1, Kärntner Str. 22
Petit-point needlework	Maria Stransky, 1, Hofburg-Passage 2
Shoes made to measure	Materna, 1, Mahlerstr. 5

A valuable souvenir: decorative objects of Augarten porcelain

Angerer & Góschl, 1, Kleeblattgasse 4	Souvenirs
Austrian Workshops, 1, Kärntner Str. 6	
Boutique Teresa, 4, Favoritenstr. 58	
G. Schreiber, 1, Schottentorpassage	
Gans, 1, Brandstätte 1	Table- and bed-linen
Gunkel, 1, Tuchlauben 11	
M. A. Kügele, 15, Hackengasse 7–9	
Schindler Weben, 1, Salzgries 3	
Zur Schwäbischen Jungfrau, 1, Graben 26	
Schönbichler, 1, Wollzeile 4	Tea
Kober, 1, Graben 14–15	Tin figures
Dux, 1, Schottengasse 9	Toys
Kober, 1, Graben 14–15	
Spielkistl, 3, Landstr. 2	
Birkenhütte, 9, Nussdorfer Str. 26–28	Traditional fashions
Hubertus, 3, Landstrasser Hauptstr. 67	
E. Kettner, 1, Seilergasse 12	
Lanz, 1, Kärntner Str. 10	
Loden-Plankl, 1, Michaelerplatz 6	
Lower Austrian Home Industries, 1, Herrengasse 6	
Resi Hammerer, 1, Kärntner Str. 29–31	
Tostmann, 1, Schottengasse 3a	
Trachten-Just, 1, Lugeck 7	
Trachtenmädl, 7, Westbahnstr. 56	
Trachten-Schmidt, 1, Stubenring 16	
Backhausen, 1, Kärntner Str. 33	Young people's boutique

Shopping

In the rail stations:
Vienna North (Wien-Nord), Praterstern
Open: daily 5.30 a.m.–9 p.m. (food)

Vienna Central (Wien-Mitte), 3, Landstrasser Hauptstr. 1c
Open: daily 5.30 a.m.–10 p.m. (food)

Franz Josefs Station, 9, Julius-Tandler-Platz 2–4
Mini supermarket with chemist's
Open: Mon.–Sat. 8 a.m.–10.30 p.m., Sun. 9.30 a.m.–10.30 p.m.
Tabak-Traffik
Open: daily 5.45 a.m.–8.15 p.m. (tobacco goods and newspapers)

South Station (Südbahnhof), 10, Wiedner Gürtel 1
Open: daily 7 a.m.–11 p.m. (food)

West Station (Westbahnhof), 15, Europlatz 1
Open: daily 7 a.m.–11 p.m. (food)

Wien-Schwachat Airport
Supermarket
Open: Sat.–Thur. 7.30 a.m.–7 p.m., Fri. 7.30 a.m.–8 p.m., Sun 10 a.m.–6 p.m.

Filling stations (with 24 hour service):
Shell-Center South, 10 Triester Str. 6a–8
Shell-Center West, 14 Hadikgasse 128–134

In the city:
AKH-Expresso, 9, Lazarettgasse 14
Open: Mon.–Sat. 6.30 a.m.–9 p.m., Sun. and public holidays 9 a.m.–9 p.m. (food, chemist)

Bücher Hirtl, 3 Landstrasser Hauptstr. 2a (in AEZ)
Open: Mon.–Fri. 7 a.m.–7 p.m., Sat. 9 a.m.–6 p.m., Sun. 11 a.m.–6 p.m. (books)

Feinkost Patzak, 19, Nussdorfer Platz 3
Open: Tue.–Fri. 7.30 a.m.–1.30 p.m., Sat. 7.30 a.m.–8 p.m., Sun. and public holidays 2–8 p.m. (delicatessen)

Hairdressers:
Hair Style W. Jost, 8, Josefstädter Str. 54
Open: Mon.–Thur. 9 a.m.–6 p.m., Fri. 9 a.m.–6.30 p.m., Sat. 9 a.m.–3 p.m.
Mod's Hair, 1, Krugerstr. 17
Open: Mon. 10 a.m.–6 p.m., Tue., Wed. 9 a.m.–6 p.m., Thur. 9 a.m.–8 p.m., Sat. 8 a.m.–2 p.m.

Janele in the Bärenmühle, 4, Operngasse 18
Open: daily 6.30 a.m.–7 p.m. (food)

Mobilmarkt, 11, Grenzackerstr. 2
Open: 24 hours a day (food, mini-drugstore)

Schwarz, 13, Auhofstr. 133
Open: Mon.–Sat. 6.30 a.m.–8 p.m., Sun. 11 a.m.–8 p.m. (food)

Zur Grüne Hütte, 2, Prater 196 (entrance Ausstellungsstr.)
Open: daily 7 a.m.–10 p.m. (good selection of food and frozen food, chemist)

See entry

Visitors to Austria who purchase goods to take home with them can reclaim the Mehrwertsteuer (value added tax) of up to 32% if the account amounts to at least 1,000 Austrian schillings. In this case the seller must make out a bill in the name of the purchaser showing the amount of tax, and fill in form U34. Both documents and the goods themselves must be produced to the Austrian customs officials when leaving the country. After export the documents must either be sent to the store from which the goods were purchased or to the Austria Tax Free Organization, Biberstrasse, A-1010 Wien. The tax will then be returned by cheque or other means. At some frontier offices of the ÖAMTC motorists can obtain immediate repayment of the tax on production of the bill and form U34.

Sightseeing Programme

The recommendations below are designed to help first-time visitors to Vienna to make the most of their stay in the city.

Places of interest which are described in the A to Z section of this guide are printed in **bold type**.

To get a first flavour of Vienna and to find out where the most important sights can be found, the visitor is recommended to make a tour on foot through the inner city. The starting point is the **Staatsoper** (State Opera House), on the corner of the Ring and Kärntner Strasse. Behind the Opera turn left into Philharmoniker Strasse, where the famous **Hotel Sacher** is situated. On the Albertinaplatz can be seen the equestrian statue of Archduke Albrecht on the top of the **Albrechtsrampe**, while in the street the celebrated "Fiaker" (see Practical Information, Fiaker)wait for their clients. Now continue through Tegetthofstrasse to the **Neuer Markt** (New Market) with the Donnerbrunnen (or Providentia Fountain); here stands the **Kapuzinerkirche** (Capuchin church). Now follow the Plankengasse on the left, turn left again into Dorotheergasse, where the **Dorotheum** (see also Practical Information, Auctions) has its premises and regain the Augustinerstrasse. On the left stands the **Augustinerkirche** (church of the Augustines), the exterior of which is quite plain. Nearby lies **Josefsplatz** with the monument to Joseph II; one of the finest squares in Vienna, it is bordered by the **Österreichische National Bibliothek** (Austrian National Library), the **Spanish Riding School**, the **Palais Palffy** and the Palais Pallaivicini. A passage in the far corner of the square leads to the **Hofburg** (for plan see page 79). In the "Alter Hofburg" (Schweizerplatz) is the entrance to the Treasury and the Hofburg Chapel, where the Vienna Boys' Choir can be heard on Sundays. The Schweizer Tor (Swiss gate) opens on to the square called "In der Burg", where there is a monument to Francis II. On the right stretch the buildings of the Reichanzleramt (Imperial Chancellery), while the upper end of the square is taken up by the Amlalienburg – these two buildings house the Emperor's Apartments – with the Leopoldinische

Trakt (Leopold range) on the left. A passage links the square with the area of the Neuer Burg, where the **Ephesos Museum** and the **Museum für Völkerkunde** (Austrian Folk Museum) are to be found, and Heldenplatz (Heroes' Square) with equestrian statues of Prince Eugene and Archduke Karl. Leave the Heldenplatz through the Burgtor onto the **Ballhausplatz**, where now stands the Bundeskanzleramt in which Imperial foreign policy was once decided. A pleasant stroll northwards through the **Volksgarten**, where the memorials include one to the Empress Elisabeth (Cissy), brings the visitor into Bankgasse which should be followed for a short way, passing the **Palais Liechtenstein**, and then turn right into Abraham-a-Sancta-Clara-Gasse which leads into the Minoritenplatz. Dominating the square is the **Minoritenkirche**. Proceed through Landhausgasse and (on the right) Herrengasse past the **Niederösterreiches Landesmuseum** to arrive in Michaelerplatz, which is framed by the Michaeler range (with steps up to the Hoftafel, Silberkammer and apartments), the **Hofburg**, the **Michaelerkirche,** and the Art-Nouveau Loos House. In the Kohlmarkt street it would be pleasant to pause and pay a visit to the **Café Dehmel**, the former confectioner to the Royal and Imperial Court, before strolling on into the **Graben**, which leads into **Stock-im-Eisen Platz** and **Stephansplatz**, beneath which the medieval Virgil chapel was excavated; here rises the **Stephansdom**, the cathedral and symbol of Vienna. As a break from sightseeing a stroll through the best known shopping street in the city, **Kärntner Strasse** is suggested. If only one day is available for sightseeing the afternoon should be spent either at **Schönbrunn** or at the **Belvedere-Schlösser**, which house the Austrian Baroque Museum, the Museum of Medieval Austrian Art and the Austrian Gallery of 19th and 20th c. Art. The palaces are situated in a magnificent park, an ideal place for a brief rest. In the evening sightseeing can be continued. The DDSG (see Excursions, Boat Trips on the Danube) organises from mid-May until late September evening excursions with music on the Danube; however, the visitor who would like to see another side of Vienna and experience something of the traditional "Wiener Gemütlichkeit" – almost untranslatable but akin to the French "bonhomie" – might visit one of the numerous Heurige inns (see Practical Information, Heuriger) or a "Beisel", for example the **Griechen** (Greek) **Beisel** (see Practical Information, Restaurants). Night-owls must take care not to disappear in the "Bermuda Triangle" (see Practical Information, Night-life).

Two days

A two-day stay will provide an opportunity of exploring more thoroughly some of the places mentioned in the one-day programme. In the morning it is very pleasant to see the Lippizaner horses being put through their paces (see **Spanish Riding School**) in the **Hofburg**. If the visitor has already seen this perhaps a visit to one of the larger museums would be rewarding. If the choice falls on the **Kunsthistorisches Museum** (Museum of Art History) or the **Natur Historisches Museum** (Natural History Museum) then it would be convenient to continue walking along the Ring in the direction of Dr.-Karl-Renner-Ring and Dr.-Karl-Lueger-Ring, passing the **Parlament** (Parliament Building), the **Rathaus** (Town Hall), the **Burgtheater** and the **Universität** to the **Votivkirche**. An alternative is to turn right at the Burgtheater into Löwelstrasse/Teinfalterstrasse and reach the open space called **Freyung**, with the Austria Fountain; here the **Schottenstift**, the **Schottenkirche** and the Café

Central in the **Palais Ferstel** invite the visitor to pause for a while. From here continue along Heidenschluss Strasse to the square and church of **Am Hof**; the square is surrounded by old town houses and palaces. The Bognergasse leads back to the shopping centre around the Graben and Kärntner Strasse. Take the opposite direction from the Art and Natural History Museums along the Opernring and turn right at Robert-Stolz-Platz to reach the **Akademie der Bildenden Künste** (Academy of Fine Arts) and via Marktgasse come to the **Secession** (art gallery), where Klimt's "Beethoven Frieze" is now again on display. From here it is only a few steps to the lively and colourful **Naschmarkt** (also flea market on Saturdays) which is surrounded by cafés, theatres, nightspots and snackbars. On the opposite bank of the little River Wien Treitlstrasse leads to the **Karlskirche**; on the left near the church stands the **Historische Museum der Stadt Wien** (Vienna City Historical Museum). In Dumbastrasse which branches off Karlsplatz is the **Musikvereinsgebäude**, and in **Karlsplatz** itself the Art-Nouveau Pavilion of the City Railway (Stadtbahn). The Wiedner Hauptstrasse leads back to the **Staatsoper** (State Opera House). A drive in a Fiaker (see Practical Information, Fiaker) provides a different perspective of the sights of Vienna.

The evening can be spent at a theatre, a concert or at the opera. For theatre lovers the choice ranges from the **Burgtheater** to the politically critical avant-garde productions (see Practical Information, Theatres). The musical life of the city is equally comprehensive (see Practical Information, Music).

In addition to the sights mentioned above, there is also the oldest quarter of Vienna, behind the cathedral, waiting to be explored. Follow Rotenturmstrasse and come to the **Hoher Markt** on the left; here can be seen the impressive Anker Clock, while underground are Roman remains dating from the earliest period of the history of Vienna. The Neihardt Frescoes (see **Graben**) in the Tuchlauben are the oldest secular paintings in the city, and in the **Judenplatz**, reached along the Jordangasse, stands the house called "Zum grossen Jordan". If the sunnier side of Vienna is preferred a detour can be made to the **Danube Island** (see also Practical Information, Swimming Baths), with its many recreational and leisure facilities.

Three days

The afternoon could be taken up by a visit to **Kloster Neuburg** in the Vienna Woods. On the way there along the Wiener-Höhenstrasse beautiful views can be enjoyed (see Practical Information: Excursions, Wienerwald).

As the end of a third day in Vienna approaches, one of the best ways of taking leave is to visit the **Prater** in the evening and admire the views of the city from a cabin on the giant wheel.

Sport and Recreation

Walzer-Spezialstunden: tel. (Mon.–Fri. 8 a.m.–4 p.m.)
5 14 50-257

Dancing

Fit & Fun, 3, Landstrasser Hauptstr. 2a; tel. 7 13 61 65/6
Fitness Center Donaupark, 22, Arbeiterstrandbadstr. 122;
tel. 23 36 61
Fitness-Center Schönbrunn, 13, Schönbrunner Schloss Str.
52; tel. 83 53 01

Fitness centres

Swimming Baths

	Fitnesscentre Stadtpark, 1, Johannesgasse 33; tel. 75 77 75 Olympic, 16, Hasnerstr. 63; tel. 4 92 10 16 Sportschule Heimlich, 3, Ungargasse 4; tel. 7 13 36 18 and 7 13 80 93
Football grounds	Praterstadion, 2, Krieau; tel. 2 18 08 54-0 Stadion Hohe Warte, First Vienna Footballclub, 19, Hohe Warte; tel. 36 61 36 and 36 61 06
Golf	Golf-Club Wien, 2, Freudenau Str. 65a; tel. 2 18 95 64
Horse racing	Trotting course, Trabrennbahn Krieau, 2, Pratergelände; tel. 2 18 00 46-0 Tram: 1; Underground station: Praterstern (U4) Season: September to June Racecourse, Galopp Rennbahn, 2, Freudenau 65, Pratergelände Information: Wiener Rennverein, 1, Josefsplatz 5; tel. 5 12 25 38-0 Bus: 81A Season: Spring and autumn
Ice skating	Donaupark-Eishalle, 22, Wagramer Str. 1; tel. 23 04 74 Eislaufanlage Engelmann, 17, Syringgasse 6-8; tel. 42 14 25/6 Eisring-Süd, 10, Raxstr. /Windenstr. ; tel. 6 04 44 43 Stadthall, 15, Vogelweidplatz 14; tel. 9 81 01-0
Sauna/Swimming	See Swimming Baths
Squash	Fit & Fun, 3, Landstrasser Hauptstr. 2a; tel. 7 13 61 65/6 Squash-Haus Penzing, 14, Linzer Str. 183; tel. 9 42 45 12 and 94 85 51 STS (Squash-Tennis-Sauna), 3, Baumgasse 83; tel. 78 82 01 Squash Center Hernals, 17, Hernalser Hauptstr. 13; tel. 43 86 27
Tennis	Isfo-Tennis-Center, 10, Heubergstättenstr. 1; tel. 67 97 73 Tennis Center La Ville, 23, Kirchfeldgasse 5; tel. 8 04 67 37 Tennishallen Edmund Herzig, 11, Leberstr. 82; tel. 74 34 40 Tennisplätze Arsenal, 3, Arsenalstr. 1; tel. 78 21 32

Swimming Baths

Covered baths (most with saunas) **Information**: (opening times) tel. 15 35	Amalienbad 10, Reumannsplatz 23 (beautifully restored Art Nouveau baths) Dianabad, 2, Lilienbrunnengasse 7–9 Hallenbad Döbling 19, Geweygasse 6 (also open-air bath) Hallenbad Floridsdorf 21 Franklinstr. 22 Hallenbad Simmering 11, Florien-Hedorfer-Str. 5 (also open-air bath) Jörgerbad 17, Jörgerstr. 42–44

Rodauner Bad (no sauna)
23, An der Au 2

Theresienbad
12, Huferlandgasse 3

Thermalbad Oberlaa
10, Kurbadstr. 14
(See A to Z Oberlaa Health Centre)

Angeliebad
21 (on the upper Old Danube)

Open-air baths

Bundesbad Schönbrunn
13, Schönbrunner Schlosspark

Freibad Baumgarten
14, Hackinger Str. 26a

Freibad Donuastadt
22, Portnergasse 38 (also covered bath)

Freibad Grossfeldsiedlung
21, Oswald-Redlich-Str. 44 (also covered bath)

Freibad Hadersdorf-Weidlingau
14, Hauptstr. 41

Freibad Hietzing
13, Atzgersdorfstr. 14 (also covered bath)

Gänsehäufel
22, Moissigasse 21 (artificial waves)

Kongressbad
16, Julius-Meinl-Gasse 7a

Krapfenwaldbad
19, Krapfenwaldgasse 65–73

Laaer-Berg Bad
10, Ludwig von Höhnel-Gasse 2

Liesinger Bad
23, Perchtoldsdorfer Str. 14–16

Neuwaldegger Bad
17, Promenadegasse 58

Ottakringer Bad
16 Johann-Staud-Str.11 (also covered bath)

Satzbergbad
14, Am Satzberg, Steinböckengasse 100

Schafbergbad
18 Josef-Redel-Gasse 2

Schwimmbad Pratersauna
2, Walsteingartenstr. 135

Taxis

Stadionbad
2, Prater, Krieau

Strandbad Alte Donau
22, Arbeiterstrandbadstr. 91

Strandbad Stadlau
22, Am Mühlwasser

Theresienbad
12, Hufelandgasse 3 (also covered bath)

Popular bathing places

Only a few minutes from the city centre (e.g. by U1) lie Vienna's most popular bathing places on the Old Danube (12km/7½ miles of beach) and on Danube Island ("Copa Cagrana"; 40km/25 miles of beach, naturist areas, summer discos) with boating facilities, sailing schools, bicycle rental, restaurants, barbecue sites, etc. Many events take place in summer. Information from Verein ARGE Alte Donau, 1, Stubenring 8–10; tel. 5 14 50-257.

Taxis

Taxis ply for hire from official ranks or they can be ordered by telephone (radio taxis). Hailing a taxi in traffic, even if the "frei" sign is illuminated, is officially forbidden, but in practice this is possible in quiet streets.

Radio taxis

Tel. 3 13 00, 4 01 00, 6 01 60, 9 10 11
For journeys to the airport and outside the city; tel. 31 25 11

Taxi ranks

Corner of Opernring/Operngasse; tel. 56 52 05
Babenbergerstrasse/Burgring; tel. 93 23 55
Hoher Markt/Marc-Aurel-Strasse; tel. 63 04 98
Dr.-Karl-Lueger-Ring, 14; tel. 5 33 12 60
Stubenring; tel. 5 12 32 36, etc.
Other ranks (without telephones) include those at Petersplatz, Kärntner Strasse/corner of Mahlerstrasse (on the left, near the Opera).

Fares

In the city fares are calculated on the taximeter (basic price plus price per km); a small supplement to cover inflation is added.

Telephone

Calls abroad can be made from all public coin boxes. For local calls 1 ÖS coins are required and for long-distance calls 10 ÖS coins.

Charges

A telephone call to the United Kingdom costs 14 ÖS per minute; to the United States and Canada 40.50 ÖS per minute. After 6 p.m. and at week-ends from noon on Saturday long-distance calls are cheaper.

Telephone codes

To Vienna from the United Kingdom: 010 43 222
To Vienna from the United States and Canada: 011 43 222
From Vienna to the United Kingdom: 00 44

From Vienna to the United States and Canada: 001
In dialling an international call the zero prefix of the local code
should be omitted.

See Useful Telephone Numbers   Telephone service

Theatres

A free survey of theatrical programmes is available from the   Advance programme
Vienna Tourist Board (see entry); details also appear in the list   details
of events (see Programme of Events) which is published every
month.

Tickets can be booked in advance (see Advance Booking) or   Tickets
direct at the theatres.

Akademietheater   Federal Theatres
3, Lisztstr. 1; tel. 5 14 44-29 59
Burgtheatre company

Burgtheater
See A to Z

Kammerspiele
1, Rotenturmstr. 20; tel. 5 33 28 33-0
Satire and comedy with the company from the Theater in der
Josefstadt

Theater in der Josefstadt
8, Josefstädter Str. 26; tel. 4 02 51 27
Light comtemporary productions

International Theatre (performances in English)
1, Porzellangasse 8/Müllnergasse; tel. 31 62 72

Kleine Komödie in Theater am Kärntnertor
1, Walfischgasse 4; tel. 5 12 42 80
Contemporary comedies and thrillers

Vienna's English Theatre
8, Josefsgasse 12; tel. 4 02 12 60
Plays in English

Volkstheater
7, Neustiftgasse 1; tel. 93 35 01-0
Contemporary drama; sometimes avant-garde productions

Akzent-Theater   Small theatres
4, Theresianumgasse 16–18; tel. 5 01 65-3304   (selection)

Ateliertheater am Naschmarkt
6 Linke Wienzeile 4; tel. 5 87 82 14

Drackengasse 2 Theater/Courage
1, Fleischmarkt 22; tel. 5 13 14 44

Ensemble Theater im Treffpunkt Petersplatz
1, Petersplatz 1; tel. 5 33 20 39 and 5 35 32 00

Experiment am Lichtenwerd
9, Liechtensteinstr. 132; tel. 31 41 08

Theatres

Freie Bühne Wieden
4, Wiedner Hauptstr. 60b; tel. 5 86 21 22

Jura Soyfer Theater
7 Spittelberggasse 10; tel. 5 26 31 95

Komödie am Kai
1, Franz-Josefs-Kai 29; tel. 5 33 24 34

Kulisse
17, Rosensteingasse 39; tel. 45 38 70

Original Pradler Ritterspiele
1, Biberstr. 2; tel. 5 12 54 00
Romantic plays

Schönbrunner Schlosstheater (July and August only)
13, Schloss Schönbrunn; tel. 82 94 66

Serapionstheater im Odeon
20, Taborstr. 10; tel. 24 55 62

Theater beim Auersperg
8 Auerspergstr. 17; tel. 43 07 07

Theater Brett
6 Münzwardeingasse 2; tel. 5 87 47 87

Theater "Die Tribüne" in the Café Lantmann
1, Dr.-Karl-Leuger-Ring 4; tel. 63 84 85

Theater-Forum
9 Porzellangasse 50; tel. 31 54 21

Theater Gruppe 80
6, Gumpendorfer Str. 67; tel. 56 52 22

Theater im Künstlerhaus
1, Karlsplatz 5; tel. 5 87 05 04

Theater Spielraum
15, Palmgasse 8; tel. 87 35 25

Cabaret

Kabarett in Amerlinghaus
7, Stiftgasse 8; tel. 56 33 95

Hernalser Stadttheater Metropol/Metropolino
17, Hernalser Hauptstr. 55; tel. 43 35 43

Kabarett & Komödie am Naschmarkt
6, Linke Wienzeile 4; tel. 5 87 22 75

Kabarett Niedermair
8, Lenaugasse 1a; tel. 4 08 44 92

Spektakel
5, Hamburgerstr. 14; tel. 5 87 06 53

Theater Kabarett Simpl
1, Wollzeile 36; tel. 5 12 47 42

Son et Lumière in Schloss Belvedere
(in summer daily from 9.30 p.m.)
3 Prinz-Eugen-Str. 27; tel. 5 12 56 85
(evening booking office tel. 78 39 44)

See Music

Time

Austria observes Central European Time (one hour ahead of
Greenwich Mean Time; six hours ahead of New York Time).
From the end of March to the end of September Summer Time
(two hours ahead of Greenwich Mean Time; seven hours
ahead of New York Time) is in force.

Tipping

It is customary to tip waiters, hotel room-maids, taxi-drivers,
hairdressers, etc. 10–15% of the bill. A tip is also expected even
when (as in restaurants) service is already included in the bill.
Do not, however, tip the self-styled "parking attendants"
(called in Vienna "Türlschnapper" = little door snappers) who
hang around the car-parks used by tourists.

Travel documents

Visitors to Austria who are citizens of the United Kingdom, the
United States or the Commonwealth require only a passport to
enter the country. No visa is required unless the visit exceeds
three months or the visitor proposes to work in the country.

National driving licences and car registration documents from
the above countries are recognised in Austria and should be
carried. Foreign vehicles must bear an oval nationality plate. It
is advisable to carry an international insurance certificate
("Green Card").

See also Motoring

When to go

Vienna has much to offer at any time of year. In spring the
temperature is pleasant for strolling about the city and making
visits to places of interest; the café gardens are already open
and the Vienna Spring Festival provides the first cultural high-
light of the year. The festival weeks are continued in summer by
the "Wiener Musik Sommer" (see Festivals; Events) and it is in
summer that there are numerous opportunites for swimming
and bathing (see Swimming Baths; and A to Z, Danube Island)
and for interesting excursions in the surrounding area (see
Excursions). Autumn is the time for tasting the new wine (see
Heuriger) and sees the opening of the theatrical and concert
season (see Theatres, Music), while winter offers further musical events, especially the fashionable balls.

Youth Hostels

Central information office

Österreichisches Jugendherbergswerk (ÖJHW)
Helferstorferstr. 4, A-1010 Wien; tel. 5 33 18 33

Wiener Jugendherbergswerk
Mariahilfer Str. 24, A-1070 Wien; tel. 93 71 58-0 and 93 71 67-0

Hostels

Jugendgästehaus der Stadt Wien–Hüttelsdorf–Hacking
Schlossberggasse 8, A-1130 Wien; tel. 82 15 01
Open: all year; 277 beds

Jugendgästehaus Wien–20 Brigittenau
Friedrich-Engels-Platz 24, A-1200 Wien; tel. 33 82 94-0
Open: all year; 334 beds

Jugendherberge Wien–Myrthengasse
Myrthengasse 7/Neustiftgasse 85, A-1070 Wien;
tel. 93 63 16-0, 9 36 90 35
Open: all year; 225 beds

Jugendherberge Hostel Ruthensteiner
Robert Hamerlinggasse 24, A-1150 Wien;
tel. 83 46 93 and 8 30 82 65
Open: all year; 77 beds

Schlossherberge am Wilhelminenberg
Savoyenstr. 2, A-1160 Wien; tel. 45 85 03-0
Open: from March to October; 164 beds

Useful Telephone Numbers at a glance

Emergencies
    Ambulance   144
    Breakdown (24 hours a day)
        ARBÖ   123
        ÖAMTC   120
    Chemist on duty   15 50
    Doctor on call (24 hours a day)   141
    Fire brigade   122
    Police   133

Information
    Airline information   77 70-22 31/2
    Austrian-Information   5 87 20 00
    Bus timetable (ÖBB)   7 11 01
    Cinema programmes   15 77
    City information (Vienna)   43 89 89
    City tours ("New Vienna")   40 00-8 10 50
    Complaints (tourist office)   43 16 08-0
    Danube trips (DDSG)   2 17 10-0
    ÖAMTC traffic information   15 90
    Rail information (central)   17 17
        Long distance (south)   15 53
        Long distance (west)   15 52
    Theatre programmes   15 18
    Timetable information   15 37
    Tourist-Information Vienna   5 13 88 92 and 5 13 40 15
    Youth-Information   5 26 46 37
    Weather   15 66

Embassies
    United Kingdom   73 15 75-79
    United States   31 55 11
    Canada   63 66 26-28

Airline information (reservations)
    Austrian Airlines   7 17 99
    British Airways   65 76 91
    Pan Am   52 66 46
    TWA   68 00

Lost property
    Central office   3 13 44-0
    Central office of the ÖBB (railways)   58 00-0

Taxis   3 13 00, 4 01 00, 6 01 60
Telegrams   190

Telephone International Dialling Codes
    to United Kingdom   00 44
    to United States or Canada   001

INDEX

Notes

Notes